UN
FAIR
MIND
SHARE

UN FAIR MIND SHARE

A CMO's guide to community-led marketing in a product-led world.

DEREK E. WEEKS

The internet addresses, phone numbers, and company or product information provided in this book are offered as a resource. They are not intended in any way to be or to imply an endorsement by the author or publisher. Furthermore, neither the author nor the publisher can guarantee the accuracy of the information presented, as these details may change over time.

Quantity sales: Special discounts are available on quantity purchases by corporations, associations, universities, and others. For details, please get in touch with us at hello@unfairmindshare.com using the subject line "I like bulk discounts."

Book cover design by Derek E. Weeks and Melissa Schmidt

Interior illustrations by Derek E. Weeks and Melissa Schmidt

Interior design by Derek E. Weeks and Marian Hartsough

www.unfairmindshare.com

Title: Unfair Mindshare: A CMO's guide to community-led marketing in a
   product-led world.
Name: Weeks, Derek, author. | Weeks Derek E.
Description of the book: First Edition. | Bethesda, MD

ISBN: 979-8-9882751-0-7 (paperback)
ISBN: 979-8-9882751-2-1 (hardcover)
ISBN: 979-8-9882751-1-4 (ebook)

Subjects: Branding (Marketing), Marketing, Customer Relations, Business
Classification: Library of Congress Control Number: 2023917547

The views and opinions expressed in this book are solely those of the author and do not represent, reflect, or express the views or opinions of any former employers, affiliated organizations, or other individuals. Readers will encounter mentions of Sonatype, a notable entity in the field. References to Sonatype are purely illustrative. It's crucial to clarify that Sonatype has not contributed to, nor endorsed, the insights and perspectives shared within these pages. Furthermore, the author has made every effort to ensure the accuracy of the information provided in this book but does not warrant or guarantee its accuracy, completeness, or applicability to any specific situation. The examples and case studies presented in this book are for illustrative purposes only and are not intended to disclose any former employers' proprietary information or trade secrets. Similarities to real companies, organizations, or individuals are coincidental and unintentional. The author disclaims any liability for any actions taken or not taken based on the contents of this book.

Printed in the United States of America

To Rosie, Connor, and Natalie.
—D. W.

PRAISE FOR UNFAIR MINDSHARE

"In the modern era, people crave connection. Companies fostering thriving, self-sustaining communities not only gain a substantial competitive advantage but also forge enduring connections, creating value for years. *Unfair Mindshare* is a tour de force in the art of attracting and engaging today's buyers. Derek Weeks illuminates how community-led marketing can become a CMO's secret weapon for driving significant pipeline and revenue growth. This book is a game-changer packed with strategic insights and fresh perspective."

—**Dan Tyre**, CEO, Tyre Angel,
HubSpot

"Derek masterfully unpacks the critical role of community-led marketing in a modern, orchestrated B2B marketing plan. *Unfair Mindshare* serves as a strategic blueprint, providing step-by-step guidance for aligning community initiatives with both demand generation and brand strategies. If your marketing team is not part of the community conversation, you're starting from a position of disadvantage. This book equips CMOs with the tools to shift from this vulnerable stance to one of considerable advantage, optimizing plans to drive tangible results."

—**Terry Flaherty**, Vice President & Principal Analyst,
Demand Services,
Forrester Research

"Unfair Mindshare masterfully engineers a seismic shift in marketing, propelling the conventional playbook into a new era of community-led strategies. Building upon traditional product and brand marketing strategies, Weeks introduces a paradigm that helps businesses rise above the market noise. A courageous approach, grounded in real-world case studies, which makes it all the more compelling. Viva la revolution!"

> —**Paul Muller**, Co-founder, Denting the Universe
> and former Worldwide VP Marketing,
> Hewlett Packard

"Derek Weeks' *Unfair Mindshare* is a masterclass in community-led marketing. With his three-fold approach to marketing strategy, he demystifies the process and provides transparent, actionable advice. This book is a treasure trove of insights for any marketer."

> —**Matt Heinz**, Founder/President,
> Heinz Marketing
> and Host,
> Sales Pipeline Radio

"Unfair Mindshare is the definitive guide to community-led marketing. Derek Weeks is a seasoned expert, whose 'been there, done that' expertise and comprehensive understanding of the synergy between product, brand, and community yield a book that's both inspirational and educational. Above all, it's brimming with actionable insights. This book is an indispensable read for the modern marketer."

> —**Kathleen Booth**, SVP Marketing & Growth,
> Pavilion

"Unfair Mindshare has redefined my perception of what's possible in community-led marketing. Weeks unveils innovative methods that align perfectly with our current landscape. For CMOs hungry for transformative insights, this book serves as your marketing North Star."

> —**Missi Carmen**, Chief Marketing Officer,
> Spirion

"Working alongside Derek, I had the opportunity to learn firsthand the power of community-led marketing. This collaboration not only enriched my experience as a marketing leader but also played a vital role in accelerating our company's growth and success. *Unfair Mindshare* is an essential read for all marketers looking to elevate their brand, expand their business, and punch above their weight-class in crowded markets."

> —**Matt Howard**, CMO, Virtru and former CMO, Sonatype

"Having collaborated with Derek on community-led initiatives for over a decade, I knew this book would be something special. It has exceeded even my high expectations. If you're a committed marketer or CMO, *Unfair Mindshare* will revolutionize how you think about community-led marketing, delivering a unique competitive edge for you and your team."

> —**Mark Miller**, Executive Producer, Sourced Network Productions

"Derek Weeks has been an invaluable thought leader when it comes to leveraging communities to drive business growth. This book provides practical guidance on integrating community, brand, and product marketing to achieve *Unfair Mindshare*. It's an essential read for any B2B marketing leader looking to accelerate success."

> —**Jim Shilts**, Head of Marketing, North American DevOps Group (NADOG)

"Derek Weeks has given marketers a powerful model to understand how community-led marketing complements traditional product and brand marketing. He provides a comprehensive blueprint on how to build, manage, and nurture communities the right way. If you're looking to leverage communities in your marketing, *Unfair Mindshare* is the book you've been searching for."

> —**Alec Cheung**, 4-time CMO and VP of Marketing and Co-host, The Marketing Share Podcast

"*Unfair Mindshare* is a thrilling success story and a practical guidebook for community-led marketing. It aims to help marketing teams stand out in crowded marketplaces. Derek Weeks provides key insights to give CMOs an edge in mastering community-led marketing. It embodies an all-encompassing strategy that transforms brands from a soft whisper into a resounding roar. His unconventional yet effective techniques are a must-read for modern CMOs."

> —**Shashi Bellamkonda**, 4x CMO/VP of
> Marketing and Principal Research Director,
> SoftwareReviews

"In a product-driven universe, Derek Weeks brilliantly lights the path for CMOs to harness the gravitational pull of community-led marketing. This book is full of actionable insights, enriched by real-world examples, insight, and inspiration. *Unfair Mindshare* is an essential must-read for marketing leaders looking to elevate their strategies."

> —**Karen Gardner**, 3-time CMO and SVP of Marketing

"It's edifying to read a well-researched book that elegantly bridges the gap between community building and marketing. *Unfair Mindshare* not only provides an effective framework, but also provides marketers with a practical toolset to comprehend and implement a community-led approach. Congratulations to Derek for crafting such a comprehensive, captivating, and invaluable guide. If you're a marketer contemplating long-term demand generation and community strategies, make this book your next read!"

> —**Ann Longley**, FRSA, Digital Strategist
> and Community Lead,
> Something New Together

"Derek Weeks' *Unfair Mindshare* is a game-changer. His unique integration of community-led marketing with traditional product and brand strategies offers business leaders a fresh, significant edge. This is a must-read for any marketing or sales leader looking to drive exponential growth."

> —**Scott Stockton**, Chief Revenue Officer,
> CTO.ai

"*Unfair Mindshare* is a rich compendium of insights for anyone striving to build thriving communities. Derek Weeks' experience and understanding of the intersection between marketing and community building is unmatched. As someone who's been in the trenches of community leadership, I highly endorse this comprehensive guide."

— **Heather Foeh**, Sr. Director, Customer
Marketing & Communities,
6sense

"Derek is my reliable guide in the tsunami of marketing trends, leading me back to the solid shores of genuine interactions and relationships. His experiences, born from a commitment to bold action, reshape marketing possibilities. *Unfair Mindshare* is a testament to his innovative approaches, providing readers with pragmatic blueprints to enrich their marketing strategies and drive tangible results."

— **Eric Bourget**, CEO & Founder,
HalfSerious

"Derek Weeks masterfully illustrates the power of vibrant communities in driving business growth in this book. Through rich examples and insights, he underscores the vital role of customer education and community engagement in the modern market. As companies reconsider their strategies, *Unfair Mindshare* stands as an essential guide for those seeking a competitive edge. It's not just a book; it's a key reference highlighting the synergy between community and success."

— **Adam Monago**, CMO/Founder of Monago Digit
and Head of Marketing,
JRI-Poland

"*Unfair Mindshare* is the catalyst for driving transformative marketing strategies. Derek Weeks' compelling guide has armed me with invaluable tactics to elevate our marketing game. If you're a marketing leader focused on excellence, this is your next essential read."

— **Elizabeth Irvine**, VP Marketing,
MarketMuse

"Derek Weeks taps into a profound insight that often eludes B2B tech marketers and executives—communities are far more than fervent fanbases, casually formed or serendipitously discovered, that boost brands from good to great or mediocre to good. Rather, community development and engagement is a vital, strategic endeavor that belongs at the core of marketing, not at its edges. Dive into *Unfair Mindshare* and seize not only immediate insights that can transform your next conversation, but also strategic understanding that will shape your marketing success for years to come."

— **Phil Gomes**, Chief Communications
& Marketing Officer,
Bloq

"Derek Weeks catapults us onto a thrilling journey of building a 100,000-member professional community. Through *Unfair Mindshare*, he unveils the synergy of community, brand, and product marketing that supports 10x growth. If you're a marketing leader, this book is your shortcut to understanding next-level strategies."

— **Barb VanSomeren**, Partner & CMO,
Health Mavens and Co-host,
The Marketing Share Podcast

"In *Unfair Mindshare*, Derek Weeks reframes community-led marketing with vibrant case studies and practical playbooks. In this increasingly transactional, automated world, he shows us how to cultivate the best of human behavior in modern software development and innovation: the desire to learn, engage, and help others. This book is a powerful beacon for marketing leaders seeking to build true brand affinity and drive exponential business growth."

— **Tanya Loh**, Chief Marketing Officer,
Forgepoint Capital

CONTENTS

ACKNOWLEDGEMENTS

Maya Angelou once proclaimed, "There is no greater agony than bearing an untold story inside you." Since the inception of this endeavor, I realized there was a tale within me, yearning for release. Through a relentless journey, and countless hours at the keyboard, it has now found its way to paper.

This was no solitary journey, though. It kicked off many years ago in the early days of my marketing career. Numerous experiences and influencers from those moments now permeate the pages of this volume. All said and done, there's a particular group of individuals who command special acknowledgment.

First in line is my family. Rosie, Natalie, and Connor, your constant cheers and encouragement echoed even in my moments of silent writing. Lexie, our lovable Labradoodle, you taught me the art of pause—reminding me to stand up—now and again to go and play a game of fetch.

Next comes Mark Miller, a confidant, a dear friend. His insights on community-centric initiatives changed my perspective on the power of relationships that can build something monumental. The trails we blazed at Global 360, Sonatype, and The Linux Foundation, made for an amazing ride.

Pivotal amongst those who deserve acknowledgement are my friends from across the industry and colleagues at Sonatype and who along with me, served as the stewards of All Day DevOps. Shannon Lietz, James Wickett, Karthik Gaekwad, Ernest Mueller, and Andi Mann. I tip my hat to you all for believing in the vision and jumping in early to help.

Then there's the remarkable Sonatype team, encompassing Gary Bean, Paul Bosco, Alexis Del Duke, Jessica Dodson, Michelle Dufty, Janie Gelfond, Dessie Harvey, Katy Hiller, Ericka Houlihan, Shannon King, Nikki Mejer, Johnna Smith, Chip Stuart, Elissa Walters, and many more—including and Eric Bourget, Clara Charbonneau, Mary Simpkins, Jenn Sherman, Amy Talley, and Dan Whiting—who remained steadfast in their pursuit of greatness. Their unwavering faith transformed the dream of All Day DevOps into a resounding reality. Through their dedication, over 100,000 individuals were touched and inspired, profoundly reshaping our perspectives on what's truly possible.

My close friend and guide, Matt Howard, with his profound marketing acumen, deserves special mention. His insights and coaching were paramount to the success of numerous go-to-market initiatives we embarked upon, including All Day DevOps. Matt embodies the essence of leadership, where it's all about inspiring others, empowering people to become architects of change, and crafting a legacy that benefits future generations."

To the devoted crew at Global 360—Kathleen Tassa, Jennifer Troxell, Debbie Rosen, and David Kammerdeiner, thank you. You were the linchpins in a transformative movement that caught the attention of an indusry—all within a breathless eight-week stretch—and sparked an incredible community movement. That milestone, deeply etched in the annals of my professional journey, owes much to your tireless dedication.

Community leaders, take a bow! Kathleen Booth, her community endeavors, a guidebook of inspiration. Matt Heinz and Latane Conant, their relentless efforts are the heart and soul of the CMO Coffee Talk communities and continue to push the boundaries of community-led success. Jim Shilts, his mastery in marrying community-led initiatives with sales success, was a revelation to witness and write about. Jared Robin, his wisdom was the catalyst to a deeper understanding of community-led success measures.

Gianna Whitver and Maria Velasquez, the pillars of the Cybersecurity Marketing Society. Their journey is a testament to their grit and vision, rewarded by so many community connections.

To the scribes, the artists. Lynn Scheurell, an editor par excellence. Her touch polished *Unfair Mindshare* from good to unforgettable. Melissa Schmidt, the graphic design maven. Her deft talents gave this book and its brand a new face.

Guiding hands and sharp minds: Christopher Justice, Tanya Loh, and Bob London. Their insights were the stars guiding my way to a completed manuscript.

And lastly, a toast to Metallica and Philz coffee. Their rhythm and aroma were my constant companions on this journey.

Inspired by true stories and marketing triumphs.

UN
FAIR
MIND
SHARE

We're Not Reinventing Marketing

"Let them in. It's dark outside."

"How many of them are out there?"

"At last count, 35,000 people."

"Then, let's give them what they came for."

The massive crowd wasn't coming to see us. Instead, they were there to uplevel their skills, meet new people, and find inspiration. A while back, we noticed our community did not have a good place to gather so, working with a couple of friends, we built them a forum. Once we opened the doors, the community created an amazing experience for themselves.

With the help of several colleagues and friends, two people within our marketing team energized a vast community that would transform how software was created by thousands of businesses. The community provided a forum for people to learn, connect, and grow. That forum attracted more than 30,000 people each year for six years running. And our work in this community helped our business achieve unfair mindshare.

Building that community was less about luck and more about doing something audacious. One of the critical elements in our approach that helped us achieve this massive scale was something savvy marketing leaders have employed for years: We focused on *them*, not us.

Working on community-led marketing efforts was familiar to me. As a marketing leader for large and small software businesses, I had been evolving these concepts for over three decades (and continue to do so). I had come to realize that the combination of product, brand, and community efforts led to better marketing outcomes.

Product and brand marketing attracted audiences that were already looking for solutions. Community-led marketing introduced a new scale of reach and participation within a market.

In building and participating in communities, we made several discoveries, including that:

- Being helpful became a viral accelerator,
- Demand generation and brand awareness reached higher peaks,
- Our knowledge of the market and buyers compounded, and
- Our influence reached the escape velocity required to catapult our businesses from a market participant to a market maker.

Community-led marketing helped us achieve unfair mindshare.

Being helpful became our viral accelerator.

As a Chief Marketing Officer (CMO), imagine the scenario of bringing a new vibe to marketing your employer's company. Everyone from the Chief Executive Officer (CEO) to the head of sales to the engineering team raves about the work marketing does in growing visibility and audience. Marketing transcends from being the ugly cost center that spends lavishly on overly promotional content to delivering the fuel that boosts business into a high orbit of performance.

Even more, imagine your reputation in the industry likewise skyrocketing because of your marketing strategies and initiatives. The community is buzzing. Competitors are wondering how you did it. And company board members are bragging about your moves to their peer investor community.

That has been my experience. As a CMO, I've taken a less-traveled road that others were afraid to take or were unaware was available to them, and that path made all the difference.

Every B2B start-up or scale-up CMO dreams of capturing enormous attention in their markets, and while some have achieved it, others run into challenges along the way. They share stories of their products, company, and people thousands of times, but their words don't resonate as much as they'd hoped with target audiences. The hooks they crafted to grab attention just don't hook. The company's growth is good, but could be better. The marketing team expends tremendous energy, but the momentum doesn't meet stakeholders' expectations. The plan was to achieve the escape velocity to zoom their business beyond the competition, but that dream never materialized.

CMOs are supposed to be experts in gaining the market's attention, and failing to do so attracts the wrong kind of attention inside their businesses. More often than not, their teams emphasize products and features over customer value, use cases, and desired outcomes. It can leave a CMO frustrated and exhausted. They were shooting for the moon, but got stuck in low-earth orbit.

This book is not about scrapping marketing as you know it. Instead, as a CMO, marketing leader, or head of community, this book will help you approach community-led marketing as a 1 + 1 = 3 strategy. In fact, you'll continue with the tried-and-true marketing and demand-gen efforts you are already pursuing, then add a community layer to be most effective.

There are incredible books already available that focus on building and running communities. However, those books don't do enough to tie the community efforts back into the rest of the marketing engine you are responsible for running as a CMO. Their position often approaches community efforts

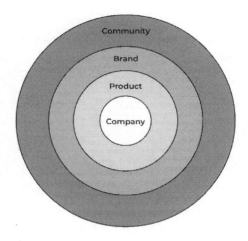

as an island. This book differs in that it's about integrating the marketing you're responsible for across three orbits: Product, brand, and community.

Blending product demand, brand, and community-led approaches at different businesses have helped marketing leaders, as well as myself, to generate unfair mindshare, accelerate growth, and transform the value of marketing for our employer companies.

Throughout this book, you'll read stories from my experiences in growing communities as part of an overall marketing strategy. You'll also read experiences from others who have advanced practices for community-led marketing, including companies and communities like 6sense, All Day DevOps (ADDO), CMO Coffee Talk, Chef Software, Cognism, CommonRoom, Commsor, Cybersecurity Marketing Society, End User SharePoint, Global 360, Heinz Marketing, The Linux Foundation, Lululemon, North American DevOps Group (NADOG), Pavilion, RevGenius, Salesforce, Sonatype, and Yoder Smokers.

You'll get to meet CMOs and community leaders like Jono Bacon, Kathleen Booth, Marc Cluet, Latane Conant, Alice de Courcy, Heather Foeh, Leslie Greenwood, Matt Heinz, Carrie Melissa Jones, Gene Kim, Erica Kuhl, April MacLean, Mark Miller, Jake Randall, Jared Robin, Rosie Sherry, Jim Shilts, Adrian Speyer, David Spinks, Scott Stockton, Gianna Whitver, and Mary Thengvall.

Pursuing product demand, brand, and community leads to better outcomes for CMOs. Combining these three elements will enable you to understand more about your markets and ideal customers. You'll have expanded access to data about the communities you serve. Enriched, relevant, and meaningful content will be developed, and its reach will surpass any of the traditional approaches you have taken previously. When demand, brand, and community initiatives combine, marketing becomes an even more exciting and rewarding career.

If you are not familiar with community-led marketing, you'll read detailed stories of leaders achieving successful outcomes for their businesses. You'll learn about a framework of three marketing orbits to help you understand how products, companies, and communities can be integrated into a common marketing motion for greater bottom-line returns.

Beyond storytelling, you'll get practical guidance on organizing community-led marketing in your team. We'll cover how to position, integrate, and budget for it. Sample playbooks will reveal how community-led efforts drive massive participation and build unfair mindshare while enhancing your core demand-generation practices. Finally, like all modern marketing approaches, we'll walk through various ways to measure the impact and report on community-led initiatives to help inform and sustain year-over-year investments.

You'll discover how to avoid common traps if you are new to community-led marketing. Traditional marketing approaches don't work the same when working in the community-led orbit, so we'll review some guardrails that can help keep your business and people in good favor. Furthermore, you'll find a simple model to help you assess the health of your community-led efforts.

B2B marketing is a competitive sport. You are either vying for attention in crowded markets or trying to drum up interest in the earliest stages of a new market segment. Over the past thirty years, as a four-time CMO and VP of Marketing, I have always sought the most efficient ways to rise above the noise, capture attention, and gain unfair mindshare over the competition. As a result, my successes include leading marketing initiatives that transformed companies lost among the noise within crowded markets into industry leaders that became top of mind. I co-founded and operated one of the largest communities for software development professionals. And I also led grassroots community-marketing efforts that captured the global attention of markets within a couple of weeks.

In my experience, one of the best ways to generate lasting impact in markets is to embrace the communities being served. Deep empathy with members of those communities, along with the knowledge, inspiration, and connections they seek, led my teams and me to combine traditional demand-generation and community-led approaches in a way that became the envy of our peers. We won industry awards for the work. We grew our businesses and accomplished favorable business outcomes through strategic acquisitions along the way.

More importantly, our work felt more meaningful. It was a blast coming to work every day. Our marketing teams were respected not only by our colleagues, but by our communities at large. So much so that our efforts led IT leaders, software developers, business executives, cybersecurity pros, academics, channel partners, and industry influencers to join our efforts as people who were going after the same thing—to build better and stronger communities for our industry.

The stories told and lessons shared in this book are legendary. Those who worked in them typically reflect upon them in two ways: *"What an incredible ride"* and *"I still have to pinch myself that that was real."* The approaches we took were simple, yet calculated for specific outcomes as success, and revealed common patterns of engagement and practice.

When you turn the page, you'll move through an adventure of how we produced the world's largest online community conference in just 75 days. It took the leadership of two colleagues, a small budget, and five industry friends to kickstart this community—and eight years later, it is still actively running and contributing to the industry.

CHAPTER 1

How We Built Unfair Mindshare

It's 2:59 AM. The sky outside is pitch black. Seven of us are in the office, and there is a definite buzz. In a few seconds, we would open our doors to 13,451 people.

When we kicked off the project just 75 days ago, none of us imagined this many people would show up. Our goal was to bring 1,000 people together.[1] We surpassed that milestone a month back.

"3. 2. 1. We're going live now," Mark said.

The dream of an All Day DevOps (ADDO) community came together. After that, there was no turning back. Over the next 15 hours, our small team would help thousands of people in 52 countries across our community learn more about new approaches to modern software development.

The community was not just showing up as an audience to a large production—they were participating as the main actors in the performance. Fifty-four people in the community volunteered to educate an industry by sharing their experience, producing 54 presentations, and recording over 30 hours of educational content. Thousands of others would share their experiences in the community Slack workspace.

In the Beginning

In the 18 months before going live on air for the ADDO virtual conference, my colleague, Mark Miller, and I had traveled to, participated in, and sometimes spoken at over 40 conferences and community meet-ups in the DevOps arena.[2] At these events, attendees were sharing knowledge and soaking in information.

In addition, leading-edge software engineering teams were learning to transition from traditional waterfall development to DevOps practices. Engineering teams in the community were trying to figure out how to transform their practices and tooling from one or two waterfall-style software releases yearly to ten (or more) deployments daily. Those who had achieved it were in small teams within Amazon, Netflix, or Etsy. Everyone else was eager to learn how to do it too.

In *Crossing the Chasm*[3] terms, we were in the early days of the market where innovators and technology enthusiasts thrived. Few practitioners existed in this space, but many people talked about it. Meet-ups in Detroit or Dallas might bring twenty people together for an evening. The most prominent conferences in this burgeoning arena attracted 600 to 800 people.

DevOps people were our community, our tribe. Traveling allowed us to meet many people and begin establishing relationships that would become critical later. We became good friends with people like John Willis, Damon Edwards, James Wickett, Nathen Harvey, Patrick Debois, and Gene Kim, who were there from the community's earliest days. We also met relative newcomers in the DevOps scene like Shannon Lietz, Paula Thrasher, Courtney Kissler, and Andi Mann. The "hallway track" (where people meet between sessions) at these conferences was abuzz with information, best practices, and newly forming friendships.

While on the road, we were able to exchange perspectives with others in the community and contribute to the overall uplift in the market. Mark and I learned from those we met, they learned from us, and we shared our knowledge from the presentation stages to reach the greater audience in attendance. The more time we spent with the community, the more we realized what people wanted and how they would learn and benefit from a more deliberate, cohesive community.

Two Patterns Emerged

After some time on the nascent circuit, the cities and conferences would change, but the roster of speakers, leaders, and thought provocateurs was more familiar each time. That was the first pattern that emerged—we shared the same story repeatedly as we met with different local communities.

The second pattern came in meeting people from companies like Disney, Intuit, Oracle, Walmart, and Lloyds of London. The conversations would go something like this.

"It's great meeting you. How many colleagues are you here with?"

"There's just two of us."

"How many people are in your DevOps practice or software engineering team?"

"Oh, there are about 700 of us in total."

Was this the best way to facilitate learning? Two people flew to some distant city, attended a conference with valuable, relevant, and leading-edge content, absorbed all they could in the time they had, and reported on what they had learned to 698 colleagues when back in the office. Something in this formula needed to be fixed. It was simply not efficient for the knowledge exchange within a community focused on scaling software engineering to never-imagined heights in practical terms. In an ideal world, all team members needed to attend these learning events if their companies were invested in moving the DevOps needle.

The Need for a More Inclusive Community

One thing that rings true of all in-person conferences and community gatherings is that they were *exclusive* experiences. In the tech industry, only a couple of software engineers at each company would ever get a travel and conference budget approved. For tens, hundreds, or thousands of others at their firm, reading a conference summary email from a colleague or stumbling upon a blog was the only opportunity they had to learn about this rising new world order.

Altogether, the significant efforts in producing an event and bringing people together were building a community, but the impact on the industry was too gradual.

Mark and I came up with a different approach. We imagined the opportunity on a different scale.

"Mark, what if we assembled the people who we've met on the conference speaking circuit and brought them together for an online conference?" I asked him.

"We could educate everyone in the world on this stuff."

That was our originating idea—it was just that simple. Do something more for the community in which we were active and interested members.

Mark was all in. We established our mission. We were out to educate anyone who wanted to learn more about DevOps. We didn't know how many people were seeking knowledge in space, but we could feel the industry's energy coming alive. Interest in the topic was growing every day. And we wanted to include anyone in any role who wanted to learn more about DevOps.

We also recognized that, with the global population connected online and in social media channels, people who were once siloed could now self-organize into communities of interest without being restricted by geography or other limitations. In this case, all they needed was a way to facilitate connections and a forum in which to gather.

Develop the Plan and the Promise

Back when Microsoft's SharePoint had achieved massive interest in the market, Mark and some friends organized a "follow-the-sun" conference hosted online featuring speakers and an audience worldwide. He brought know-how on how to engage a global community with our mission. That was the inspiration for ADDO that came to me for this burgeoning DevOps community.

Admittedly, I initially thought of having about ten speakers online for a few hours. Mark was always one to think bigger...much bigger. Over the next few months, we refined our vision and planned to build something amazing. Because ADDO would be a significant undertaking, we would need help.

The best place to search for talent to build and lead a community forum would be from within the community itself. The relationships we had built over the past 18 months elevated our posture. The net result is that we enlisted the help of five friends (Andi Mann, James Wickett, Karthik Gaekwad, Ernest Muller, and Shannon Lietz) from the industry and shared our vision with them. They bought into the concept and agreed to help us produce a new forum for our community.

On November 15th, we would bring together 54 speakers over 15 hours across 15 time zones. The concept was simple. The forum ground rules were simple.

- It's online.
- It's free.
- No vendor pitches allowed.

The digital venue meant that, no matter where an attendee lived or worked, that person could join with an internet connection—no flights, hotel rooms, or travel budget needed.

It was free because we wanted no barriers to entry—no credit card or budget approval was required. No vendor pitches were allowed because they were a turn-off for any crowd. No one wants to sit through 15 hours of pitches for products or services. People wanted to learn, not hear from someone schlepping products. At the time, nearly every conference hosted across the community allowed vendor pitches in some form; we had to be explicit that our community conference was different.

We set these ground rules out of respect for the community. We were building the kind of conference that people in the community wanted; these ground rules helped establish our brand promise to the community.

Unlike large organizations that run events as their business, we wouldn't need to operate by the same rules. We would be online from the beginning, so we didn't need to sell tickets or vendor sponsorships to cover the cost of staff, food, union workers, or venue rental. We would be online from the beginning, like Mark's previous "follow-the-sun" conference.

There was no expectation that we would promote the community conference as a corporate thing. Of course, there could be corporate and/or personal benefits that would come from association with the conference, as our employer connections were obvious. However, we insisted our companies not be front and center because we were building this community for the people of the community. It was about them, not us.

Our previous community-led experiences showed us that our corporate brand(s) would benefit in the long run when we treated the community members right. Building a new community forum would expose our employer to a more significant portion of the market—a portion of which might become future customers. In addition, the more time our team spent with the community, the more we could learn and use in refining our approach to the market.

Fund the Effort and Organize the Team

To support ADDO, we invested in resources like a website, a community channel, digital promotions, a basic community tech stack, and word of mouth to support our work in the community.

Mark and I adopted principles from our past work together when managing the community. For example, one of the ground rules of community-led marketing was to minimize the promotion of any company brands and outbound marketing that might conflict with the community's interests. We knew when we focused on our community's interests, the time and relationships we invested in would help build an affinity for the company where we worked.

Wave 1 of Community Growth — Announcing Our Intent

Influence came in waves, and the first one hit the shoreline on September 1st—at t-minus 75 days.

To pull off the conference, we needed 54 speakers. The seven core organizers put the word out on our personal social channels, and we listed the call for papers on papercall.io. Incredibly, we had our first speaker submission that same day. Woot!

Then something strange happened. People came to us saying, *"This looks like a great idea. How can I register for the conference?"*

"Register?" we were thinking. *"For what?"*

At that time, we had a concept for a community conference and a date to host it. There were no speakers, no agenda, and no way to register for it. We had planned to get a decent pool of speakers and an agenda together before promoting the conference.

We should have thought further ahead, but we weren't event management pros. We were just a small band of people trying to do something good for our tribe. But we learned quickly, and we were nimble.

We didn't have a conference website, so Mark put up an Eventbrite widget on alldaydevops.com that asked for an email address. It could not have been more bare bones. We informed any visitor to the site that we would email them in October (about six weeks in advance of the conference date) once we had more information about confirmed speakers.

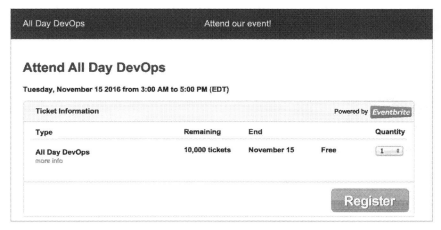

When our community event was barely out of its ideation stage, people wanted to register. We quickly placed an Eventbrite widget on our website to capture interest.

By mid-September, 80 people had registered.[4] This first wave of interest caught our attention—we were on to something big. While we were more concept than a conference, more than 300 people had registered to join us by the end of September.[5] The value registrants recognized was tangible: The community was building something for itself.

It was time to build a website.

Wave 2 of Community Growth — Email Blasts

Our creative agency turned around the site design in four days, and it went live on day five. It was a simple site. All it needed to say was 54 speakers, 15 hours, online, free, and no vendor pitches. The agency picked an open source picture of a young boy screaming into a microphone to represent our ADDO brand.

On October 10, at t-minus 60 days, we started promoting the first 20 speakers our team had selected to attract more attention. The next day, the company where we worked, Sonatype, sent its first email promoting the conference and encouraging people to register. The company was playing its part in helping get the word out about our community conference. Then came our next amazing surprise...

The first email our team sent for ADDO triggered hundreds of registrations. In any career, there are days that are rare and truly special—that day was one of them. It started like a typical day, and then *boom*—instant validation of

The original website for the ADDO community conference showcased our mascot, a screaming boy named "Bobby."[6]

our work. Even though we thought we were onto something, the email response was much higher than we initially imagined possible. We were already making a foothold into something significant and worthwhile.

By mid-October, we were 45 days into our 75-day journey. Our original goal of 1,000 registrants had been surpassed as one thousand six hundred people had registered.[7] We were in unknown territory. This was the first time anyone in our industry had ever put together something of this scale, and there was still a month of potential registrations ahead.

Wave 3 of Community Growth — Calling CMO Peers

By relying only on our small band of five external community members and the support of our company, ADDO might have been perceived as another corporate event. We had to reach beyond our circle for help in getting the word out. It became obvious and relatively easy to look for a couple of community sponsors.

Having crossed paths and built connections at events over the past two years with several DevOps industry CMOs, I called on five of them. None of us competed with one another directly on the technology side of things, but all our firms served the community in some way.

I explained we were assembling an online community conference to educate as many people in DevOps roles as possible. Their buy-in was swift and they agreed to help us spread the word. For each of them, we would add their company logo to the ADDO website to recognize their community support.

By October 20th, at t-minus 40 days, 2,700 people had now registered.

The Internet Broke

To continue the adventure, at t-minus 24 days from our *online* community conference, with thousands planning to attend, something went wrong.

"The internet is down on the entire eastern seaboard of the United States. We're all in the dark," Mark said.

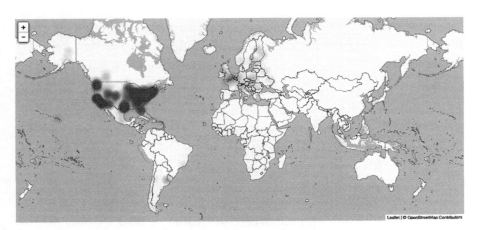

A map of internet access areas experiencing problems tied to a significant botnet attack on October 21, 2016, and featured in The New York Times. ©OpenStreetMapContributors.[8]

Simultaneously, we all thought, *"This is not good. With no internet, we have no ADDO."*

That was the day when Mirai malware compromised 55,000 IoT devices to trigger a massive, distributed denial of service attack (DDoS).

We took it personally. Here we had invited everyone to the start of a big online community, and there was no internet. We were dead in the water.

Fortunately, regular internet service resumed later that day. But for the time between realizing the internet had broken and its return to service, it was a white-knuckle feeling. We had no backup plan for a major region of the internet going down. Access to everyone was only feasible if the internet worked.

Wave 4 of Community Growth — Engaging the Locals

It started over breakfast. Mark and I were attending a conference in London on October 20th when he had an epiphany. He looked at me and asked:

"Would we be doing anything differently today if we wanted 15,000 people to participate in ADDO?" [9]

I thought for a couple of seconds and responded.

"Yes."

At that time, we had just shy of 3,000 registrations. Mark's epiphany was to grow that number by FIVE times—in the next 25 days! Imagine how insane that sounded! Simple mental math showed we would need many more friends to help us spread the word.

As luck would have it, the DevOps London meet-up group would host an event at the conference later that day. We knew Marc Cluet, who headed that community, and he was at the event. We met up with Marc, told him about the community conference, and asked if he could help us get the word out. Like us, the London DevOps meet-up was trying to help people in the community learn from one another. As members of the same global community, we had a common mission.

> ## Community is not about the actions of a select few. Community is about the motion of many.

The London DevOps meet-up had about 5,000 members at that time. Marc committed to spreading the word about ADDO at his evening event as well as sharing information about the conference via his email list.

That sparked the next wave of effort from the ADDO organizing team. We built unfair mindshare by working symbiotically with local communities that benefited as much as ADDO did. We reached out to stakeholders in the community who ran meet-ups or had a following in the DevOps arena.[10] We asked our friends at the Open Web Application Security Project (OWASP) for help. We also asked several groups to help promote the conference: London's Continuous Delivery meet-up, the DevOps Norway meet-up, Atlanta's Java User Group community, Agile Orlando, Cloud Austin, Devopsdays Kansas, and Devopsdays Berlin. Industry friends from SOASTA, Perfecto Mobile, Cloud 66, Contino, Modev, Newt Global, and others also joined to help us spread the word.

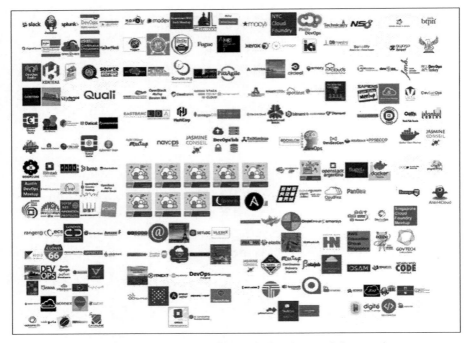

Community groups worldwide helped spread the word about free DevOps education for all. Groups helping out had their logos featured on ADDO's community website.[11]

The value of this growing community value came from offering access to free, high-quality speakers from around the world. For example, if you were running a DevOps community meet-up in Las Vegas, you might need help attracting top-name or geographically distant speakers to your local events. With ADDO, they could offer their local community more expertise at no cost. Placing a community meet-up logo on the ADDO site was a small gesture of gratitude and showed the wide span of interested organizations.

With the help of these industry friends, by November 6th, registrations jumped over the 6,000 mark with community members representing over 52 countries. We were at t-minus nine days. Registrations were pouring in at 250 per day. If that continued, we might have a chance of hitting 10,000 participants.

Wave 5 of Community Growth—Getting the Parties Started

Word of mouth was key to increasing registrations. Our promotions in late October had encouraged people to register themselves and then register their teams. We were looking for opportunities to serve the "other 698" people from those companies who typically send two or three employees to a conference. The good news is that people will find a way to get together even when you have no venue. That became apparent with one pivotal phone call.

An industry friend, Andre (his name has been anonymized), reached out to me. He was a software engineer at a large U.S. bank encouraging their teams to learn more about DevOps practices. Andre was not an executive from the business. Rather, he was a quiet engineer, always looking for new opportunities to learn. And he was calling me with an idea.

"Would you mind if our bank broadcast the ADDO community conference in auditoriums in our New York, Austin, and Seattle offices? We want all our software engineers to participate."

"That would be awesome! Yes, please," I said.

"Do they all need to register?" he asked.

"Officially, no," I said.

Shortly after this call, Mark Miller posted about a similar community effort in our ADDO conference Slack workspace:

"33 people just registered for a viewing party in London."[12]

The London DevOps meet-up had secured office space to invite their members to watch and discuss the community conference sessions.[13] Even more, community members formed viewing parties, and we encouraged others to do the same.

Devopsdays Cuba, the DevOps meet-up group in Las Vegas, a large insurance company in Dallas, and other parties began to spring up. Large telecom, energy, consulting, electronics, entertainment, and financial services businesses were all encouraging teams of employees to reserve conference rooms, gather, and watch together. Our aim to help the "other 698" in offices world-wide was coming to life.

By November 10th, t-minus six days, ADDO had jumped to over 10,000 registrations.

> *Sidenote:* The viewing parties continued to evolve over the years. By the second year of running the conference, the ADDO website featured over 180 viewing parties.[14] We had even heard of one viewing party at State Farm where they had encouraged over 600 people to participate, sponsoring food, handing out t-shirts, and providing vendor pitch-free content to their software development teams.[15]
>
> A few years later, the same small band of managers at State Farm helped us recruit 4,000 of their IT employees to participate in the conference.[16] Employees could watch together in conference rooms or auditoriums and then discuss what they had learned in a specific session, determining what practices, tools, or lessons they could apply internally. Again, we were enabling self-organized learning on a global scale.

Wave 6 of Community Growth — Encouraging More Involvement

In the first year of running the conference, the idea of viewing parties came late in the organizing process. People were showing up in teams and we wanted to encourage that further. So, we put two plans into action.

First, any company or community meet-up group hosting a viewing party could be listed on the conference site. Some of these viewing parties were private corporate events, which gave those companies visibility for their support of educational opportunities for software engineers. Other viewing parties were open to the public. All we asked was that those parties manage their event registration, so they would know how many folks were showing up in case they would order refreshments for their local community members.

Second, we wanted to understand better how we were reaching the "other 698" at companies. While not all participating companies had over 700 software engineers, we wanted to recognize those organizations helping advance their employees' careers. Our offer: If any company got 20 or more employees to register for the community conference, their company name and logo would be added to the conference website on the "Club 20" page.

CLUB 20

Club 20 members are those who put DevOps first. Over 20 people from these organizations registered for All Day DevOps 2020, and they continue to be active in the community year-round.

If your company has a big DevOps tribe, start planning to get your name on the leaderboard next year.

1ST PLACE	2ND PLACE	3RD PLACE	4TH PLACE
State Farm	Tesco	Sonatype	IBM
502	106	93	82
ATTENDEES	ATTENDEES	ATTENDEES	ATTENDEES

RANK	COMPANY		ATTENDEES	
1	State Farm	StateFarm	2392	CLUB 500
2	Northrop Grumman	NORTHROP GRUMMAN	708	CLUB 500
3	Macquarie	MACQUARIE	443	CLUB 100
4	Keurig Dr Pepper	Keurig Dr Pepper	370	CLUB 100
5	PepsiCo	PEPSICO	298	CLUB 100
6	Sonatype	sonatype	265	CLUB 100
7	TJX	TJX	257	CLUB 100
8	Standard Bank	Standard Bank	221	CLUB 100
9	Walmart	Walmart	206	CLUB 100
10	TCS	TATA CONSULTANCY SERVICES	137	CLUB 100
11	IBM	IBM	128	CLUB 100
12	HCL	HCL	98	
13	Accenture	accenture	97	

Companies with 20 or more employees registered for ADDO were featured on the conference website.[17]

The idea took off. Club 20 sparked a new kind of community-activated behavior.[18] DevOps leaders, managers, and internal champions were now trying to get their businesses on the list. The list reflected company investment in DevOps education for their employees and the recognition that these companies might be worth checking out for future career moves. In a burgeoning market, DevOps skills were hard to find for employers, and those who showed an investment in building talent had an easier time recruiting new employee expertise.

Some of the cool things that came from Club 20 resulted from the champions who made it their mission to activate their employer companies. A friend at a large financial services firm asked his Chief Information Officer (CIO) to invite everyone in the DevOps and developer practice to the conference leading to hundreds of their employees signing up. In another instance, two food and beverage competitors sparked a friendly competition by trying to see who could get more DevOps pros from their businesses participating in the community conference; each encouraged hundreds of colleagues to join in their respective in-house viewing parties.

> **Unfair mindshare was not achieved through a single voice or company.**

Each annual ADDO conference meant featuring large numbers of organizations on the Club 20 leaderboard. The champions not only brought more people into the community, but many were also recognized internally by their companies with, promotions due in part to their ADDO community leadership.

The same was true for community meet-up groups that wanted to encourage greater participation in their local markets. The meet-up leaders would promote the viewing parties in their local areas to encourage more of their members to gather in person for the added benefit of personal networking mimicking the value people find at in-person conferences.

Flip the "Go Live" Switch

It was 2016. TechCrunch had reported[19] that Uber was the world's largest taxi service but owned no cars. Facebook was the world's most popular media owner but created no content. And Airbnb was the world's largest provider of accommodations but owned no real estate.

At the same time, our team at Sonatype—in collaboration with friends in our industry—had created ADDO. We were about to run the world's largest community conference but had no venue. Essentially, we built the community, not by having them come to us, but by delivering an attractive and appealing forum to the community. While the idea of a large-scale virtual conference was replicated—years later—numerous times during the pandemic years, in 2016 no one had done what we were about to pull off.

"Good morning, good day, good evening. Wherever you are, welcome to ADDO."

It was 3:00 AM on November 15th. Total registrations for our community conference hit 13,451. It was time to deliver value to the community.

The community built and delivered the presentation content. The day split into three tracks. Fifty-four speakers from the community would grace our digital stage over the next 15 hours. That day, ADDO community speakers would generate over 30 hours of free educational content for anyone who wanted to learn about DevOps via a range of perspectives, insights, and practical tools.

Tracks were live-streamed, and every session was recorded for binge-watching later. All three conference tracks were moderated by our community organizing leaders in Washington D.C. (me, Mark Miller, Shannon Lietz), Austin (Karthik Gaekwad, James Wickett, Ernest Mueller), and Denver (Andi Mann).

Encouraging Conversations

One of our friends, Chris Corriere, from Atlanta, suggested using Slack for community attendees to chat with one another, meet the speakers, and exchange information. Chris designed a way for community members to jump on the platform by entering their email.

On the day of the conference, countless conversations were initiated in Slack. Every attendee had access to ask questions of every speaker. Every attendee had access to every other person in the community. Questions were answered. New connections were made. Sample code was shared between engineers.

Friendships were formed. The community wasn't just watching . . . people were participating and engaging.

Slack delivered persistence, which was critical to the community-building value of the conference. Communities that build value through content and connection with other members have greater longevity.

After the conference, the conversations and connections on Slack remained there. The community could remain active even when the conference was over. Those who made connections during the conference knew where to find one another again. Slack's search feature enabled them to find people, files, or code.

Persistence meant that value created and shared was preserved.

Unlike physical conferences where people arrive and leave, participants formed lasting relationships and had an ongoing discussion forum. Regardless of location, people could connect.

Slack also brought a second face to the conference. Community members shared selfies from their homes and offices. "Hello," was shared by countless members with their accompanying country flag emoji. No matter where they were, people could see them. Everyone was welcomed and celebrated.

At one point, I remember vividly urging Shannon Lietz from Intuit to get up and take a break from moderating the DevOps security track. But instead, she refused to get up because she was having too much fun. She said, *"Do you know how many connections I am making with brilliant people? I'm not leaving my post. The Slack forum is too good."*

There Was No Exhibit Hall for Sponsors

ADDO was intended to be an educational event for our community rather than a product or company event. One of the three rules for the conference was "no vendor pitches," and we delivered on that promise.

ADDO offered no online exhibit hall for three reasons. First, traditional exhibit halls are rampant with vendor pitches, and the ADDO brand promise was not to allow them. Second, there was no swag to give away. And third, virtual exhibit halls are often impersonal and distract from the actual value of the event as delivered through speakers sharing valuable knowledge and experiences.

Measure Community Success

We were all amazed that year one of the conference community forum attracted so much attention and praise and achieved 13x the original participation target. Post-conference surveys revealed that most community attendees were satisfied with the experience, and nearly every attendee wanted to participate again. The community conference also achieved a significantly higher world-class net promoter score (NPS) than Apple's or Amazon's NPS.

In year two, the conference was expanded from a 15-hour program to a 24-hour format. This allowed registrants to participate in the conference at local reasonable hours, no matter their geography, by going to the 24-hour format. And amazingly, a few folks around the world choose to stay up around the clock for the full 24-hour experience each year.

The 24-hour format also led to a more extensive speaker base and tracks. The conference came to feature 180 speakers annually, which would produce over 90 hours of community-generated content. ADDO would see countless session views of the community content. Attendees would share tens of thousands of message exchanges in the Slack workspace each year.[20] Today, thousands of members continue to participate in the Slack workspace.

Over the next five years, Mark and I continued to organize and run ADDO. The annual conference drew in over 30,000 attendees each year, and our membership swelled to over 100,000.

ADDO provides a great example of building a robust community. Throughout this book, you'll hear many other stories of how teams of people built their community-led efforts. As you read on, you'll learn how to build, organize, execute, integrate, and measure your own community-led initiatives.

As an added bonus for you, at the end of each chapter, I'll share an expert tip. These tips are inspired by real-world experiences and are meant to educate, motivate, or spark an idea. Here's the first one for you.

EXPERT TIP: INVITE OUTSIDERS

When starting a community-led marketing initiative, invite people from outside of your business to take part. If writing a blog, invite others to contribute to or proofread it. If organizing a panel discussion, invite community members to join or ask your community who should sit on the panel. If starting a meet-up in your local area, invite a couple of people from your community to be part of the core organizing committee. When you start with community involvement by default, the thing you build is more likely to resonate with your target audience.

CHAPTER 2

Where CMOs Must Invest in Marketing

A well-known African proverb reads:

> *"If you want to go fast, go alone.*
> *If you want to go far, go together."*

Creating a thriving community embodies that wisdom. It is exhilarating and rewarding. It's also a lot of work and takes a significant time investment. However, more work must be done to extract the maximum value for your business.

This is where the magic lies. As a marketing leader, you'll need to merge community-led initiatives with other marketing and business operations. Just as demand generation or product marketing cannot operate in isolation, community-led marketing must likewise be interconnected with different functions. CMOs who fail to combine community-led marketing efforts with other business areas may struggle to secure the budget and resources needed to sustain their community. The more you integrate community-led efforts with other parts of your business, the more value you can derive from them.

Community-led initiatives can bolster your business's demand generation, content marketing, sales, customer success, product development, and other areas to produce exceptional marketing outcomes. Integration of these endeavors and assessing their results will help support the investments necessary to maintain thriving communities year after year.

> **CMOs who fail to combine community-led marketing efforts with other business areas may struggle to secure the budget and resources needed to sustain their community.**

To help you better understand this integrated marketing approach, I'll introduce you to three orbits in marketing. The most sophisticated B2B marketing teams operate in these three orbits: Product, brand, and community. You can think of the three orbits as marketing maturity levels. Product-led is the most fundamental effort for a marketing team, and as they mature, brand- and community-led initiatives are added into your go-to-market initiatives. Each orbit builds upon the other and is not mutually exclusive.

How CMOs Approach Marketing Today

Every marketing team operates in a product-led orbit. As CMO, you own this orbit. Your business offers products and services, and it is your team's responsibility to promote them. In this orbit, everyone interacting with your marketing efforts is a potential lead, you're always trying to close a deal, and your business controls 100 percent of the narrative. Your website product pages, your demand-gen programs, product announcements, and your product demos all support this motion. Most of your marketing budget and resources are directed here to help the business grow through new and repeat customers.

The next marketing orbit is brand-led. Brand-led marketing efforts promote your company, its customers, and your partners. This orbit helps reassure potential customers that your company is a safe bet. At the same time, it reiterates to your existing customers that they should renew or expand their investments with you. Your user groups, solution architectures, website, partner programs, and portfolio messages operate in this orbit. While you don't control the entire narrative, you often invite participants in this orbit to speak on your behalf, where endorsements can be implicit or explicit. This is an orbit where your team maintains significant control, and as a marketing leader, you generally allocate 10–15 percent of your budget here.

No matter what company, industry, or geography you work in as a marketing professional, you always work in the first two orbits. The go-to-market paths here are well traversed. As we proceed through this chapter, we'll cover the first two orbits in more detail, but the aim of this book is not to educate you on all their nuances. The two orbits are defined here only to help differentiate more easily from the less familiar community-led orbit.

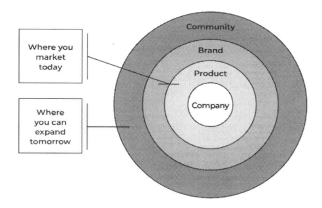

The Leading Edge of Marketing / Orbit 3

First, let's get a quick glimpse into the third orbit of community-led marketing. This is the orbit where you can expand marketing initiatives effectively as you deepen relationships in your industry.

Community-led marketing approaches the furthest bounds of your market where participants share a common interest. Marketing in this orbit is no longer about your company and any products or services it may offer. Community participants are part of your market, but in this orbit they are seeking connections, information, and inspiration. They build relationships, exchange knowledge, and work to level up their skills and experiences.

Here, you don't control the narratives in this orbit as your marketing team's participation shifts from promoting to listening and contributing. Your Orbit 3 team members serve as trusted peers and help facilitate exchanging information and sharing experiences. Participation in this orbit is self-motivated to level up as practitioners and professionals.

The audiences here are also much larger than in lower orbits. Remember, the most significant community-led motions can attract 10x to 1,000x the number of participants seen in the product- and brand-led orbits. Reaching this outer orbit takes time but, overall, can be less costly than lower orbits. CMOs operating in this orbit generally invest 5–12 percent of their budgets in such communities.

Each orbit has unique characteristics that can help you define the orbit you are working in as well as what you need to move into the next successive orbit. You will learn about each orbit's:

- Origin
- Purpose
- Content
- Narratives
- Team roles
- Pace
- Investment profile

We'll cover the community-led orbit in much more detail in the next chapter. For now, let's get into the attributes of the first two orbits.

The Product-Led Orbit / Orbit 1

Every CMO manages a product-led orbit. It is fundamental to any product or service organization that offers a solution to the market. First, you talk about your company and position it in the market. You introduce new products and platforms and show off their latest cool features. Your pitches are filled with statistics that back up why your product or business is a great solution for your market, and you produce logo splash slides revealing all the name-brand customers who purchased from your company.

You Are 100% in Control

You create and manage this marketing orbit for your business. Everyone in the market who visits your orbit is a potential lead that can be further nurtured and qualified. You and your team spend a lot of time figuring out how to highlight and enhance a pain point the company believes its target audience has to solve. You control 100 percent of the narrative here that is detailed in all your positioning decks, creative briefs, and ideal account and customer profiles (IAP and ICP).

Self-Promotion Dominates

This is where your team devotes substantial effort to creating purpose-built content. It is self-promoting by nature and seller-centric. When your buyers want to buy, this is the content that nurtures them through to the finish line. Your webinars, datasheets, website, sales presentations, and corporate podcasts fly around in this orbit. Any business with a potential intent of buying from you will find this content, free or gated, on your site or through personal engagements with your teams or stakeholders.

In addition to purpose-built content driving demand, you might also work for a product-led growth company where product use drives demand. The more people who find your product helpful and tell others in their networks about their experience the more customer and revenue growth will be achieved.

Product-led Marketing (Orbit 1)

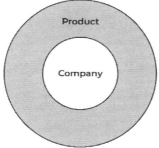

Companies self-create the product orbit to promote and sell their offerings.

Working in product-led orbits is easy because everyone in the company is focused there. Engineering teams are focused on getting new products, features, and user experiences out the door. Product marketing teams are busy collecting market feedback for engineers and detailing what the product does to enable their sales team for better conversations and conversions. Demand-generation teams are busy building the qualified pipeline to hand over to sales. Sales teams are busy selling the products on the price list and the roadmap. Product-led orbits are comfortable because everyone at the company is building, talking about, or selling the same things. As a result, everyone feels like they're on the same page.

Most importantly, this is where every B2B company and its Board measures success or failure. The company sells a product and generates revenue to support continued growth and operations. The degree of profit is the determination and level of success.

How the Market Sees the Orbit

The market sees product-led orbits differently than you do. B2B customers are inundated daily with emails, promotions, and salespeople all pitching their solutions. Every solution will save time, lower costs, and improve business outcomes. For buyers, trying to identify the signal through the noise is a daily challenge. They don't need just the one solution you may offer to get their work done. They are looking for broader, integrated approaches that fit with their people, culture, and processes.

While product-led orbits are comfortable inside corporate walls, competition is fierce in the market. For example, the Marketing Technology Landscape does an annual review of available products. In 2023, martechmap.com represented 11,038 products available to CMOs and their teams for consideration. When every product-led marketing team says faster, cheaper, and better, they are each correct—and they all sound the same. As MarketingProfs Ann Handley recently remarked, *"When we all sound the same, we're invisible. "*

MartechMap an initiative by chiefmartec & MartechTribe

2023 Marketing Technology Landscape   May 2023

Chiefmartec's landscape image for 2023 includes over 11,000 vendors.[21]

visit martechmap.com to search, sort & filter

It Speaks to the Marketer vs. the Buyer

Let's address the elephant in the room. Your product-led marketing teams produce an abundance of content. That content is required to help customers self-educate on your solution. Because too many marketers in this realm don't speak directly with customers and users, there is a disconnect that is apparent in the content. The content conveys the language of the marketer, not the buyer. As such, the buyer is left as the interpreter in the purchase transaction.

Content produced by the company (or produced for the company for a fee) supports the traditional sales cycle, which many, if not most, buyers today view as untrustworthy. They recognize vendors will only mention the good or best things they do. Buyers weave through the exercise, trying to determine what a solution truly does or does not do. And to make things more challenging for potential buyers, your best content in this orbit is often locked behind a form.

> **"Your self-promotion is more
> annoying than you think."
> —Jessica Stillman**

Another way to easily spot marketing teams working in product-led orbits is via company social media channels. Posts resemble billboards for products, webinars, and whitepapers. Your product-led marketers narrowly share blog posts about your product, a new analyst paper featuring your company, or a local event you are hosting. To amplify the message even more, they ask their marketing and sales colleagues to like or share their posts, hoping it can reach an even broader audience—mainly because they have only a few followers who are paying attention. In the words of Jessica Stillman, *"Your self-promotion is more annoying than you think."*[22]

Success Measurements Are Traditional

The measurements for B2B product-led marketers are traditional and rely on numbers. How many people visited a website, downloaded the latest product whitepaper, or tripped enough nurture triggers to convert as a marketing-qualified lead? It's not necessarily about sincere two-way engagement or progressive behavior preferences that refine experience going forward but on how many people elected X asset or took Y action. More mature organizations will track what led prospects further through their pipeline to report on marketing-influenced bookings and win rates.

There is nothing wrong with product-led marketing orbits—all B2B companies and marketing teams play here. It's mandatory as product sales support the heart of your business. You have to talk about yourself sometimes, but, like all things in life, balance and perspective are required. This is where Orbit 2, the brand-led marketing efforts, benefits your business.

	Product-led marketing
Origin	Self-created
Purpose	Promote and sell product
Marketing perspective on the audience	Everyone is a lead Always be closing
Content	Self-created
Narratives	100% control, your voice Less trusted
Who does the work	Your team
Pace	Things move fast Short-lived campaign
Community Perspective	Rent access
Investment Profile	70 – 80% of the budget Near-sighted

Characteristics of Orbit 1 product-led marketing

The Brand-Led Orbit / Orbit 2

You have likely attended sponsored conferences like HubSpot's Inbound, Salesforce's Dreamforce, or even your own company's user conference. The moments created during these events are magical. People meet face-to-face for the first time (or reunited), new connections are (re)forged between employees and customers, branded swag is everywhere, selfies are snapped, and bread is broken as attendees share a meal together. The marketing, customer success, product engineering, and sales teams in the sponsoring companies work their tails off to create an incredible experience for everyone. FOMO (fear of missing out) is real for those people left back at home.

> The *herd effect* is real: Individuals follow others and imitate group behavior rather than deciding independently based on their own information.

Generating Escape Velocity

The energy from your customer and partner community builds the escape velocity from product-led orbits to brand-led orbits. These communities do not spontaneously generate out of the ether; instead, your company purposely builds the community to better promote the business and its brand through the voice of others. The customer and partner participants are handpicked to support your narrative. You invite them to share their perspectives, products, practices, and powerful relationships they've built with you. And you help them with language they can use to describe their experience.

The Herd Effect

The brand-led orbit expands knowledge sharing within your installed base on product best practices and also attracts new partners. Orbit 2 reassures potential customers the value bets they are making on your solution have a more substantial chance of paying off than other solutions because others in the community have chosen your solution and are accompanying them

Brand-led Marketing (Orbit 2)

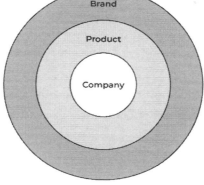

*Companies self-create the brand orbit to promote
their company and product communities.*

on their journey. The *herd effect* is real: Individuals follow others and imitate group behavior rather than deciding independently based on their own information.

Brand-led orbits reinforce all the value statements, benefits, and product features described by your team in Orbit 1. Here, the narrative is not 100 percent controlled by your team, but the acts are scripted and rehearsed. Customers invited to speak on stage at user conferences, during roadshows, webinars, or in case studies do so for a purpose. They've agreed to speak on your behalf, bringing more credibility to your story. Their voice is regarded as more independent and trustworthy than your own, and most importantly, it's viewed as an authentic representation of brand and product value.

Everyone in Orbit 2 knows the customer has had to go through multiple approval hurdles to share their story. The boss, the corporate communications team, the lawyers, and the compliance officers all needed to sign off on the participation ahead of time. So, it is inferred that anyone going through that much effort to tell their story with your brand must truly be convinced of the value your product or service delivers.

Collaborative Content Development Takes Longer

Your brand-led marketing team will need to coach others in the organization about the brand boundaries and guardrails established in an agreement. For example, the content can only be used in certain places, customer logo uses are restricted, and recordings of presentations—if permitted—have parameters set on whom they are shared with and for how long. Case studies that take months to produce due to extensive edits and approval paths strain the timing of your go-to-market plans.

Endorsements are powerful, and they are hard to get. The customer has to be in a good mood, and the product needs to be in solid working order for their business. Complex renewals, product outages, reorganizations, and approval chains can all wreak havoc on securing the needed commitment, and the timing of such requests is almost always a sensitive subject. Most marketers have been there, running the gauntlet to capture the prize.

Content Is More Valuable in This Orbit

The content produced in this orbit is gold. A great customer endorsement is repeated thousands of times in different accounts by sales representatives pursuing their next deal. The best pieces secure prime real estate on your home page, in your blogs, and in corporate videos.

The content produced here is a product of the customer's experience. The less your team prescribes what to say, the more authentic and valuable it will be. For example, a recent Dixa study found 79 percent of customers put as much weight on customer reviews as they do personal recommendations. The study also found, on average, reviews produce an 18 percent uplift in sales.[23]

Brand-Led Orbits vs. Community-Led Growth

You might be reading this with the idea that brand-led orbits are equivalent to what many refer to as community-led growth (CLG) or community-led marketing. However, there are distinct differences worth discussing between the two concepts.

Zapnito.com defines community-led growth as *"the process of turning a product's users into its best advocates, who go on to share their experiences using the said product with their peers. This helps brands in several ways: Promoting a product and recommending it to their peers."*[24]

Other mentions by builtin.com and venture capital firm Greylock tie the product-led growth (PLG) movement to the similarly named community-led growth (CLG) movement. *"The phrase is a play on 'product-led growth,' which is a go-to-market strategy in which companies make their self-serve products the main vehicle for acquiring, activating, and retaining users. Community-led growth 'acts as a multiplier on top of product-led growth,"* wrote Corinne Marie Riley of Greylock.[25] CLG creates a flywheel of active members strengthening the community.

Community-led growth acts as a multiplier on top of product-led growth.

We should not rush to use brand-led and community-led marketing as interchangeable terms. While your brand and community audiences will ideally be similar, this book describes these approaches as different strategies. Here

---

weekstweets ✔
@weekstweets   •••

The talk:
"We have a community-led growth strategy."

The reality:
"The only people we cater to in our 'community' are our customers."

The best marketing teams go beyond their customer base to embrace like-minded members across a broad community.

#marketing #customerledgrowth

In reality, many "community" initiatives are focused on a single company's products and brands.[26]

in Orbit 2, your brand's audience is built upon your ideal customer profile, and your business manufactures the connection to the audience. If your business went away tomorrow, the brand community would go with it. Communication and collaboration in this realm are business-to-customer.

Your Company Created Orbit 2

As we'll explore in the next chapter, community-led marketing is made up of member-to-member interactions. Your company may help facilitate some of those interactions, but your employees and investment are not required to sustain the community. Where your company has built its brand-led orbit and invited others to participate, community-led orbits were created by their members. Your employees can join these communities—and even help facilitate interactions—but the orbits operate best when they reflect the needs of their members.

For example, suppose your company builds solutions to support a form of marketing automation. In that case, you can bolt on a community forum for customers, partners, and prospects to gather and exchange information. But those marketing professionals in your target audience likely rely on more than just your solution for their organization. The global community of marketing professionals (beyond your company's community) has its own needs, with members investing in upleveling their practitioner status and looking for opportunities to gather and connect with like-minded people.

> **Your brand-led community is not the only community your members participate in—it represents only part of their professional world.**

When operating in Orbit 2, remember the following key point. Your brand-led community is not the only community your members participate in—it represents only part of their professional world.

	Brand-led marketing
Origin	Self-created
Purpose	Promote the company
Marketing perspective on the audience	Everyone is a customer Expand after land
Content	Co-create with customers
Narratives	Hand-picked participation More trusted
Who does the work	Your team + customers
Pace	Influence moves slower Longer-lived value
Community perspective	Build forum
Investment profile	20 – 25% of the budget

Characteristics of Orbit 2 brand-led marketing

This is where community-led marketing comes into play. When you harness it in the right way, community-led marketing can unlock massive value, accelerate sales cycles, and distance your business from the competition. More on that in the next chapter . . . first, here is a quick review of brand-led Orbit 2 marketing characteristics.

EXPERT TIP: ENCOURAGE OTHER TO ENGAGE

The most successful brand-led communities focus on getting their customers and partners to engage with one another. The majority of content developed and exchanges shared in these communities originate with their members vs. the employees of your business. Focus your efforts on encouraging the engagement of others rather than measuring how much your own team engages. There is a good reason for this approach. First, when your own engagement outweighs that of the community, the content and exchanges will represent less of the community's voice and more of your company's voice. Second, you can control how much your employees participate, but their participation does not necessarily guarantee the optimal outcome of a community that needs to thrive on its own exchanges.

CHAPTER 3

Launching Community-Led Marketing

In 1997, Steve Jobs shared his enduring wisdom with Apple's community at their Worldwide Developers Conference:

> *"One of the things I've always found is that you've got to start with the customer experience and work backward for the technology. You can't start with the technology and try to figure out where you're going to try to sell it. And I made this mistake probably more than anybody else in this room. And I got the scar tissue to prove it.*
>
> *And as we have tried to come up with a strategy and a vision for Apple, it started with 'What incredible benefits can we give to the customer? Where can we take the customer?' Not starting with, 'Let's sit down with the engineers and figure out what awesome technology we have, and then how are we going to market that?' And I think that's the right path to take."*[27]

The same perspective applies to community initiatives. We must start with questions like *"What incredible opportunity can we provide the community?*

Where can we take the community?" Your answers will be very different than if you started with, *"Let's sit down with the marketing team and figure out what awesome product promotion we have and then how are we going to present it to our community?"*

Just as Jobs suggested an outside-in approach to developing great products, community-building benefits most from this same outside-in perspective.

Orbit 3 is where marketing gets interesting. Part of the reason why is that marketing's reach can be significant. The relationships formed and knowledge exchanged in this orbit can have a long-lasting impact and represent a significant upside for your business.

Regarding go-to-market activities, the initiatives we'll cover here are new territory for many marketing executives. Therefore, we'll spend more time describing the orbit fundamentals before delving into how best to integrate them with your traditional lower-orbit marketing motions.

CMOs whose teams venture into this high orbit can impact their markets more with fewer competitive headwinds. The smartest teams then link efforts in all three orbits to accelerate demand and grow brand awareness.

> ## CMOs whose teams venture into this high orbit can impact their markets more with fewer competitive headwinds.

Marketing strategies in the third orbit expand your business through participation, not promotion. In Orbit 3, your community-led marketers are stewards of a community of interest. This is the superpower of Orbit 3. Community-led marketing initiatives enable you to grow faster, help more people, and distance yourself from the competition by energizing a community of practice.

Before getting into all the characteristics of community-led marketing, let's launch into Orbit 3 by exploring a story about an amazing group of people that meets weekly.

Witness a CMO Gathering

Nearly every Friday morning at 8:00 AM ET, you can find me in the CMO Coffee Talk community call. I've been joining my CMO peers there for more than two years and find incredible value in the conversations, connections, and shared insights. I often listen and occasionally share helpful information when it can add value to the conversation. There are some awesome CMOs on that call each week; that said, we all realize we have more to learn and want to explore opportunities to refine our work and teams.

The CMO Coffee Talk community is a great example to represent Orbit 3 in our story about community-led marketing. For that reason, I'll spend some time talking about that community, its origins, and its purpose. Like the ADDO example, its roots are in the community, but its value stretches across all three marketing orbits.

The Origin of CMO Coffee Talk

CMO Coffee Talk came about through a collaboration between Heinz Marketing and 6sense. Heinz Marketing is an agency that specializes in sales and marketing services that deliver measurable revenue results. 6sense is a company that builds account-based marketing (ABM) software for marketing teams. Both companies offer products and services that are well-regarded in the market, and their businesses have grown rapidly over the past few years. They also have a fantastic customer and partner ecosystem that raves about their experience with the companies, their employees, and their products.

Both teams invest a lot of time, effort, and money in promoting their products and services to their markets. In other words, they are great at product- and brand-led marketing—Orbits 1 and 2. Heinz Marketing and 6sense don't just stop there. They have invested heavily in Orbit 3 community-led marketing.

The origins of the community stemmed from a series of CMO Breakfast events that Matt Heinz had been hosting for years prior to the pandemic. At the beginning of 2020, Heinz Marketing set up a new 10-city CMO Breakfast tour with 6sense as a sponsor. They worked their way through the first eight cities and then the COVID-19 pandemic shut them down.

Like many marketing programs at the time, the CMO Breakfast tour decided to go virtual. They invited CMOs to join them online. They wanted to inspire CMOs to become better at their jobs by sharing information and insights from industry experts and peers. This was the start of the CMO Coffee Talk community.

They could have chosen any of a number of different segments in the marketing industry to start with, but they made a smart move to build a community around the economic influencers in their market: the CMOs.

Heinz Marketing and 6sense set out to create a movement around better education for CMOs. The movement would include inviting subject matter experts to share information while encouraging CMOs to share their experiences within a safe community of peers.

CMOs are given many opportunities to connect in various online and in-person forums, but many have strings attached. Whoever is organizing the effort is always trying to sell some new product or service from their company. Such interactions feel more like an elongated sales call than a community gathering because the sponsors are not truly working in Orbit 3.

Creating a Forum for CMOs to Gather

The CMO community existed but needed better connectors and facilitators. Heinz Marketing and 6sense took it upon themselves to coalesce a community of CMOs who wanted to uplevel their skills through peer relationships and knowledge sharing. Put simply, that is the CMO Coffee Talk community.

There are several different branches of this community forum, including weekly Zoom meetings, the occasional afternoon happy hour, a Slack workspace, specialized meet-ups at industry events, and in-person gatherings.

One of my favorite initiatives in the community is a weekly-hosted forum called the First Sip Club. Every Friday morning, CMOs like me gather on a Zoom call where we discuss a wide variety of topics.

- Your first 100 days as a CMO
- Sales enablement strategies, tactics, and examples that work
- Making marketing attribution work at your company
- Best practices for collaborating with your Chief Financial Officer (CFO)
- Partner marketing best practices
- Understanding equity options, comp package pros and cons
- Modern marketing organization chart trends
- Pricing power—what companies get wrong, who owns it, packaging, and more
- Preventing employee burnout

6sense CMO, Latane Conant, and Heinz Marketing President, Matt Heinz, jointly host the call. The only attendance requirement is that you have to be a CMO. Attendance is free and hosted online, removing any barrier to participation.

Latane and Matt do not create the core content in these weekly CMO calls. The content and information exchanges are produced by its members and invited guest speakers. The content is authentic, personal, and highly trusted because there are no pitches, sponsors, or vendor marketing influences.

The Community Offers Specific Brand Promises

CMO Coffee Talk operates under a few basic promises. The first promise is that the forum is free from vendor pitches. In the two years I have attended the Friday morning First Sip Club, they've never pitched 6sense or Heinz Marketing to anyone as part of this weekly forum. While 6sense and Heinz Marketing are actively pitching ABM solutions and services outside of this forum, those topics are not permitted in our weekly pitch-free zone meetings. It goes against their brand promise to community members.

Second, you don't need to be a 6sense or Heinz Marketing customer. I've never been a customer of theirs, and yet I am welcome to participate every week. For the CMOs who have joined, it's a family, a therapy group, and a professional collaboration network like no other. The forum allows us to connect, share insights, and ask questions in a confidential, trusted environment.

Third, First Sip Club meetings are never recorded to ensure greater trust in the community. What happens in First Sip Club stays in First Sip Club.

Fourth, everyone is encouraged to participate. The meetings almost always feature a guest speaker from the community or industry. The speaker initiates the topic with a 10-minute talk sharing their perspective, and then the conversation opens up to the group. Attendees ask questions and the guest answers as well as other attendees. A flurry of chat messages is exchanged. It's amazing. Like-minded people are sharing knowledge, experiences, and helpful content with others trying to level up in their profession—not to mention the frequent virtual high-fives and laughs.

Beyond the weekly calls, members can reach each other in a unique CMO-only channel in the community Slack workspace (b2b-cmo-roundtable. slack.com). Helpful slides and strategies are shared there in a "swipe-file." Book and blog recommendations are shared in a "reading list." Even charities are supported in a "CMOs-give-back" channel. In addition, the Slack workspace fosters persistence—offering a location where CMOs can connect outside of the Friday First Sip Club meetings.

6sense and Heinz Marketing do not talk about their companies in the First Sip Club. As ADDO did for DevOps pros, they did not create the population of CMOs who exist around the world, but they play an essential role in the community. They provide a platform for CMOs to gather, share, build peer relationships, and help one another. With this comes the benefit of relationships—they build trust within their community by being helpful. I'm sure they also win more business with CMOs because of their role in bringing the community together.

The CMO Coffee Talk community constantly gives and provides while asking nothing in return—other than encouraging all its members to participate even if that means simply tuning in to listen regularly.

CMO Coffee Talk is not the only marketing community I participate in, but it is among the very best and most active. Although I still listen to podcasts, read books, attend industry conferences, and join local meet-ups to stay current, CMO Coffee Talk is community-led at its heart. That makes a huge difference in where I spend my time and build relationships.

CMO Coffee Talk is a terrific example of community-led marketing. We'll use the rest of this chapter to dive into Orbit 3's attributes and dynamics.

Shift Your CMO Mindset

In Orbit 3, we marketers must shift our mindset from creation to participation, which sometimes means facilitation as well.

Kathleen Booth, SVP of Marketing and Growth at Pavilion, summarized community participation nicely when she said the following:

"Lots of people talk about community-led growth, but few companies know how to do it. I'm not talking here about building your own community— although that can be a very effective strategy. I'm talking about leveraging communities that already exist to drive demand for your product or service.

No, it is not enough to simply sponsor a community.

No, it is not enough to just do webinars.

No, it is not enough to post promotional offers within community chats.

No, it is not enough to sponsor that community's events.

All these things are valuable, but they are pieces of a larger puzzle. Community-led growth is 'organic.' To make it work, you need to be a true member of the community, not just a sponsor or a partner. Your team should be in the community alongside other members, participating in conversations and being helpful, with a 'give-first' mentality.

Most companies won't do this because it's a long game. This is all the more reason why those who do it well will be the ones whose brands get mentioned and who get the 'at bats'."

Orbit 3 community-led marketing requires you to think of yourself first as gathering, supporting, and empowering people to be active. In this orbit, you are not a primary creator of content people will consume. Instead, you are a facilitator of connections and trusted conversations. Sometimes, you are a content creator; other times, you are a cheerleader of content creation. It's less about you engaging with your community and more about members of the community engaging with each other.

> **Sometimes, you are a content creator; other times, you are a cheerleader of content creation.**

The smartest marketing leaders not only play a leading role in their external communities but also connect their Orbit 3 motions with internal initiatives. They build feedback loops that help others in the company better understand what is happening in the market. They also look for opportunities to connect community-led activities with brand and demand-generation initiatives that support their business' continued growth.

Continue Promoting Your Product and Company

You are not alone if you're telling yourself that pursuing an Orbit 3 community-led marketing initiative feels awkward. Engaging in the market and not talking about your products or services is the antithesis of marketing and everything you've been trained and hired for by your company.

Let's face it: As a CMO, you've made your living promoting and growing your business by following the unspoken mantra: *"Always be pitching."* But if you are honest with yourself, you understand it is more challenging to form trusted relationships in the market when your audience assumes you are only engaging to benefit yourself/your company.

Additionally, your CEO, Chief Revenue Officer (CRO), and Board all want you to be promoting the business to accelerate growth. If no one talks about your business, you'll have no business. The focus is on money now, now, now vs. money now and later.

As mentioned earlier, the best marketing leaders operate in all three orbits. You cannot stop investing in product and company go-to-market initiatives for your business. That would result in the end of your CMO stint. However, the journey of adding a third orbit is about expanding your approach into the market by reaching new people and offering even more value in ways that can differentiate and distance your business from the competition.

Include All Orbits for Peak Marketing

Community-led marketing strategies complement product- and brand-led initiatives by engaging a community of practice with similar interests to your business. Where your Orbit 1 and 2 strategies promote your products and services to target enterprises and ICP, Orbit 3 aims to unite people with the same specialization or interest.

You and your team rightfully spend most of your time in Orbit 1: Product-led marketing. You describe your product, address customer pains, and highlight how your company and solutions can improve the customer's world. Orbit 1 is required of all marketers.

You also invest time and effort into Orbit 2. Brand-led marketing supplements product-led efforts by inviting external voices within your community to reinforce Orbit 1 promises. Here, customer and partner voices reassure buying and renewal behaviors while celebrating wins they've achieved with your solution(s).

Orbit 3 strategies play to a much larger community than the ones built around your product and company. The approach requires your marketing team to take the lead in building relationships, facilitating communities of interest, connecting people, exchanging knowledge, and helping them uplevel their current practices.

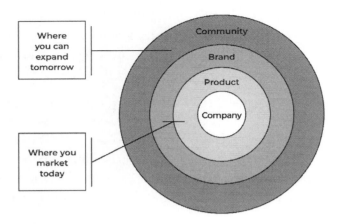

It's essential to recognize that just as the product- and brand-led orbits are not mutually exclusive, the same goes for community-led orbits. Community-led marketing acts as a multiplier and amplifier on top of product- and brand-led marketing. The best marketing leaders integrate all three orbits in their go-to-market plans.

Now, remember the outside-in perspective of the community mentioned at the beginning of this chapter? The community-led orbit is not something that gets built as an outcome of maturing your product- and brand-led orbits to the next level. The community-led orbit starts best with an outside perspective where your team asks, *"What incredible opportunity can we provide to the community? Where can we serve and lead the community?"*

The community-led orbit is not something that gets built as an outcome of maturing your product- and brand-led orbits to the next level.

More often than not, the community will shape itself if given the right relationships, forums, encouragement, and support. It will build and share its content and create incredible opportunities. When done right, the community will ask, *"Where can we take ourselves, and what incredible opportunities can we build and share with others?"*

Define Orbit 3 Characteristics

Let's get into defining characteristics of Orbit 3 community-led marketing.

As you now know, your company does not need to create a community in Orbit 3 because the community at large already exists. That said, the community might require better facilitation for members to get more value out of their participation. Additionally, just because the community exists does not guarantee efficient interactions and exchanges. Exchanges might need to be more efficient. The content might need to be more accessible. And achieving such outcomes might require taking on a leadership role in the community, or taking the lead on creating a new segment within the community to serve an unmet need.

For example, there may be a hundred local meet-ups worldwide for CMOs, but there may not be a national or international community for those same people to get together. For ADDO, the burgeoning DevOps community already existed, and conferences were held across the world. The conferences were incredible but exclusive, catering to those who lived near or who could afford to travel to them. We took the step as facilitators to bring more people together in a more inclusive digital environment with minimal barriers to entry. We were a catalyst the global community needed.

The Purpose of Communities

The purpose of communities in Orbit 3 is to get people together who want to further their education and career development. The community benefits from improved networking and collaboration around an area of common interest; engaged community members spark discussions and share knowledge.

Another important distinction about community-led orbits is the absence of competition. Members of the community are trying to help one another uplevel as practitioners. Competitors only surface where there is selling or an offer promotion, and self-promotion in communities is frowned upon. Self-promotion or pointing at competitors' weaknesses erodes trust in this orbit and should, therefore, be avoided.

The Role of the Community-Led Marketer

We should also recognize not all members of a marketing team need to participate in community-led orbits. In fact, only a small portion of the marketing team needs to invest time in being continuously active in the broader community. However, just as marketing teams have specialists for demand generation, communications, product marketing, and brand development, Orbit 3 requires the support of community-led marketers.

Where product-led marketers live by the mantra *"always be closing,"* the community-led marketer lives by the mantra *"always be connecting."* Orbit 3 marketers are building long-term relationships in the community that will deliver value over time. Community building is a long-game investment. It takes time to forge relationships and build trust.

> **Where product-led marketers live by the mantra "always be closing," the community-led marketer lives by the mantra "always be connecting."**

Like any other relationship in life, it is hard to just pop into a community one day and establish long-lasting and influential relationships among its members. Building trusted relationships between members can take many months. Engagements with the community have to be consistent, and exchanges have to be valued from all sides. However, once established, those strong relationships can smooth the path to making other connections or supporting additional influence in a market. You become a trusted entity who can move more freely within the community because you've invested time in building a reputation that reflects the community's values.

Community-led marketers listen to the market to learn who holds what expertise. Then they facilitate connections between people to share that expertise. They share common interests, have common values with other community members, and get involved in actively helping people bridge connections that could be helpful or interesting.

The community-led marketer also understands that not everyone is a lead. Outreach in Orbit 3 that starts with the intention of *"How do I get my community to buy my product or service?"* immediately places community members in a lead funnel and is a turn-off. Instead, the community-led marketer networks in the community as a trusted peer, often serving as an industry advocate. They rarely talk about company products or brands externally. However, they frequently facilitate discussions and content creation on best practices, trends, or methodologies—subjects that are relevant, interesting, and timely for community members.

For example, I once assembled a couple of DevOps reference architecture sets to help the software engineering community where I worked. The reference architectures were featured in various blogs or presentations developed by members of this community, but I combined them into a common set that recognized the creators. Those DevOps reference architectures were shared online, with no form required for viewing or downloading. They've now been viewed over 270,000 times.[28][29][30] Community members found the deck helpful, shared it with others, and helped accelerate its viral uptake.

The CMO's Role in Connecting Orbits

One day, a friend of mine, Karl (his name has been anonymized), called looking for some advice. Karl was leading an effort with a couple of friends in the video game industry to write a book. Each of the chapters in the book would be written by a different person in the community, each of whom would share their experiences and advice for working in highly distributed, remote teams.

Once published, the book would consist of 12 chapters, each written by developers and development team managers in the video gaming community. The book would be made available for free to any developers in the community who wanted to download it. In addition, the plan was to share the book through mentions in their existing Discord and Reddit communities.

While the book was coming along nicely, Karl's CMO stated that he didn't quite understand why Karl was spending so much time working on a book that had nothing to do with their products or company. The only thing the book and the business had in common was their link to the video game industry.

Internally, the demand-gen team did not understand the book's purpose either. To them, Karl was a community leader off on his own, doing something that benefited the community and not the company. Every day the demand-gen team showed up to work, they focused on promoting products and generating leads.

For clarity, Karl asked the demand team what they would consider a successful lead generation campaign. They said any activity generating 500 leads or more would be significant for them at their stage of growth.

A short while later, the book was finished, published, and ready for promotion. Karl worked with the demand gen-team to pull together an email to promote the book's release. They also included promotions of the book through a variety of posts on social channels and created a few banner ads to advertise on different industry media sites.

To the demand-gen team's surprise, the email, digital, and social campaign generated 2,500 requests for the book and new top-of-funnel leads they could further nurture toward qualification. In its first three months of promotion, it achieved 5x the performance of other successful promotional emails the demand-gen team had sent previously. Even when the content was available elsewhere for free, it still supported strong lead results for the demand-gen team.

> **Just because CMOs have community marketers and demand-gen marketers reporting to them does not mean the two are always in sync when integrating marketing efforts and campaigns.**

One of the challenges facing this marketing team was that they needed to connect the work in their outer orbits with the work in their inner marketing orbits. While the CMO was mature enough to recognize his company would benefit from community marketing, he had yet to recognize the team efforts needed connective tissue. Just because CMOs have community marketers and demand-gen marketers reporting to them does not mean the two are always in sync when integrating marketing efforts and campaigns. It's the responsibility of the organization's CMO or other senior marketing leaders to help connect the dots to improve their overall return on marketing investments across the three orbits.

The CMO and other marketing leaders must play a key role in connecting orbits for their team. Specialization of product-, brand-, and community-led marketing roles does not guarantee team members know how to collaborate best. Therefore, marketing leaders need to identify potential connections and operationalize behavior.

Connecting the demand-gen and community-led efforts for the video game development book may sound intuitive, but those connections were not evident for those working in a specific orbit. Therefore, as in Karl's company, be prepared for marketing executives to establish communication streams between one orbit and the next to make the most of each endeavor.

Establishing Feedback Loops Across the Organization

In addition to playing a supporting role in demand-gen operations, community-led marketers can also provide near-real-time feedback loops to product engineering teams. Community-led marketers are often attuned to what the top active people or influencers in the community say and what sorts of things they value. Feeding the information back into the organization can help engineers and executives prioritize new features, introduce new products, or pursue acquisitions or partnerships to accelerate business growth.

For example, your engineering team may be considering a series of new features for a software as a service (SaaS) offering. Your community-led marketers might know people in the community with experience in implementing those features—or perhaps who have failed at implementing those features. Community-led marketers can connect your engineering people with those experts to better guide the development effort toward success. Once implemented, the community-led marketer can share the story of how some community members influenced the direction of specific product features—thus completing the feedback loop.

Community-Led Content Creation

Content creation is a critical component of community-led marketing. In this orbit, content is generated by community members and obviously from a user-centric perspective. The content will reflect personal and professional experiences, promote knowledge, share successes and failures, and exchange information. Content that originates in the community is viewed as more authentic and highly trusted by its members.

Content, in this context, comes in many different forms. It can be documents, ideas, conversations, videos, documentation, training, books, conference presentations, industry reports, infographics, webinars, or other forms of information sharing.

You or your team members will create some of the content in this orbit as part of your role and contributions to the community. However, in Orbit 3, the balance of content creation effort shifts from internally to externally developed.

For example, in our ADDO community, nearly 100 percent of the content was generated by people in the DevOps community, and not Sonatype employees. Organizations like Pavilion and RevGenius, which have developed communities to serve sales and marketing professionals, also leave most of the content creation and exchanges to their members. Sometimes it just takes the right community leaders to establish the right exchange forum, and the community will bring the content.

Promotes your product and company	Helps people in the community
Product-led marketing	Community-led marketing
Brand-led marketing	

Content generation in three orbits

While it should go without saying, content in the community-led marketing orbit cannot be gated. In the community orbit, gating content immediately places people in your demand-gen funnel, pulling people into a lower orbit. When the intention is to be open and helpful in the community, personal information gates are not viewed positively. Gates throw up barriers, block interactions, and stunt the sharing that is critical to community growth.

Now that you understand the marketing team's roles and content responsibilities tied to community-led marketing, let's shed light on the role of community members.

The 1,000-Hour Rule

Members join a community to connect with like-minded people. They desire shared experiences, want to find new information, deepen what they already know, contribute to peers, and pursue expertise. The community is self-motivated to level up as practitioners in the space. The vast majority will join to listen in via apt lurking vs. a more active role. There is nothing wrong with that—we all benefit from listening in our communities.

That said, a small percentage will actively contribute, and of those, an even smaller percentage will lead. This is the sweet spot for community-led marketers. The more an individual contributes, the more trust that individual builds with the community. As trust grows, deeper relationships are formed, and more new connections are established.

> **To be trusted as a contributing community member, I recommend finding at least one person on your team who can contribute twenty hours a week to the effort. At this level, marketing executives should budget for 1,000 hours a year—over 80 hours per month.**

But make no mistake—building trust and relationships takes time. An industry colleague, Dr. Ibrahim Haddad, Vice President, Strategic Programs (AI & Data) at the Linux Foundation, once told me, *"If you want to make an impact in your target community, find the person who will contribute 100 hours a year to the effort. That will get your foot in the door,"* he explained. Without

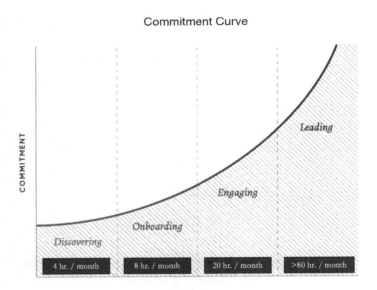

Commitment Curve

The Community Commitment Curve, as shared
by Carrie Melissa Jones, with added emphasis on
suggested time commitments for community participation.[31]

contributing at least 100 hours a year, your role in the community will be seen as an observer.

Even more, contributing 100 hours may get you started, but I would argue that leading and influencing a community takes at least 1,000 hours a year. When it came to the DevOps community, I invested over 1,000 hours in building relationships and contributing content before we came up with the idea for ADDO.

To be trusted as a contributing community member, I recommend finding at least one person on your team who can contribute twenty hours a week to the effort. At this level, marketing executives should budget for 1,000 hours a year—over 80 hours per month. Community-led influence isn't free, but the return on investment can be tremendous when connected with the first two orbits. The 5x performance on Karl's book download requests is one of many examples that you'll hear of throughout this book.

Communities Can Build Their Own Momentum

"We launched regional meet-ups for the Cybersecurity Marketing Society a few months ago," Gianna Whitver told me one afternoon. *"To our surprise, our community quickly took it a step further. They wanted even more connections and community and took it upon themselves to begin hosting their own local meet-ups for the Society."*

Gianna, who co-founded the Cybersecurity Marketing Society in 2019 with Maria Velasquez, explained that when given the opportunity or are inspired to do so, people will begin to self-organize. The community's energy creates momentum that cannot be stopped (and should not be restrained).

	Community-led marketing
Origin	Already exists; needs catalyst
Purpose	Educate, collaborate, inspire Always be connecting
Marketing perspective on the audience	Not everyone is a lead
Content	Personal experiences
Narratives	Don't sell Highly-trusted
Who does the work	Community members You inspire and cheer
Pace	Trust takes time Longest-lived value
Community perspective	Participate and lead
Investment profile	5 – 12% of the budget 1,000+ hours

Summary of Orbit 3 community-led marketing

Today, the Cybersecurity Marketing Society is a community home to more than 2,000 professionals. Members interact through several forums, including a Slack workspace, and a growing number of in-person events. While Gianna and Maria spent countless hours in the earliest days of the society to spread awareness and grow their membership, every new member today joins as a referral from existing community members.

The more time members spend in the community, the more they will take ownership of its activities, outcomes, and growth.

Frame Next-Orbit Success

"Why isn't s/he talking about us?"

"Aren't we paying her/his salary?"

These two questions are emblematic of organizations that have failed to connect the dots between their three orbits. When product- and community-led teams can't see the connection or fail to find ways to measure collaborative impact, company investments in the community are harder to justify.

Community-led marketing requires long-term investment. The connections and trust needed to operate in community-led marketing orbits are not manufactured overnight. Relationships must be nurtured to strike the right influence and build sufficient trust.

> **Community-led marketing can only be successful when it connects all the way back to the product-led orbit.**

Furthermore, community-led marketing can only be successful when it connects all the way back to the product-led orbit. For example, a community-led event generates content, connections, or forums for the product-led teams to leverage. Not every community-led action needs to be leveraged, but the value is questioned when orbits aren't connected occasionally.

Investments in this realm are not insignificant. According to Insight Partners, 73 percent of marketing leaders allocate some portion of their people and program budget to brand- and community-led marketing. Their average share of marketing spend falls between 7–12 percent annually, which is a reasonable investment for long-term impact.[32]

While ample evidence shows that companies planning for and making long-term investments generate more value and growth, marketing executives face overwhelming pressure to deliver quarterly results above all else. CMOs can be successful at ignoring this pressure for a time but buy-in from your executive peers for community-led initiatives is essential for long-term success.

> **If not framed strategically or measured properly, even the smallest percentage of spend can be cut to meet quarterly or annual earnings expectations.**

With solid support from their CEO, peers, and board, long-term investments in the community will be easier to defend. This is especially true when it comes to periods of an economic downturn that bring discretionary spending into focus. If not framed strategically or measured properly, even the smallest percentage of spend can be cut to meet quarterly or annual earnings expectations.

Now that you understand the three orbits and the relationship between them, we'll dive further into the rules around community-led engagement. When done right, everything flourishes. When done wrong, the drag coefficient can be enormous—crashing the best-intended plans or even preventing them from ever taking off.

EXPERT TIP: INTEGRATE, MEASURE, AND INVEST

Three different practices can help protect the long-term investments required for successful community-led marketing. First, the three marketing orbits must be aware of one another to build value between them quickly. Second, CMOs must find a way to measure, even in a rough way, the impact of community-led marketing on their product- and brand-led orbits. Finally, their C-level peers must recognize that a small portion of marketing budgets should always be focused on generating longer-term impacts in the market.

CHAPTER 4

The Rules of Community-Led Engagement

Two years after we started the ADDO community, a company in the same market decided they wanted to get in on the community action. FastCorp's (their name has been anonymized) marketing and evangelism team came up with the idea to host a community and conference we'll call DevOps The Gathering (also anonymized).

Even though we had founded ADDO, we never felt that anyone in the DevOps community making contributions or leading an effort was imposing on our turf. In reality, our values meant we encouraged others to get involved and often helped them succeed. But DevOps The Gathering was doomed to fail from the start.

Why? There are several reasons that become teachings for what not to do for success in Orbit 3. While they billed the forum as a community initiative, they controlled the entire narrative. All their keynote speakers were executives of FastCorp or widely recognized reference customers of the company. Fast-Corp employed the entire organizing staff for the forum, and they were not collaborative with others in the community who could volunteer to help.

They controlled the content and the narrative. In short, they were using "community" words but speaking the language of vendors.

It doesn't take long for a community to sniff out imposters, and FastCorp's efforts were easy to identify by these tell-tale signs. As anticipated, the community never blossomed into what had been imagined. The marketing team was blamed for poor execution, and company leadership steered the budget away from any community initiatives in the next budget cycle—focusing instead on more traditional product and brand marketing.

Understand the Basics

Any marketing team can pursue an Orbit 3 community-led marketing strategy, but there are some essential ground rules to follow. Abide by them, and you can flourish. Ignore them, and you'll weigh down—and potentially kill—any momentum your team (and community) has invested in building.

Community-led marketing has no insurmountable barriers to entry, but the best approaches require committing time to make connections, build trust, and support meaningful exchanges. In this realm, the more you participate, the greater the rewards.

> **Community-led marketing has no insurmountable barriers to entry, but the best approaches require committing time to make connections, build trust, and support meaningful exchanges.**

In this chapter, we'll visit a few of the basic ground rules for engagement. Once you know those, we'll walk through some of the things you want to remember for day-to-day operations.

Finally, we'll discuss the need for marketing leaders to help guide interactions between the three orbits. When everyone understands the rules of engagement, the communication between orbits is more fluid, and trust in the community is maintained.

Rule #1: Don't Talk About Yourself

"You shall not pass!" Gandalf pressed as he battled Balrog in the *Mines of Moria.*[33] The well-known quote from the movie *The Lord of the Rings: The Fellowship of the Ring* aptly applies to many rules for getting started in community-led marketing initiatives.

Follow the rules and you can "pass" into the community-led Orbit. Ignore them and you'll find yourself forever stuck in the two lower orbits.

These rules have been developed over years of community-building initiatives that I have either led or observed from others and then applied myself.

> ### Community-led marketing is like a first date. If all you talk about is yourself, there won't be a second date.

While it's ideal that you follow every rule in this chapter, none stands out more than:

Don't talk about yourself.

(A.k.a., it's about them, not you.)

I've often said that community-led marketing is like a first date. If all you talk about is yourself, there won't be a second date.

Getting Messaging and Content Right

The first thing I do when evaluating any community-led marketing initiatives is to check against the organization's messaging and content to ensure it is separate. Community-led marketing should be free of any product or company messages. This is not an orbit of self-promotion but one of collaborative and inclusive participation.

Here, the messaging and content should be about community concerns, ideas, and lessons that range far beyond what any business might offer. The content helps to solve problems, share insight, offer opinions, and provide guidance.

Sure, your company's content and messaging cover those things for your product or service, but the community's needs are more extensive than what any one company can offer.

The community seeks expertise and education. They want solutions that extend beyond one vendor, product, or set of services. They are looking for advice that is not tainted with vendor pitches and want to collaborate with others who are trying to solve similar problems or gain specific experience. The focus of any particular vendor's products, services, and expertise is too narrow for Orbit 3.

Marketing leaders and their teams failing to abide by the community-led rule of "don't talk about yourself" will drown any community-building momentum.

The Audience Is the Content

Latane Conant, co-leader of the CMO Coffee Talk community, once told me, *"When it comes to community, you have to think of the audience as the content."* When pulling together the weekly Coffee Talk conversations programs, they often invite an expert from marketing or other communities to speak on a topic. But here is where the magic happens for all us attendees: We create the "content" of the community through our dialogue.

Let's say the topic of the week is tech stacks. CMO Coffee Talk will invite an expert to the forum who will introduce that topic for ten minutes. Then the conversation opens for group participation. Typically, many questions and engagements then follow, like:

- I am starting to evaluate new customer support platforms that support multi-language audiences. I wonder if anyone has an RFP/RFI template they are willing to share. If someone has information that might help, they add it to our Slack #swipe-file channel.

- Has anyone found an alternative to ZoomInfo? The audience then chimes in with experiences they like about ZoomInfo and others who have tried alternatives. Someone else might chime in with the latest pricing info they received.

- Another community member may mention their unique experience as a CFO prior to being a CMO. They might then share perspectives that help other CMOs in our community better communicate and plan with their colleagues in the finance department.

As a community, we gather each week to listen, learn, and exchange insights with our peers. Answers might be provided during the weekly forum or afterward through Slack or LinkedIn channels.

Even though Latane Conant and Matt Heinz are the two forum organizers, no one expects them to be the lead content developers for the community. We all recognize that the content in the community comes from our member interactions and exchanges. When the content originates in the community, it is more helpful, authentic, and valued than when vendors develop and share content.

Aren't We Paid to Talk About Ourselves Though?

While it may seem obvious to avoid pitching your products and services in this orbit, practicing this rule is more difficult to implement than most people think. As marketing professionals, we are hired to promote our businesses and products. We understand the outcome of those promotions, close deals, and pay the bills. The work of community-led marketers is attributable to the bottom line, but the return on investment does take longer to materialize.

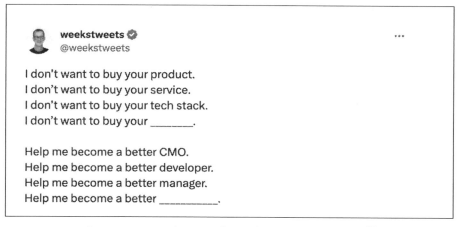

Community mindset: "Help me become a better…"[34]

Always Be Connecting; Building Vendor-Neutral Relationships Improves Brand Affinity

Community-led marketers are in the motion of *"always be connecting"* and *"always be helping."* They focus on what the community needs and help them attain it. They might create content themselves that moves the community forward. They might introduce community members to others who have specific expertise. And they might collaborate with community members to build something that benefits others.

The community-led marketer improves your business's brand equity by serving the community, not promoting your company or product. Helpfulness builds connections and trust, while self-promotion weakens connections and erodes trust.

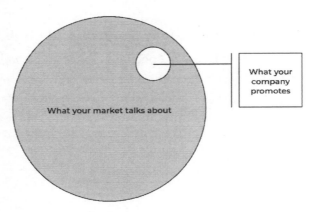

The more relationships you build in the market, the more success your company will enjoy. While executives and sales teams build relationships with potential clients and existing customers, they are not building key relationships with community leaders who can influence market consideration for your products and services. Those deeper relationships are built from the hallway and back-office talk in the community that tells others, *"They are trustworthy,"* *"You should consider doing business with them,"* or *"I would stay away from that company. They are not good people."*

This is where community-led marketing can play a key role. It's why many businesses have hired well-known influencers in their markets, to accelerate the formation of those relationships.

By comparison, traditional B2B product-led marketing is more transactional. It does not attempt to build relationships; it leaves that responsibility to the sales organization. Instead, product-led organizations focus where they are measured — the number of incoming engagements triggered and the number that convert into meaningful business this quarter and next.

Brand Benefit

It might seem counterintuitive to not brand a new community-led effort under a company name but it's the strategy I recommend. The issue with using your business name for a community-led initiative is that it creates an expectation that community members are there to discuss your business. Basically, it's perceived as "direct hit" selling, which is a turn-off for most consumers.

In community-led marketing endeavors, company- and product-specific branding can act as a hindrance as it can imply that the content and community members need to be connected to your business. For example, if you were hosting an event like the Alexa Live Developers Conference, attendees would expect to interact with others with direct experience with Amazon. A community-led initiative benefits more from a unique brand independent of the product and company name.

To illustrate, let's continue with the Amazon Alexa example. Alexa is Amazon's cloud-based voice service available on more than 100 million devices from Amazon and third-party device manufacturers. With Alexa, developers can build natural voice experiences that offer customers a more intuitive way to interact with the technology they use every day. Instead of branding their community-led initiative as "Alexa Live Developers," branding around a category or ideal customer profile (ICP) name, such as "Voice Developers" would be more appealing to the target audience.

Taking this approach could enable their marketing team to attract a much larger audience because the latter appeals to any developer working with voice technologies, while the former targets developers specifically interested in using Amazon Alexa. If Amazon followed this advice, they could likely attract developers using other competitive voice-related technologies like Siri, Eleveo, Voiceflow, and Jovo.

When community members benefit from their participation, your company brand naturally reaps rewards through affinity. This affinity is often achieved organically through the visibility of community-facing employees as initiative leaders. Additionally, supporting the community by using shared spaces, experiences, and history—all within a vendor-neutral environment—improves the perception of your company as a brand to be trusted in the market.

Moreover, your efforts in the community can distinguish your corporate brand from competitors. While other companies focus on their products, solutions, or company, your brand stands out by investing time in helping the community grow, enlisting the support of others in a collaborative way. In a community-led setting, the first interaction many people could have with your company would then be an experience of value that is free of charge and without a vendor pitch. This initial touchpoint can set your brand apart in a business landscape saturated with corporate and product promotions.

It's Easy to Spot the Community Imposter

It's sometimes easiest to demonstrate the *"Don't talk about yourself"* rule by offering examples that break the rule. So, let's explore a couple of scenarios where you can see this concept in action.

First, imagine you are invited to attend a "community conference" for marketing executives. The program offers experts to discuss topics including conversational marketing, personalized content experiences, experiential marketing, social media trends, and artificial intelligence.

The topics sound promising. The event is being held at a prestigious venue. And you have that time open on your calendar.

Now imagine you review the speaker roster for the event:

- Bill Stout, CEO at Pipeline Corp.
- Mary Rishi, CMO at Pipeline Corp.
- Dwayne Barron at SVP Customer Success, Pipeline Corp.
- Heidi Klaus, CTO at Pipeline Corp.
- Bruce Mittwoch, Director of Product Marketing at Pipeline Corp.
- Jane Green, CMO at Drummer (a Pipeline Corp customer)
- Scott Simple, VP of Marketing at Holding (a Pipeline Corp customer)

We've all seen this game before. The promise of community pulls us in, yet the organizers can't help but position themselves at the center. This type of event is not an Orbit 3 gathering and would be better positioned as a brand-led marketing effort in Orbit 2.

It's Easy to Spot a Product Pitch in the Wrong Forum

Another indicator of community-led marketing gone wrong can be seen in event forums. Imagine the first speaker at a community event for marketing gets up and talks about three new trends in marketing. The next speaker gets up and talks about negotiating a better salary in her next role. The third speaker—your company's community ambassador—gets up and talks about how great your company's conversational marketing tool is and its incredible latest features. As soon as they start product pitching, the audience begins tuning them out and checking their phones for the latest email from colleagues back in the office.

Your company's speaker is the dud of the event because the community didn't want to hear about your products. Instead, they wanted to level up their experience and improve their craft.

Your marketing team member talking about their company or product is fine as long as the activity is framed in the right orbit. When your employees masquerade in a different orbit, everyone else notices. And when they do, it diminishes your brand. Therefore, keep your product pitches in the product- and brand-led orbits where they best resonate and are more appropriate.

Community Is Not a Sales Channel

Popular lyrics from a Luke Bryan song say:

> *"You're a buzzkill every time you come around*
> *Why are you still showing up and bringing me down?"*

When everyone is hanging out, being happy, learning something, and finding inspiration, no one appreciates a buzzkill. If you form a community to help others, keep your product and sales pitches away. In Orbit 3, a product or sales pitch screams: *"They care only about themselves. They are not here for us."*

Later in the book, there are chapters dedicated to helping marketing teams nurture community relationships over time into demand-generation cycles. There's also a chapter on community-led sales where you can read about my friend Jim Shilts' experience building massive communities that supported his sales initiatives.

In any case, rest assured that when operating in Orbit 3, no one can treat the audience as a sales channel. The moment anyone experiences an unwarranted sales pitch in this realm is the moment they become determined to move out of your community.

Rule #2: Keep Your Brand Promises

Community-led promises help attract people to your cause. "No vendor pitches" was one of our first brand promises to our ADDO community. This meant "no vendor pitches" leading up to, during, *and* after the community conference. The promise was critical to persuading the community to see the genuine nature of our offer to buy into it. The promise summarized that, *"We're in this for you, not for us."*

The CMO Coffee Talk community makes a similar promise. Every Friday morning in the First Sip Club, attendees are reminded, *"There are no vendor pitches here."* The organizers make CMOs a brand promise that they're investing time to help us improve as professionals instead of creating an opportunity to build a lead funnel and attempting to sell us their products.

We made three core promises for ADDO: Free, online, and no vendor pitches. Each of the promises attracted people to engage. When they experienced the value of the community, they stayed. Many members invited others in their circles to participate, recognizing it as a safe and trusted community brand.

Over six years, the community and its conference evolved in many ways, always serving community members' wants, needs, and preferences. Over that same period, our commitment to the three core promises never changed, and the community rewarded those commitments with their continued participation and engagement. Annual surveys revealed the overwhelming majority of our community participants were satisfied with their experience, and nearly all of them were highly likely to continue or deepen their participation.

When vendors are known to be behind a community-led initiative, the community's concern about sales pitching never goes away. Unfortunately, so many vendors have broken their promises and filled inboxes with spam that it is harder for any community with company support or affiliation to maintain trust. The concern can be minimized when you stay true to the community mission—but one false step can ruin years of trust very quickly.

As a marketing leader, I can recollect countless times when someone in our product-led demand-gen team asked me about sending a company- or product-specific promotional email to members of the ADDO community. Typically, it was usually one of the newer members of the team who didn't have sufficient background on the community, didn't know the relationships we had developed, and/or the defined community brand promise. Whether the request came from the newest demand-gen team member or a fellow executive, the answer was always "no."

Saying "no" is not always easy. Everyone in the business is under a lot of pressure to meet their numbers, and direct access to a very loyal community can be an attractive audience to engage with a product-led offer. However, breaking promises can require years of rebuilding trust *if* it can ever be regained. As the proverb teaches, breaking someone's trust is like crumpling a perfect piece of paper . . . you can smooth it out, but it's never going to be the same again.

> **As the proverb teaches, breaking someone's trust is like crumpling a perfect piece of paper . . . you can smooth it out, but it's never going to be the same again.**

A simple way to think about keeping your promises is to put yourself in the shoes of a community member. Ask yourself if that community member—you—would send the email, promote the roadshow, or share the news about a new product feature. If the answer is no, stick to your community promise. Shift the email back into the product-led orbit where it is expected. Preserve the sanctity of the brand promise because second chances are hard to come by in any relationship but especially the one you have built with your community members.

Rule #3: Say "Yes"

This is one of my favorite rules in community-led marketing. The following is a memorable dinner experience to show you why it's both profound and powerful.

One evening, we gathered a number of people in the ADDO community for dinner in London. Many of us had been in town for a large industry conference, so we took the opportunity to connect with some of our local peers. Sumit Agarwal from Broadridge Financial attended the dinner and happened to be sitting right next to me. Sumit was one of the inaugural ADDO conference speakers in 2016.

During our dinner conversation, Sumit says, *"You know what you really need to make ADDO better? You need a Cultural Transformation track at the conference."*[35]

"You are absolutely right. I couldn't agree more," I responded. It was true that anyone leading a DevOps transformation needed to understand the cultural impact of the move upon their organization. Now here's the catch. I told Sumit that we could add the track to the community conference, but the only way to achieve that was to have him run it.

Remember, ADDO was not built by a large band of employees at Sonatype but by the community at large. Anything new brought to the DevOps community needed to be community-supported. By having people in the community lead and run the initiatives they suggested, member involvement would grow. More importantly, having someone like Sumit run the cultural transformation track would better match the community's expectations for value and authenticity. So, by saying, "yes" to Sumit, we are saying, "yes" to the community. Everyone benefitted.

Here are a few more examples of how following the rule of "yes" led to amazing results.

Chris Corriere at AutoTrader suggested setting up a Slack workspace for conference attendees. *"Great suggestion, Chris. Can you set that up?"*

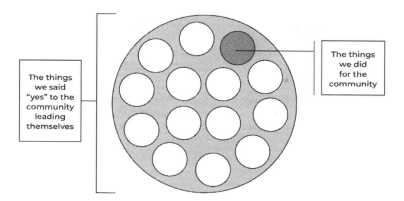

Mike Rosado at Microsoft wanted to gather people from DevOps Cuba and promote the conference in Spanish to Central and South American community members. *"We love that idea, Mike. If you want to lead that, you have our support!"*

Claire Moss at Home Depot was a Twitter (now X) pro when it came to live tweeting at industry conferences. When she suggested live tweeting for the 24 hours of ADDO, she was clearly the best leader to make it happen.

We were never going to be able to justify adding tons of people to our company payroll to support the community-led effort. Applying the "rule of yes" enabled us to deliver a more authentic and valuable experience for everyone in the community. Each year that we organized the conference, there were about 50 volunteers actively supporting the conference production both on-air and behind the scenes. The vast majority of these people had volunteered their effort, and in fact, had suggested the role they were performing. The ADDO community was better because of them.

I should also add that not everything suggested always worked out. The "rule of yes" did not guarantee success. For example, one year, someone suggested we add a track for government stories for the community conference. We added the track to the agenda, and the person suggesting it took the lead on it. For whatever reason, the track never materialized as we had expected. But that was ok because we tried it, which honored the spirit of both ADDO and innovation. No blame was assigned but, the following year, we collectively decided not to attempt a repeat.

Rule #4: Mobilize the Middle

Communities are always evolving. People come and go as priorities in their professional and personal lives shift. However, there are usually a few stand-outs that hold the spotlight.

When you are actively engaging in your community, it is easy to spot the top influencers. At conferences, they are gracing the keynote stages. On news and social media sites, their posts and quotes are garnering the most attention. Their books have become best sellers, and they are contributing time to build-ing community events and other gatherings. None of these folks started at the top of the mountain. They all pursued the journey for their own reasons and invested the time needed to grow their skills, experience, and connections. They also made it a priority to share their knowledge with others.

> **Once you have your core community leaders in place, you must mobilize the middle.**

At the same time, we made a point to recognize when others were just taking their first strides in the community. We were always on the lookout for the people taking those first steps—knowing we were once in their shoes.

On the speaking circuit, we would always look out for the yet-unknown locals who successfully found their way through a conference's call for papers (CFP) process and up on stage. In social forums, we would keep our eyes out for the frequent humble contributor or the person who wrote one blog that caught everyone's attention. These professionals were telling amazing stories, had a dynamic presence, or shared a diversity of thinking that the community had not yet experienced. And we wanted to give them a stage.

Jake Randall at Common Room has a similar rule that he applies to commu-nity interactions: *"Go find the people who your community loves hearing from, not just the most well-known folks. Look at the unknowns who are getting a lot of responses from their posts and invite them to be part of what you are building and hopefully take an active part."*

Community builder and founder of Chief Evangelist Consulting, Leslie Greenwood, came up with a nice label for this type of effort. It is something she calls *"mobilizing the middle."*

The "middle" in ADDO's case was made up of people like Mykel Alvis (then at Cotiviti) who delivered raw, unbridled suggestions for how to look at technical problems and cultural transformations. Others like Bryan Finster (then at Walmart) were challenging his team and the industry to experiment hands-on with new approaches rather than just read about them online. Folks like Jennifer Petoff from Google were lifting the technical tide on one coast of the community but deserved to be heard nationwide and even internationally. We also connected with women like Vandana Verma who were well known in one part of the world, but we wanted to support her by helping her share her perspectives with a global audience.

To be clear, we didn't make those folks successful. We simply played a part in moving them further up the mountain via the ADDO community. We placed them on a global stage where they could attract even more of the recognition they deserved. We also celebrated their contributions by telling others in the community, *"You have to come and meet her because she is working on something that might elevate your idea,"* or *"You should go read the thing he pulled together. It might help you over that hump."*

We were busy making connections, giving yet-unknowns deserved visibility, and celebrating their journeys along the way. It was not about us—it was about them. When we focused on the community above ourselves, the community thrived.

As a marketing leader, it is always incredibly rewarding when you discover a yet-unknown talent on your team. They contribute to the achievement of the overall team, and as you commend, celebrate, and elevate them, your brand wins. Members benefit from the same approach in community-led initiatives.

One caveat: At the same time you are looking for not-yet-known talent, a single community member's journey could be just beginning. Emphasizing rising stars can inspire, but might also intimidate, others in the community. Unknown community members who desire to be more active might think, *"I could never be that good. I can't offer as much as they do."* Others might be thinking, *"The things I know about don't seem as impressive as what the top influencers are sharing."* So, it's important your community create the space and support they need to grow into being a rising star and future speaker/influencer.

Rule #5: Be in It for Them

In his book, *The Accidental Community Manager*, Adrian Speyer writes, *"Please remember you shouldn't tell people how you want your community to be. You should ask what they need from the community to be successful at these goals, and then take their input and work to create a space that helps them achieve those outcomes."*[36]

The great thing about communities is that they bring together a bunch of like-minded people who can drive real change. If you ask for help that benefits the community at large, there is a good chance you will get it.

When Mark Miller asked me, *"Would we be doing anything different today if we wanted 15,000 people to participate?"*—the answer was not, *"Yes, let's work more hours."* We needed more friends to help.

As previously mentioned, our first move after that conversation was reaching out to Marc Cluet, who helped organize the London meet-up group. He agreed to help us by informing thousands of their members about ADDO. Over the years, many other community groups and companies pitched in, just like Marc, to get the word out and invite people to benefit from the community.

Sometimes this approach requires a different mindset. In the community-led orbit, your team members need to shift their ask from their standard business-to-customer interaction to one of the member-to-member exchanges. In fact, across my community building experiences, I can't remember an instance where anyone ever declined to help, if they were already active in the community. The difference was being in it for them, not us.

Rule #6: Give Without Expectation

Community-minded folks give generously. If someone needs help and has good intentions, you make connections. You don't need to ask for anything in return. You give without expectation, and your karma points accumulate.

Adam Grant, the author of *Give and Take*, echoed this sentiment when he wrote: *"The best Givers give in ways that are thoughtful and courteous, and they aren't worried about receiving something in return from whomever they're giving to. When they give, they believe karma will come back around for them through other means."*[37]

> "The best givers give in ways that are thoughtful and courteous, and they aren't worried about receiving something in return from whomever they're giving to. When they give, they believe karma will come back around for them through other means."
> —Adam Grant

In contrast to the Givers, Grant describes a group more akin to product-led marketers that he calls the Matchers. Grant writes, *"Matchers give and expect immediate reciprocity. They want to see results shortly after their time of giving."*

You have experienced encounters with Matchers. Think about all the times product-led marketers have asked you to scan a tradeshow badge in exchange for a t-shirt, complete a form fill in exchange for a whitepaper, or submit your credit card in exchange for a free trial. Now think about how you felt about the Matchers vs. how you would feel after a Giver shared a resource, introduction, or cool tool with you. That difference is part of the power of community.

There is a time and place for both Givers and Matchers. Great marketing teams should have a balance of both . . . but for our purposes here, Givers make a significant difference in the success of community-led marketing programs.

Rule #7: Localize Community Relationships

"We're bringing 180 DevOps experts to your office on November 15th," was one of the lead promotions we used for years with ADDO.[38] Unlike a traditional industry conference, ADDO never had a single physical location for people to gather. At the same time, we never lost sight of the value people could get on a local level.

We understood that individuals wanted to learn about DevOps, and that the most successful transformations required teams of people to collaborate within their organizations. Therefore, instead of inviting individuals to the conference, we encouraged teams of people to participate. "We're bringing 180 DevOps experts to your office" was a call to action that encouraged people to think about how they could take advantage of our community experts across their teams.[39] If 180 DevOps experts truly were showing up, what might your business do to prepare for receiving their knowledge?

This "180 DevOps experts" call to action flipped traditional product-led marketing motion on its head. Instead of a *"come to us"* motion, ADDO was positioned as *"we're coming to you."*

> ### Instead of a "come to us" motion, we positioned the community as "we're coming to you."

The same call to action was complemented by our encouragement for community members to host viewing parties at their offices. The community recognized from the beginning that self-learning paths could be complemented by group-learning experiences with both being served by the same community-led platform. Energizing local audiences to engage others helped further amplify our reach.

When I think about other virtual conference experiences I have seen over the years, they usually miss the benefit of group learning by focusing more on the individual. Imagine how many more people would participate in Hub-Spot's Inbound, Salesforce's Dreamforce, or Adobe's MAX from their own offices if those companies encouraged marketing teams to reserve a conference room, plan out their agendas, and watch together as a team. Those teams could then discuss what they learned, talk about how they could apply their learnings in their companies, and get on the same page faster to accelerate fresh results.

Rule #8: Moderate Lightly

Communities are not for you, the marketer. Communities are for the members—it is *their* space.

Your community has something to say, so let them. In forums where your community gathers, they want to learn from one another. The conversations will center on what they need and the value they are seeking. Remember that forums are not restricted to conversations about your product or company but, instead about topics that are relevant, timely, and compelling for your members. So, let them flourish.

Where moderation has a light touch, you will get a much better sense of what the community truly cares about. As a marketing organization, the narratives shared in the community forums are invaluable in terms of market research on what your ideal customer truly cares about day-to-day. Listen in and learn.

As a real-world example, let's look at conversations in community forums like Slack or LinkedIn Groups. Moderation is important in these forums to ensure that members aren't bothered by "pitches." There are always people who join large communities to pitch their products, company webinars, events, or job postings. For most of the community, these posts are noise that has to be sifted through. When there is too much noise, community members will look for alternatives that offer a better value-to-noise ratio.

A good friend of mine, Daniela (her name has been anonymized), moderates a large developer community on LinkedIn with more than 165,000 members. For years, she has worked to maintain the high quality of content in the forum for its members. As a result, the group gets thousands of new-member requests each month.

She occasionally posts in the group to remind people of the basic "no vendor pitches" moderation rule. Here's one recent example:

> *"Today, I deleted 105 job offerings and recruiters from the moderation queue. These are people who don't believe the rules of the group apply to them. Believe me, the rules DO apply to EVERYONE! Thank you to those who contributed useful content recently. It's very much appreciated."*

Light moderation in member forums helps maintain trust across the community by demonstrating that you respect their time. Establish your light moderation rules, share them on a regular basis, and remind people that you are enforcing them.

Light moderation should not be confused with a light hand when it comes to management. If you are an active participant, leader, or admin in a community forum, continuous attention is needed. There is always someone in the community who does not want to play by its rules or may not yet realize there are moderation rules.

If conversations are not monitored actively, conversations in the community can degrade quickly. Encourage your community-led leaders to play an active role while also asking community members to call out bad behavior.

Rule #9: No Velvet Ropes

Gene Kim, at IT Revolution, introduced this rule to his community of tech enthusiasts. It's a simple rule that I've also seen implemented within the CMO Coffee Talk, Pavilion, the Cybersecurity Marketing Society, and other communities.

When Gene implemented this rule in his community, he wanted to ensure that everyone was on a level playing field when it came to participation and access. He did not want to create barriers between the groups that might imply elite, intermediate, or beginner status. He understood that everyone could learn from each other in the community and that all contributions were welcome.

As a result, incredible connections are made, and awesome ideas are shared. Communities work best when access is not restricted to a select few.

Rule #10: Commit to Diversity

Playing off the old adage, *"With great power comes great responsibility,"*[40] we understood that *"With a great community comes great responsibility."* Community-led marketers understand that diversity and inclusiveness matter. Research shows:

- 57 percent of consumers were more loyal to brands that commit to addressing social inequities in their actions (*Deloitte*).[41]

- 38 percent are more inclined to trust brands that "effectively embrace diversity in their marketing" (*Forbes*).[42]

- Organizations in the top quartile for gender diversity are 25 percent more likely to show above-average profits than companies in the fourth quartile. (*Financial Times*).[43]

When leading community marketing initiatives, make Diversity, Equity, and Inclusion (DEI) part of your DNA. Commit to inclusion and show it in your actions. Like everything else in Orbit 3, when you do it right, the outcomes will speak for themselves.

You should not only make sure your community eliminates barriers to entry, but also demonstrate inclusiveness in your community promotions and outreach. Highlighting diverse community groups and members as participants helps to reinforce and communicate your commitment.

Marketing leaders who want to see their community-led initiatives thrive should actively commit to building trust, fostering learning, and working against discrimination. Taking concrete measures to ensure greater diversity and inclusion will help the community, your brand, and your business thrive.

Rule #11: Welcome Competitors

When leading product or company-specific marketing campaigns, no marketer appreciates participation by their competitors. You don't want the competitors on your mailing list, attending your webinars, or participating in your user conferences.

However, when it comes to community-led initiatives, welcome everyone. It's a community, and when someone is part of it, access should not be restricted. Expect your competitors to join but, like everyone else, make sure they play by the basic rules of engagement. If you are leading the community properly, your competitors will likely be jealous of the trust and relationships you have established with and within the community.

Orbit 3 communities that I participate in have no restrictions on participation. For example, when I was leading marketing at the Linux Foundation, my team selected an Account Based Marketing solution to support demand-gen and sales efforts. They selected the vendor because they had years of experience working with that company and knew our needs would be met. At the same time, 6sense did not ban me from participating in the CMO Coffee Talk community; they welcomed me regardless of the ABM solution my team was using. As part of the community, their openness encouraged me to contribute even more over the years.

An important rule to keep in mind when it comes to the competition is "commit 1,000 hours." The more time your community-led marketers put into the community, the more your leadership and influence will shape it. If a competitor does come to participate, they are likely never going to eclipse the effort or influence the impact of your 1,000-hour contribution. As long as they are playing by the rules, welcome everyone. Your community will respect you more for it.

Rule #12: Have a Code of Conduct

People want to feel welcome, safe, and respected when participating in a community. A code of conduct (CoC) establishes expectations for participation and behavior by your community members. Codes of conduct remind people to be friendly, patient, collaborative, inclusive, respectful, and supportive. Basically, it's a set of *"don't do things that suck"* rules.

It is important to have a code of conduct for your community, but even more important to enforce it. When it came to ADDO, our Slack workspace would be home to countless conversations. Over 99.9 percent of those conversations played by the rules, but there was always someone who didn't want to follow the simple "don't do things that suck" guidelines.

We took a straightforward approach to enforcement. If someone violated the policy by pitching their products, harassing someone, using foul language, or other can't-play-nice-in-the-sandbox behaviors, we removed them from the Slack workspace. There were no warnings or three-strikes-and-you're-out approaches. Our Slack administrators immediately deleted the violator's account.

You might think this approach is harsh, but it served our community well. Those who followed the rules had an incredible experience. Community members who brought CoC violations to our attention felt safe and respected because their concerns were addressed immediately. It's easy to spot unacceptable behavior and even easier to address it head-on.

EXPERT TIP: ASK FOR HELP

If you ask for help from your community members, there is a good chance you will get it. Asking for help increases the likelihood of receiving assistance due to human nature, empathy, reciprocity, relationship building, expertise sharing, and collaborative problem-solving. Humans are social beings and often have a natural inclination to help others. When you ask for help, it creates an emotional connection and evokes empathy in others. Additionally, people feel a sense of reciprocity and are more likely to help when they have been helped before. While not guaranteed, asking for help significantly increases the chances of finding support.

CHAPTER 5

The Rules for Scaling Your Operation

Now that we have covered some of the basic rules of community-led engagement, it's time to understand what the day-to-day journey looks like when it comes to community-led marketing. Marketing leaders and their teams who support community efforts will benefit from understanding the time, investment, technology, and practices that enable Orbit 3 to flourish. We'll start here with the most important rule for scaling the community:

Rule #1: Commit 1,000 Hours

There are generally two paths into a community for any marketing team—engage and hire. The first is to get out and engage in the community to create your own momentum.

My good friend, Mark Miller, has participated in and helped lead a number of very large tech communities. At one point, he was focused solely on serving the Microsoft SharePoint community. He didn't work for Microsoft at the time but ran a community site called End User SharePoint. The community attracted over 2.4M online visitors a year to share experiences, exchange codes, and learn best practices—and brought many more people together in person across the globe. When I asked Mark how much time he was investing in maintaining that community, he shared the following.

"For End User SharePoint, I was spending 30 to 40 hours per week. It was a full-time gig for me to run the community. In that case, it was 1,500 to 2,000 hours a year (300 days). That paid off by attracting, helping, and engaging 200,000 community members online each month."

He then added more advice for marketing executives planning to invest in community-led initiatives, *"For a community builder working for a company, it depends upon what else is in the job description. I could easily spend two to three hours a day, so 600 to 900 hours. The community efforts would be integrated into an overarching marketing strategy and not run as a standalone initiative."*

At this level, marketing executives should budget for 1,000 hours a year—over 80 hours per month. Community development takes time. As a CMO, you can't expect to build a community overnight. Establishing this expectation, along with a realistic projection of the time commitment required, with your team, peers, and Board will be important to the success of your community-led efforts.

Rosie Sherry, Community Executive Officer at Rosieland, depicted community growth through a variety of lenses with a touch of humor. As communities develop, many people in marketing get excited about the opportunities ahead, then realize it will take time to develop. The CEO and other executives also begin to understand that trusted relationships and forums developed in a community are a long game. But community managers who keep their momentum through the growth challenges are bound to see success that benefits both the community and the company.

The second path into a community can be to hire your way into it. For example, Mark Miller and I first started working together when my then-employer hired him to help us better understand and engage in the SharePoint community. He was extremely well known in the space and hiring him offered us the opportunity to accelerate our presence and brand attention in the market.

The community industry

Marketing discovers community

Web3 discovers community

CEOs discover it's a long game

Marketing discovers AI

Marketing re-discovers community

Community Success

Community managers keep going

Community managers keep going

Layoffs

Rosie Sherry, of Rosieland, depicted this view of how communities are built within companies.[44]

The move to hire Mark and engage him across all three marketing orbits paid off. He helped us complement our product- and brand-led endeavors by building community surveys, sharing market influencer research, and developing books to better serve community members. As a result, our business was awarded Microsoft SharePoint Partner of the Year three times. I even had the opportunity one year to go on stage in front of 30,000 people, receive the award, and shake hands with Steve Ballmer, who was Microsoft's CEO at the time.

Hiring your way into community influence requires the right approach. Influencers who have spent years in a community making connections, building trust, and delivering value don't want to announce one afternoon that they've gone to work for the "dark side" of corporate marketing to now pitch a product and company every day. When such influencers accelerate your presence in Orbit 3, you still have to play by the rules of the orbit. Your organization can recognize massive value from a better understanding of your audience and connections within the orbit and then tie that value back into your brand- and product-led orbits.

Rule #2: Measure Engagement

When I tell someone that our ADDO community attracted more than 30,000 registrations a year for our annual conference, it is common to see jaws drop. Even for me, it's still difficult to wrap my head around the massive engagement we witnessed—and I was there in the trenches helping make it happen.

That registration number certainly meant a lot to those of us organizing the annual forum for the industry. It provided a benchmark for us to understand the extent of our reach and impact.

On its surface, though, securing 30,000 registrations could have just been a vanity number for the marketing team to hang their hat on because it indicated traction but was not a good measure of engagement. The analogy for a product-led marketing team would be measuring 700,000 visitors to your company website each month but not tracking what journeys and content engaged those people.

Jono Bacon, community strategist and author of *People Powered,* recently remarked, *"One yardstick that many companies have is the number of members in their community. I think this is a pointless statistic. Let me tell you why: If you have 1,000 people in your community but none of them are doing anything . . . if they are not posting, replying, engaging each other to be successful—then what is the point?"*

He continued, *"A way more important metric is the number of active users. You should expect that about 20 percent of registered users will be your most active. These are people who are actively posting, replying, engaging, creating content, or speaking at your events. That is a sign of a genuinely healthy community."*[45]

To help better imagine the "measure engagement" rule, here is one example of a Discourse dashboard shared by Jono. The dashboard provides insight into a community's health by measuring user activity, signups, topics, and engagement.[46]

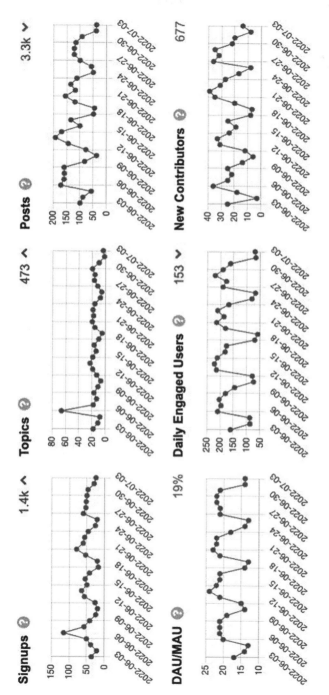

Community health dashboard. Source: Jono Bacon, Discourse blog.[47]

"You should expect that about 20 percent of registered users will be your most active. These are people who are actively posting, replying, engaging, creating content, or speaking at your events. That is a sign of a genuinely healthy community."
—Jono Bacon

For any community-led initiative, marketing leaders should place their primary focus on engagement measures across the community. Engagement metrics and trends are a great benchmark for the health of the community your team is nurturing.

Rule #3: Think Bigger

When it comes to planning community initiatives, it is important for marketing leaders to challenge their teams on their priorities and measures. Aim low, and you'll strike low. Aim high, and at least you are pointed in the right direction.

The incremental effort to attract 25,000 people is not that much greater than the effort to engage 1,000 people. If you want to move the needle—in short order—you need to think much bigger.

This same rule applied to the ADDO program itself. If we were going to host an online conference with five or ten speakers, it would not have attracted much attention. When we introduced the format of 24 hours and 180 speakers, it triggered a reaction from the community: *"This is either going to be epic or an epic failure. Either way, I'm showing up to see."*

This approach mimics what Seth Godin refers to as "Purple Cows"—that is, remarkable marketing. He notes, *"Remarkable Marketing is the art of building things worth noticing right into your product or service. Not slapping on marketing as a last-minute add-on, but understanding that if your offer itself isn't remarkable, it's invisible."*[48]

Marketing leaders should challenge their teams to focus beyond goals like getting the first ten or first 1,000 people engaged in their community. By aiming at larger, more audacious targets and asking, *"What would we be doing differently today if we wanted to achieve that goal?"* you create space for spontaneous innovation.

Great marketing is full of experiments. As a marketing leader, I encourage you to challenge your teams to run bigger experiments.

Rule #4: Build Community with Members

Engaging outside contributors from the beginning to help build your community initiatives is an essential strategy. Marketing teams building communities must understand this to be successful in their endeavors. That is, communities built by their own people, or members, are easier for others in their networks to trust. Such communities also last longer as people are invested in what they create. Communities built by their people also hone in on value better than corporate-branded communities. That means relationships in these member-built communities are more authentic, offer more efficient buy-in, and member needs are easier to discern.

> **Community participants with purely vendor-specific venues will seek more independent forums to gather in as they seek more authentic and trustworthy value.**

Community participants in purely vendor-specific venues will seek other independent forums to gather in as they seek more authentic and trustworthy value. This can drive people in communities who originally discovered local value to go elsewhere by joining larger national or international forums for their participation. It can be easier to lurk as well as dismiss offers in faceless communities.

As a B2B marketing leader, you can build a more extensive community around a market than your company can when its focus is aimed at a brand or products. Communities built around market spaces or knowledge collectives deliver more value and attract more participation than product- or brand-led communities.

Rule #5: Initiate with Value

Imagine you did not work for your company, and instead were a member of your target community. In that case, would you take the same approach in your marketing initiatives?

As traditional product-led marketers, we are trained to put forms in front of any good content or offers to capture visitor information. Forms are seen as a gateway to identifying potential warm interest and sales opportunities. We want to nurture those contacts through our pipeline, and ultimately, collect money from them.

Community engagement does not work this way. Community members help one another advance in their knowledge and careers. When you offer something of value to a community without asking for something in exchange, they'll naturally reciprocate.

When the UK consultancy 3G4G created a reference architecture for a 5G serviced-based architecture for the telecom industry, they didn't locate it behind a form. They simply placed it on SlideShare, un-gated, and received over 50,000 views of the content. They next built a video-based tutorial on the same topic where they had 79,000 people participate. That's 129,000 impressions.[49] [50]

Nothing about the content was gated by their demand-gen team. Having said that, one thing 3G4G did to connect their community-based effort to the reference architecture was to invite people to follow the company across their company's social networks. Those who did were then later exposed to the product and corporate demand-gen content and offers from 3G4G.

When you take on the mindset of a community member, your behavior will change, which will likely yield stronger engagement with members of the community.

I emphasize this point because the struggle you will face as a marketing leader is real. Product-led marketers will question why community-led marketers aren't following standard operational procedures for sharing content and inviting participation. Growth marketers will wonder why forms aren't needed for pieces of content that attract lots of attention. Demand-generation team members will question why community-led marketers aren't asking for titles, phone numbers, and state/country info from community members.

Community-led marketing is not form driven—it is engagement driven.

However, when it comes to community-led marketing, forcing those kinds of traditional marketing asks in the beginning of an engagement with potential community members erodes trust and drives people away. We saw material differences in the ADDO community impact when our behavior was community-first. Just like the reference architecture shared by 3G4G, valuable content shared without forms and avoided "vendor pitching" attracted significantly larger audiences. Imagine reporting to your executive team that your community-led marketing efforts exposed your brand to over 129,000 people. Then, following that exposure, you saw a continued increase in visits to your company website, blogs, and webinars. That kind of result can be the norm when it comes to taking non-traditional approaches to marketing with engaging and growing communities.

The bottom line: Community-led marketing is not form driven. It is engagement driven.

Rule #6: Use the Tech Stack That Works

"What does your tech stack look like?"

This is a common question for CMOs and their teams, who are constantly looking for new ways to reach audiences and scale business operations. It was also a common question when it came to how we produced ADDO.

The answer I often provided people was, *"The tech stack didn't matter."*

For the ADDO community, any technology could have performed the trick. The reality is that when your team is looking for the right stack, they should first use what is already available in-house. Why? It's simple, your team already has access to it, and they are familiar with how to use it.

For example, if you were using HubSpot to build your website and automate marketing sequences, you should use the same platform for your community. Do you say your team is using WordPress for your website? Then use that for your community website. Don't add more complexity than necessary.

Next, lean into free or inexpensive tools. When setting up a community, especially in the early days, you don't need to spend a ton of money.

Need a place to chat? Slack has a free version.

Need a place to share blogs? Medium can be your answer.

Looking for a place to host video content? YouTube can be that place.

Many of the free tools like Slack and YouTube offer almost unlimited scale on their free platforms. But before you decide on one platform or solution versus another, you'll want to look into where your team will hit a paywall.

I remember reaching out to some industry friends who worked at Slack and asking, "*If we have 25,000 people logging into your free version next month, will you have any problem handling that workload, or is there a chance that you would boot us from the free version?*"

They came back with a simple answer that confirmed: "*It's not a problem. The platform is free for anyone to use at any scale.*"

The third piece of advice I would offer is to experiment with different tools. For example, perhaps your marketing team is looking at generative AI content development tools or considering new ways to track conversations on topics across social channels that mention certain topics. Your community team and forums can act as a testing ground for these new solutions before they are adopted across your entire organization.

If you're looking for suggestions on where to start with tech stack options, here is a list of tools that community leaders and I have used to support various community-led initiatives.

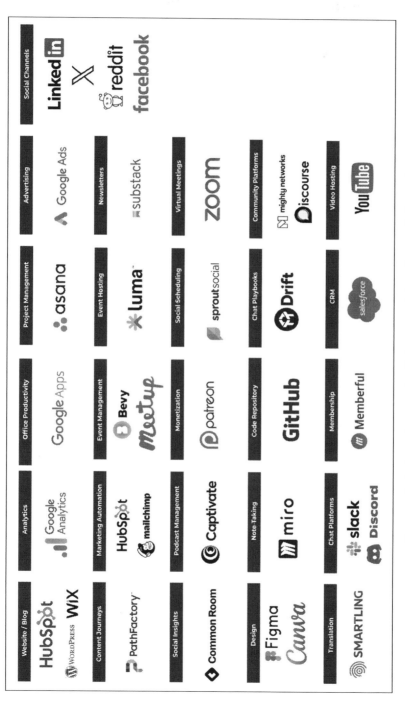

Community tech stacks come in all shapes and sizes. Start with the tools your company uses, then explore and experiment with new options.[51]

Rule #7: Avoid Spamming the Community

It pains me to add this rule, but so many marketing teams still get it wrong. When it comes to community-led initiatives, even the best teams find themselves cruising outside the guardrails.

Let's assume you've done the right things to build your community, encourage engagement, and foster collaboration. If anything could be a buzzkill for what your community-led teams have built, it is unnecessary or ill-targeted emails.

Imagine how enticing it would be for a traditionally-minded Orbit 1 marketing team to follow up on 30,000 top-of-funnel leads from a community marketing initiative. They might salivate at the opportunity to exploit that contact list for their own initiatives. Imagine all the signups they could get if they targeted the list for product, whitepaper, or company promotions.

However, to sustain community trust, marketing teams operating across all three orbits need to establish and then enforce operating boundaries. An Orbit 3 community member's participation in an activity does not—unless specifically stated—sign them up to be marketed to about a company's products or other offers. Following up with such content would be akin to spamming them—a practice no one likes and could mean fines for the company as a result.

Some marketing managers can forget that community members are actually people who joined the community with a specific purpose in mind. Those people came to the community to cultivate an interest, build skills, find support, and make new connections.

Harvard Business Review provided this perspective on getting communities right, remarking that community-led marketing *"builds loyalty not by driving sales transactions but by helping people meet their needs."*[52]

When you immediately place people in a sales funnel, you shift them from a community-led engagement to a product-led engagement. Building confidence and trust through responsible support for people's interest in community-led orbit fosters curiosity towards the product and brand, which can be further nurtured when the timing is more suitable. When people respect your brand because of how it works in the community, they are more likely to do business with you in the long run.

> **When people respect your brand because of how it interacts with the community, they are more likely to do business with you in the long run.**

For people who signed up to participate in our community, we did email them occasionally about community-related interests. We alerted them to new blogs, books, and reference architectures the community had pieced together. We also invited them to participate in community surveys about industry practices or to dive into hundreds of on-demand recordings from our previous conferences. And we also encouraged them to sign up to speak at future community conferences or to attend local meet-ups in their area. As in any relationship, the better we treated them, the more they engaged with us.

Rule #8: Honor the Spirit of Endorsements

Imagine you are hosting a field marketing event in Atlanta for customers and prospects. Your product-led marketers (field marketing, demand gen, sales) are hosting the event to build relationships and generate leads for the sales team. In order to boost the credibility of their event and grow registrations, they want to secure an industry thought leader to speak.

To accomplish this, the product-led team may enlist help from the community-led team for support in making the request to the thought leader. Assume the community marketing leader has already established some level of relationship with the thought leader and all goes well, the target speaker buys in. It's not hard to imagine the following conversation taking place.

"Hey there, thanks for getting Mr. Big to participate in our event next month," says the field marketing manager. *"Do you think we could get him to endorse our product during his presentation?"*

"I don't think that would be appropriate," replies the community manager. *"He agreed to speak at our event based on the relationship we've built over the years. He doesn't do product or company endorsements because he achieved his status by working with everyone—regardless of competitive boundaries."*

In this situation, your community-led marketer spent some social currency to secure the leader's participation. As a result, the thought leader helped boost attendance and delivered a favor to the community and your business. This is where things take a turn . . . endorsements might be offered by the thought leader naturally during a discussion at the event but dictating them is another thing. Dictating endorsements as a requirement could damage the social fabric woven into community exchanges.

I've seen many such requests play out in different forms over the years. Here are a few examples:

- *"Can we get them to like and retweet our company's social post about the event?"*
- *"Can you ask the influencer to ask their 73,000 followers to register for our webinar that features them?"*
- *"Can we tag that influencer on LinkedIn to encourage them to comment on our post?"*
- *"Can you ask them to accept our CTO's presentation at the big event that the influencer organizes?"*
- *"Do you think we can get them to wear our company swag when they are on stage speaking?"*

Unless you have contractually obligated an influencer to do these kinds of things in exchange for some form of payment, the answers all end up in the same category:

"No. That would not be an appropriate ask."

Influencers—even if on your payroll—need to be careful about whom they endorse, support, or promote. Establishing ground rules for such interactions upfront can help minimize friction for marketing teams that work with them and their community counterparts.

EXPERT TIP: THINK BIGGER

"Thinking bigger" encourages individuals to expand their perspectives and consider possibilities beyond their immediate circumstances. By pushing beyond self-imposed limitations, thinking bigger helps overcome obstacles, fosters creativity and innovation, and sets ambitious goals. It enhances problem-solving skills, promotes personal growth, and inspires others. While maintaining a balance with practicality, thinking bigger opens new possibilities, fuels motivation, and leads to significant achievements on personal and collective levels.

Any effort you begin yourself or with others will take time. When pointing yourself toward bigger outcomes from the beginning, you may be able to accomplish more with the same amount of effort that lesser outcomes require.

CHAPTER 6

Connecting Orbits for Internal Success

The unvarnished truth is you are going to have to measure the business impact of your community. This is true for all marketing leaders and community leaders.

David Spinks, the author of *The Business of Belonging*, recently shared his perspective on aligning community initiatives with the business. He said, *"The hard truth is that the marketer who builds community is probably going to get more budget than the community builder who drives marketing.*

"And I'll be honest . . . this pains me. I've dedicated my entire career to the community profession. I've spent, literally, over 10,000 hours working to carve out a corner for community builders in the world of business.

"But I've also always known that community was never going to be the end goal for businesses. Community was always going to be a means to profit. Because it doesn't matter how 'good' a business is . . . they all live by the same golden rule: You must make more money than you spend."[53]

"It doesn't matter how 'good' a business is . . .
they all live by the same golden rule: You
must make more money than you spend."
—David Spinks

Now, let's discuss the importance of connecting and integrating the three orbits of marketing.

Establish Expectations Between Orbits

Think of the rules in this chapter as guardrails for your success. The guardrails will come in handy on a number of different fronts. First, the people heading up your community-led marketing initiatives will have to live by these rules every day. Abiding by the rules will enable them to make stronger connections and establish deeper trust.

The rules are also critical to keep in mind when connecting the orbits. Work performed in the community-led orbit can benefit efforts in the product-led orbit, but the marketers in each orbit need to be clear on the rules and boundaries of engagement.

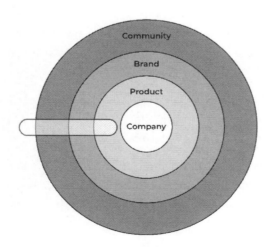

*Integrating orbits is critical to your
community's and company's success.*

Collaboration between the orbits is required for success, but teams must understand that standard operating procedures and expectations will be different in each orbit. Forms, permissions, communications, and promotions have different boundaries in each orbit. Crossing the boundaries without the right permissions or approach will erode trust and strain relationships that take time to build. And again, once damaged, those relationships may not recover even when given the time.

For community-led marketing initiatives to succeed, everyone across the organization needs to understand and appreciate the guardrails around community stewardship.

Integrate Content and Relationships Across Orbits

Relationships form the heart of community-led marketing endeavors. All the work, ideas, and rewards from communities stem from relationships developed over time. For marketing leaders, these relationships take on additional value when used to connect their product, brand, and community orbits.

Ryan Leier is a global yoga ambassador for Lululemon who lives in Vancouver. Global yoga ambassadors are part of the company's philanthropic passion projects and their efforts to build connections with the yoga community. As part of the program, Lululemon provides wide-ranging support for Ryan, including sending him to international events, supplying mats for his studio, offering a monthly gift card for product distribution, and most significantly, supporting his non-profit, Vinyasa Yoga for Youth.[54]

Lululemon's ambassador program is a significant way the brand invests in people, fostering relationships that vary by design. The program consists of three categories: Global yoga ambassadors (eight experienced yoga instructors with diverse practices), elite ambassadors (over 75 professional athletes from various sports), and store ambassadors (over 1,500 local influencers involved in personal training, yoga, running, and other active pursuits). Ambassadors are chosen based on their ability to reflect Lululemon's culture and core values, as well as their passion for elevating the world.[55]

By thinking creatively and leveraging the growing interest in yoga, Ryan and other ambassadors are able to bring Lululemon's products and services directly to their local communities, making it more accessible and engaging for people who might not have the opportunity to visit a physical store. The company's ambassador program showcases the brand's commitment to promoting a healthy lifestyle and connecting with the community that, ultimately, helps strengthen Lululemon's brand image and increase customer loyalty.

While this is just one example, there are numerous other stories of individuals working with or at Lululemon stores who have led or participated in community initiatives, furthering the company's mission to create a positive impact on the lives of people in their local geographies.

Lululemon's ambassador project starts in Orbit 3. They partner with local athletes, fitness instructors, and wellness professionals. These individuals embody the company's values and promote an active and healthy lifestyle. They support these professionals through donations, equipment, and apparel gifts that are used to benefit others. There are no specific requirements for ambassadors working outside the stores to draw audiences or generate sales. Yet these ambassadors play a very important role in the community—they build relationships, foster values, and build affinity.

Beyond the ambassador program, the company collaborates with local non-profit organizations, social enterprises, and charities to support various causes, such as mental health awareness, environmental sustainability, and female empowerment. This fosters goodwill and a positive brand image, which can translate to increased customer loyalty and store visits.

Lululemon also encourages its employees to engage in volunteer work and give back to their communities. This creates a positive work culture and generates a sense of pride among employees, which can lead to increased productivity and customer service quality. In turn, community members may be more inclined to visit and support a business that clearly cares about its community. The relationships, values, and brand affinity create relationships with the community beyond the storefront.

Through these community-led events, Lululemon also maintains an active and engaging social media presence. The company showcases its community involvement, and that further enhances relationships with local customers.

This sense of familiarity and connection encourages people to visit their stores to experience the brand's values and culture firsthand.

Giving without expectation is not limited to the company's community programs. As part of their Orbit 2 initiatives, they also host free classes and events, attracting people to Lululemon stores. The events and classes include such topics as Yoga, Pilates, or running clubs, where you might spot one of their local ambassadors like Ryan leading the instruction.

These events serve as a way to engage with the local community and create a sense of belonging. By offering these free classes, Lululemon encourages people to visit their stores, and in turn, sets the stage and increases the chances of potential customers making a purchase.

> ## Community-led initiatives begin by giving without expectation, but by also committing time to engage often with their community of prospective buyers.

Lululemon is effectively putting on a master class of community-led marketing integrated with its core marketing and promotion programs. Community-led initiatives begin by giving without expectation and also by committing time to engage often with their circle of prospective buyers. Those buyers might not be aware of the brand or have experience with it, but the brand is investing time to grow its affiliation with people and experiences in their geographies.

Lululemon does not operate its community and ambassador programs in a silo. The programs build visibility for the brand, drive foot traffic to their stores, and engage their audiences in ways beyond transactional purchases of yoga pants, swimsuits, or shoes. The approach that Lululemon uses in their business-to-consumer marketing strategies can be applied in similar ways to your business-to-business marketing strategies. Invest in the community first, build relationships with the people you want to engage with, and then draw people into your core business offerings.

EXPERT TIP: INTEGRATE EVERYWHERE

Don't approach community-led marketing as an island unto itself. Marketing teams that incorporate community-led initiatives reach bigger audiences, produce better content and experiences, and achieve unfair mindshare. As a marketing leader, you are already comfortable integrating content marketing with demand generation, or brand marketing with communications, or product marketing with sales enablement. Integrating community marketing into the other functional areas of your marketing team should be your default behavior, not an afterthought.

CHAPTER 7

Launching into Orbit 3 (Pre-Flight Checklist)

When community-led marketing is tied to product- and brand-led marketing, it thrives. But if you have never been down the path of a true community-led marketing initiative, knowing where to start can be difficult.

> **If you have never been down the path of a true community-led marketing initiative, knowing where to start can be difficult.**

An industry friend of mine works for a well-known venture capital firm. One day, he sent me an email asking if I had the time to meet with a CEO at one of his portfolio companies. The company provided a cool new solution that would help software development teams accelerate their code releases. The company was young and was just getting off the ground with a base of ten customers.

Mila (for the sake of this story, her name was anonymized), the CEO, was wondering how she could build a community around her company. She was getting some pressure from her team, her board, and other friends in the development community to start a community because that seemed to be a trend working for other better-established firms.

Starting a brand-led community at this time made little sense to me. When you only have ten customers, you are not going to have much going on in your product-led community. Imagine showing up to the next Board meeting exclaiming that your user community was seeing incredible success. Mila didn't want to be in a scenario where at the next Board meeting, she would share, *"Nine of our ten of your customers decided to participate. We have a 90 percent participation rate."* While statistically good, ten customers are too small to use as an indicator for any community growth metric.

Instead, my suggestion for Mila and her team was to invest time in the developer community in their local region around Tel Aviv. Developers Tel Aviv has 3,423 members.[56] The Israeli Unity Developers meet-up noted 2,250 members.[57] Node.js Israel has over 7,000 members.[58] These are just a few of the hundreds of pre-established communities that include people who might be interested in learning more about Mila's solutions for developers.

"Get out in the community to get a sense of what people are talking about. Spend time with them to understand their most pressing priorities," I told her. *"Once you spend enough time embedded in these communities, you will have more choices about what to do with your own community motions. First, you might find a benefit from taking on a leadership role in one of the existing meet-ups. Second, you might identify gaps not served by the local communities and then have one of your employees start and promote a new meet-up that addresses those needs."*

"When you spend enough time in the community, you'll find the right path," I told Mila.

Provide me a list of 25 developer meetup groups around the world in table form. Include a url to the group and member count.

Here is a list of 25 developer meetup groups around the world, including their URLs and member counts. It's important to note that the member counts may change over time, and you can always find the latest count by visiting the respective meetup URLs.

No.	Meetup Group Name	URL	Member Count
1	San Francisco Python Meetup Group	https://www.meetup.com/sfpython/	17,000+
2	New York JavaScript Meetup	https://www.meetup.com/NY-JavaScript/	12,500+
3	Seattle JS	https://www.meetup.com/seattlejs/	9,000+
4	London Java Community	https://www.meetup.com/Londonjavacommunity/	7,500+
5	Berlin Android Developers	https://www.meetup.com/Berlin-Android-Developers/	3,000+
6	Paris Data Science Meetup	https://www.meetup.com/Paris-Data-Science-Meetup/	6,500+
7	Tokyo iOS Developers	https://www.meetup.com/Tokyo-iOS-Meetup/	2,800+
8	Bangalore JavaScript Meetup Group	https://www.meetup.com/Bangalore-JavaScript-Meetup/	6,000+
9	Toronto Ruby Brigade	https://www.meetup.com/toronto-ruby-brigade/	3,500+
10	Madrid PHP Meetup	https://www.meetup.com/madridphp/	2,500+

Expert tip: Use generative AI tools like ChatGPT to find a list of local community groups...

Find Your Community-Led Orbit

Your company creates product- and brand-led orbits, but when it comes to community-led orbits, you find them. In Orbit 3, the focus shifts to joining in, connecting members, and facilitating outcomes.

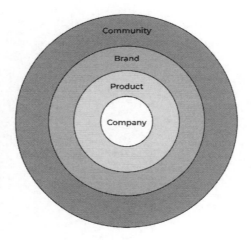

ADDO is one example of a community-led marketing initiative. At Sonatype, where All Day DevOps was founded, we did not create the global DevOps community; members of our team simply joined in to help propel the community further in achieving its interests. We played a primary role in helping community members achieve more of the things they were seeking for themselves.

Here's another example. When COVID-19 lockdowns went into effect, Heinz Marketing and 6sense took the lead in creating a forum for CMOs to join virtually. They did not create a community of CMOs around the world, nor were they the first organization to gather marketing leaders to share experiences. However, CMO Coffee Talk provided a forum for leaders that fulfilled a promise of a safe place to gather, share experiences, learn, and exchange information.

McKinsey & Company calls these kinds of approaches to marketing, *"an evolution from targeting consumer segments, which are anchored in demographics or individual need states, to targeting communities of people who share similar interests and values—communities of shared relevance."*[59]

One of the really smart things that 6sense and Heinz Marketing did in defining their orbit for CMO CoffeeTalk was focusing on their ideal buying persona. They recognized that the best buyers of their solutions would be stronger CMOs. They then set out on a mission to help support this community to become even stronger CMOs.

> **Your company creates product- and brand-led orbits, but when it comes to community-led orbits, you find them.**

The vision for their community was that it would offer an opportunity for CMOs to hang out with other CMOs who wanted to uplevel their skills, be more data-driven, hire the right people, and prioritize well. If the community delivered on its promise, 6sense and Heinz Marketing would be in contact with stronger CMOs and hold deeper relationships with them. The community would win through participation. And in the future, if the CMOs were ever considering Account Based Marketing solutions, it would be more likely that 6sense and Heinz Marketing would get an at-bat for an opportunity to win that business.

Build Your Own Segment (or Help Lead One)

One of the first decisions you will have to make is whether you are going to invest your time and resources to build a new segment of an existing community or work your way into a leadership role within an existing community.

For example, if your community-led motion was aimed at marketing professionals, there are several different paths you could explore. One might be to join an existing community segment like CMOs, cybersecurity marketing professionals, or marketers who live in your metro area. Once there, you would need to contribute enough time to that community to make your relationships and contributions pave the way into a leadership role. As a leader, you could then help guide and facilitate connections for others or help devise the best ways for the community to deliver more value.

Another option might be to create your own path. For example, maybe you live in Madrid and there is no local marketing community that meets your needs. You could then invest in creating one for Madrid that perhaps someday extends further across Spain, Europe, or even globally.

Or perhaps you work in the real estate industry, and you have not found the right forum for real estate marketers to collaborate. This means you have discovered a specific underserved segment in the overall community. This might represent your opportunity to better serve people in your industry by filling that underserved need.

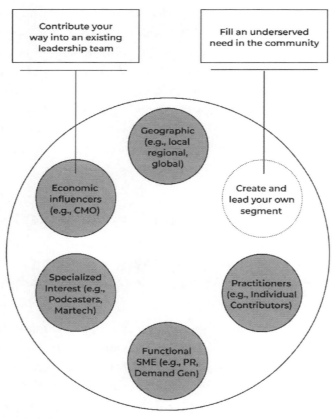

One of the first decisions you will have to make is whether you are going to invest your time and resources to build a new segment of an existing community or work your way into a leadership role within an existing community.

The path you are looking for is one in which you participate in an existing segment or create your own specific segment of interest within a broader community. Regardless of the path you decide, the effort will be similar if your organization is going to play a lead role in the community. Lead roles in communities require a commitment of at least 1,000 hours of time annually from someone on your team. As discussed earlier in the book, any less than that means you might have difficulty launching yourself into an existing community's orbit or creating sufficient momentum in your own segment.

If you have already created a brand-led customer or user community for your business, you have an idea of how much time and effort it took to set up and operate. Orbit 3 communities may take even longer if you don't already have external relationships established.

Moving forward, let's make the assumption that your business will be creating a new segment in an Orbit 3 community rather than working your way into an existing external community. We'll also assume you've spent enough time in the communities related to your market that you have a foundational understanding of what they do, what value they represent, and who participates in them.

Right-Size Your Community

When I recount the experience of building ADDO to 30,000 annual participants, CMOs and other executives are excited to learn how they can incorporate community-led efforts into their businesses. They would love to build a community of thousands of people that develops great content, shares information, and inspires one another.

It's also important to set the right expectations for success. To be successful in your community-led growth practices, you don't need to attract thousands of people. Attracting ten or twenty people can be the beginning of a great community-led effort. You get the opportunity to meet new people in your industry, build trusted relationships with them, and collaborate on projects that deliver value to the great community.

One example of a simple project to get a community started is to host a podcast series. Interview ten or twenty people about their careers and what they did to get into their current position or profession. Ask them to share advice they believe others would benefit from hearing. This is a great example of working with people to build content that is about your community and not your company or products.

To build upon this initial step, take those podcast sessions and promote them to the larger community in which your business operates. You can then repurpose the content of those interviews by splicing them up to create a blog or social media content. Small initiatives like this can be a great place to start building your 1,000-hour community investment.

Marketing leaders, especially those at smaller or growth-oriented companies aiming to build communities around their products or brands, will struggle to do so. In many cases, it is more efficient for them to look beyond their walls to the community at large. While the communities they operate in often exist, the forums to gather in don't necessarily exist yet. And that's their opportunity.

This is what we accomplished at Sonatype with the ADDO community. First, we built a forum to create space for gathering and transferring information. When we did, these self-identified DevOps people gathered to learn, share, and collaborate. As trust grew, these folks invited others to join them. The ADDO community grew to over 13,000 people in 75 days when people realized it was serving their needs first, not someone else's.

Companies like HubSpot have taken a similar approach in their market. HubSpot mastered the idea of developing content to help marketing professionals, even if that content had nothing to do with their products or platform. Marketers wanting to build an event plan, optimize a budget, understand AI-generated content, or improve social listening strategies could turn to the HubSpot blog for help. When they did, HubSpot wasn't pitching solutions or product sales. They were building brand affinity by being helpful. Furthermore, HubSpot didn't solely rely on its own marketers, it also encouraged blog contributions of content from its network of solution partners.

Understand the Three Axes of Community

One day, I was having a conversation with Jared Robin, co-founder of RevGenius. RevGenius is a community of 35,000 sales, marketing, RevOps, and customer success professionals. Jared shared his perspective on the three things he believes are critical to getting and keeping people involved in a movement. He said, *"It all comes down to brand, community, and content loops."*

Jared understood that communities are formed around a specific brand promise (e.g., the value or experience that people expect from joining a community). He also recognized that the community was made up of people who wanted to find others with similar interests to their own. And lastly, he understood that the best communities enabled information sharing and feedback loops associated with those exchanges. The more community leaders centered on each of these three things, the better the community would be.

Jared's view very closely matched my own perspective on what made communities work. The three axes I've used to describe and assess the growth and health of communities are brand promise, community relationships, and community content. The three axes can serve as a guide to helping you establish, grow, and assess the health of your community efforts.

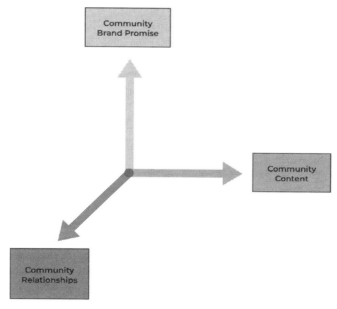

The three axes of community-led marketing. Strength in any one axis is tied to the strength of the other two.

The brand promise is what your specific community claims to offer its members. Brand promises should be short and succinct, representing what the community should expect at every intersection of their engagement. Even as the community grows and evolves, its brand promise should remain consistent. While brand promises can be implicit or explicit, it plays in your favor to be more explicit as that will help to build trust with members who you will attract. The brand promise will also serve as your community's north star (i.e., a long-term stretch goal), helping to define the guardrails of relationships and content.

Content and relationships work hand-in-hand within a community. But you might ask yourself which comes first: Content or relationships? While a community might start with content, relationships are more important. The more people who come to your community, the more ideas, knowledge, and content will be exchanged. The more people-to-people exchanges that form in your community, the more its value increases for its participants. When the community finds value, they engage more and invite others to join them. As the community grows, its members will accelerate knowledge exchanges and content development.

The content represents part of the value that rewards member engagement. Community members join movements to find content or information that their peers share. As member involvement grows, they begin to contribute perspectives or feedback to existing content and discussions. The most involved members of the community will evolve over time to share their own content or work with others to build new content that serves the community.

Example: Starting Your Community Effort on All Three Axes

Let's walk through a real-world example of the three axes. When Mark Miller and I co-founded ADDO, one of the first things we honed in on was our brand promise. Our intent was to educate anyone in the world who wanted to learn more about DevOps. The brand promise for the ADDO community conference that we landed upon early was:

- Online
- 24 hours
- Free
- No vendor pitches

For the six years that we produced the community conference, built and shared content with community members, and expanded relationships across the globe, the brand promise never changed. From the first to join to the thousands who joined us over the years, our promise of what to expect from the DevOps learning environment we created was consistent.

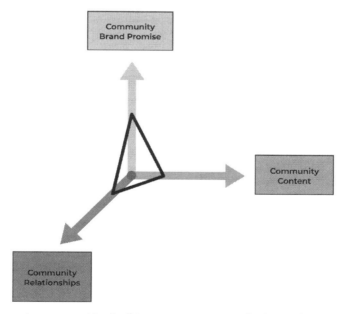

As communities build momentum, trusted relationships build. When relationships prosper, content and information exchanges grow with them.

After establishing our brand promise, we then set forth establishing relationships with different parts of the community. We first gathered a few friends to help us organize the community conference and Slack workspace. We then reached out to the community asking for people to volunteer to speak at the conference, where they would deliver content in a session or perhaps assist with some of the back-end operational needs for running the event. Next, we pursued waves of community invitations to the conference and our Slack workspace for DevOps professionals.

On the third axis—even though our community was in its formation stage—we decided not to create the content ourselves but to instead focus on a platform for the community to share what they created.

During our first year, community-originated content came in two forms. The first was in the form of 54 live conference presentations. Speakers at the community conference built and delivered vendor-neutral content that we then broadcast and recorded on YouTube for on-demand playback and binge watching. The other form of content came through countless exchanges in the Slack workspace, where community members shared ideas, experiences, content, and code, all while establishing new connections.

Even though our community conference was hosted only for one day, the relationships we built in our Slack workspace and the content we shared there and on YouTube delivered value for years to come.

Example: Growing Your Community Effort on All Three Axes

Over the years, our ADDO grew tremendously. In year two, the only change we made to our brand promise was extending the annual conference from 15 hours to 24 hours in order to accommodate 180 community speakers and extend geographical coverage. The move to the 24-hour program increased participation from India, China, Australia, and other large communities of software developers.

By sticking to our promise of "free, online, and no vendor pitches," trust in the community grew and attracted more members. In year two, our participating community grew from 13,000 to 33,000.

Our core organizer tribe also grew. New tracks brought new moderators. More speakers bought more back-end operations. A higher volume of conversations brought more need to observe exchanges, guide people to the right places, and enforce our community code of conduct.

More member participation also meant that content and exchanges were growing. Content delivered in conference sessions sparked press coverage and encouraged others to blog about their experiences. Over the years, hundreds of DevOps blogs have been published. Many of those blogs were transformed into a series of books that highlighted the work our members were doing in the community. The books and the blogs also extended our engagement with the community beyond the 24 hours of the community conference day.

Beyond the books and blogs, we also conducted annual vendor-neutral surveys of the DevOps community. The questions were built from the input of community leaders, and the survey analysis reports included commentary from members who participated in the survey.

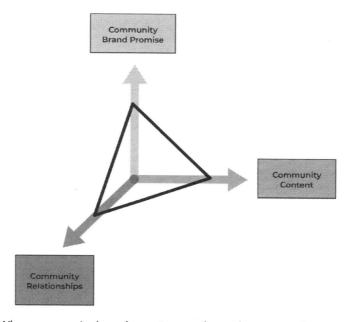

When community brand promises are kept, the community grows through trusted relationships and content/information exchanges.

We reached even more people throughout the year within the DevOps community by supporting the development of local events. Community members wanting to share more of what we brought together on a global level would organize local DevOps events, and we often supported them by helping identify solid speakers for their programs. Even though we founded All Day DevOps, we were not trying to corner the market on the DevOps community. Helping others help the community was part of our community DNA.

Boom and Bust Cycles of a Community

All communities want to maintain their brand promise to attract new and retain existing members. As membership expands and exchanges are encouraged, content and contributions should also grow.

Over time though, communities change and evolve. New leadership establishes new or different directions under the brand promise, markets grow and decline, and member needs evolve. The three axes can also serve as evaluation points for leaders to evaluate strengths, weaknesses, opportunities, and threats facing the community.

For example, did new leadership change the brand promise of the community in a way that degraded the trust of community members? Imagine a company that built a community where participation was free . . . and all of a sudden, they decided to charge for participation. That move could trigger a drop in brand trust.

Other communities might experience infighting among members or leadership that hinders member growth. No one likes to sit in the middle of political upheavals, and as such, members might focus their time on discovering new, less disruptive environments.

Beyond community leadership, your own company's leadership can hinder the success of community-led motions. If your CEO, CRO, or CFO do not see

Jay Peredo (▲,◐) ✅
@jayperedox   •••

Marketing isn't always about acquiring customers immediately.

It's also about building trust with your audience by providing constant value.

When you do it this way, you'll end up with a community of users who don't just buy your products, but also give feedback and support.

Marketing isn't always about acquiring customers immediately.[60]

value in community endeavors that take time to impact the top or bottom line positively, they may deprioritize the investments needed to keep the community afloat. On the other hand, executive teams and company culture that encourage or reward community participation may enable motions to flourish.

In other cases, the state of the overall market can have an impact on community success. In newer growth markets, excitement and hype are high, encouraging people to get involved in communities where they can learn new concepts and establish important relationships. In older or declining markets, waning attention can lead to fewer community relationships and a lower desire to share or create content.

For example, in 2022, we observed the launch of artificial intelligence-based solutions like Dall-E, ChatGPT, Midjourney, Stable Diffusion, and others. While the topic and technologies are booming today, they will inevitably be replaced by some new practice, technology, or approach. Whenever that day comes, membership in communities that are growing today will contract, content development will slow, and brand promises that brought those communities together will become less relevant.

Participation in communities varies over time

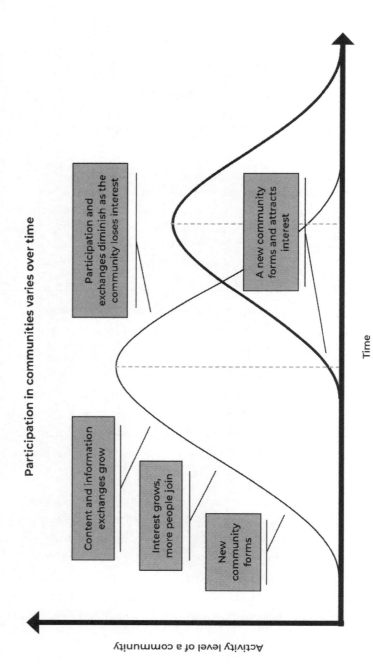

New community forms

Interest grows, more people join

Content and information exchanges grow

Participation and exchanges diminish as the community loses interest

A new community forms and attracts interest

Activity level of a community

Time

Community interest and engagement evolves over time. Communities may need to shift priorities to stay in line with member needs and expectations. Other communities will grow and compete for attention over time.

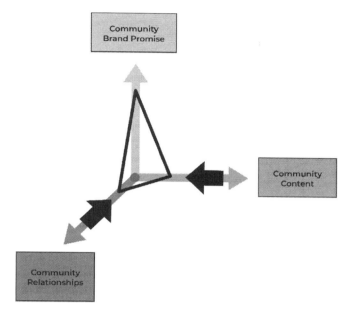

Changes in one axis impact the other two axes. For example, when trust erodes in community relationships, the volume of content/information exchanges will contract.

Position Your Community Idea

The next thing you will want to do is spend time on the whiteboard to write down your community idea. For this exercise, don't guide yourself into the mistake of defining a community idea that you think people "should" join; instead, build the community that people want to join.

With ADDO, we built a community conference that provided a forum anyone could join because other industry conferences were set up with too many barriers (cost, travel, limited access). For CMO Coffee Talk, they built a community of peers who could gather regularly to share ideas in a forum where we weren't barraged by vendor pitches, and everyone was welcome no matter where they resided physically.

Now comes the fun part. Head to your whiteboard or open your favorite note-taking application—it's time to describe your ideal community. To help you start, here are a few questions. Read through them before you begin answering them. Once you have read them all, use 100–200 words to answer each question.

- What is the community about?
- If your community didn't exist, what alternatives would they use?
- What does your community offer that others do not?
- Why would your ideal members care about those things?
- What is happening in the industry now that will make your community even more relevant?

Answering just five questions will help you discern whether you are building the forum to serve your company and customers or to serve a larger community than your organization.

> **Answering just five questions will help you discern whether you are building the forum to serve your company and customers or to serve a larger community than your organization.**

I have to admit we did not take this formal approach to define our community with ADDO. This exercise is something I picked up later in my professional experience. That said, I will use ADDO as an example in answering these questions.

Here's my stab at positioning ADDO using the five questions above (181 words).

> *We want to educate anyone in the world who wants to learn about DevOps. Prior to our community, a select few software engineers secured travel budgets to attend regional DevOps events. Others left back home or living too far from these events pursued individual self-learning paths online or in books.*

> *We want to make education accessible for all by creating a free online forum and running it for 24 hours straight. We will give everyone direct access to*

thought- and practice leaders where they can ask any questions that come to mind. For anyone who can't make the 24-hour gathering, we'll place all 90 hours of content online free of charge. We want individuals and teams to learn together from community contributors.

Software engineering teams who want to outpace their competitors and level up their skills desire this knowledge because they have already heard that industry leaders like Netflix, Amazon, and Google are adopting these next-generation engineering practices. Engineering teams and individual developers who don't want to be left behind in a fast-paced industry will benefit from this free, online, community-based forum.

Your words don't need to be perfect, but the idea of the community should be clear. In the idea above, the target audience is defined, and the industry trends supporting the need of the community are laid out.

After going through this positioning exercise, if you find yourself in the company/customer realm, you are still in Orbit 2. You need to revisit the purpose and find the escape velocity needed for Orbit 3.

If you find yourself stuck in Orbit 2, imagine several industry influencers sitting in a room. None of them are employed by your business. Then ask yourself, *"What community idea would they come up with, what value would they say is missing from the communities where they already participate, and whom would they envision needing that value?"* If none of those things are tied directly to your products and what your company offers, you are on the right track.

Create a "Happy Hour" Pitch

As a final exercise, it's now time to create your "happy hour pitch." This time, imagine you are at a happy hour one evening at your next industry event. You've already established the community, and it has had tremendous uptake. It's the buzz of the industry. There is a small group of people discussing what is working and not working in the market at large. Someone pipes up wanting to recommend the community your team built to serve that missing piece of value.

What would they say to recommend it? It's a one or two-sentence remark that tells others exactly what the value is and gets them excited to join. It's not a tagline or positioning statement. It's not how you would describe it yourself. It's a real person—an arm's length away—who became a fan of what you are doing.

For example:

> *"Hey there, do you know Gianna? She co-founded and built an online community for marketing pros in the cybersecurity arena. They have over 2,000 members who share insights with each other on Slack, but they also host in-person events on a local level. I joined it two years ago."*

Or

> *"She created a weekly CMO-only forum for people like us to have candid discussions about what's working, what's not, and things we're all trying to level up on. There's also a private Slack workspace where you can reach all the CMO community members. They even have a cool "swipe file" in Slack where we share great CMO-oriented content."*

Form Your Brand Promise

Once you have the positioning laid out, it's time to consider what specific things your community will do for its members. These are the things that will keep people coming back for more and inviting others to join them. People participate in communities for numerous reasons. They want to:

- Find their tribe
- Solve a problem
- Gain knowledge
- Share knowledge
- Develop new relationships
- Inspire them
- Hear diverse perspectives
- Discover a safe space
- Have fun

You don't have to guide every member of your community to these outcomes. The role of the community is to foster a space that encourages and enables these outcomes.

Serve Business Goals Through Orbit 3

There are a tremendous number of benefits your company can get from form-ing or helping lead the charge in a community. The benefits bring value to marketing, sales, product engineering, and customer success. The more your organization recognizes the benefits, the more employees you'll see partici-pating in or working alongside the community-led initiatives.

Some of the common benefits include the following.

- **Capturing mindshare/visibility:** The more you participate, the more top of mind your people and your business will be when it comes time for people to buy or recommend products.

- **Improving credibility:** Taking a leading role in sharing knowledge, solving problems, and connecting with others can boost the credibility of your business.

- **Understanding market priorities:** The more active you are, the more opportunities you have to listen which improves the opportunity to understand trends that could impact your business and product roadmap.

- **Attracting new customers:** Communities attract new audiences, many of whom will be curious to learn about your business. Relationships forged within a community can extend further into and influence a sales cycle.

- **Analyzing market opportunities:** Communities can represent a channel to new data that can be analyzed by your business. Things like attendance or survey data can shed light on ideal accounts and personas or market interests and priorities.

- **Impacting others:** Perhaps no greater personal benefit comes from community-led initiatives than helping others. You might directly help someone or simply facilitate people helping one another through the community.

Be Clear with Your Value

People will naturally place their eggs in more than one community basket. That's perfectly ok. It would be impossible for one community to serve all these needs for its members.

When we founded the ADDO community, there were already many DevOps communities across the globe. Over 50 DevOpsDays communities had been formed on a local level. A couple of DevOps groups on LinkedIn had formed with over 50,000 members. Some vendors had started to form DevOps communities that were more brand-centric, but still attracted a lot of attention.

Be clear with your mission, objectives, and value when it comes to community. We founded ADDO to provide the most inclusive and accessible educational space for anyone in our community. As such, we did not compete with the other DevOps communities. In fact, where we could, we did our best to collaborate with them. We prioritized providing the highest quality experiences for our members, and they stuck with us for it.

The same holds true for the multiple marketing communities in which I participate:

- **CMO Coffee Talk** provides an excellent weekly session and Slack workspace that provides incredible insights and connections.
- **Pavilion** provides access to a wealth of information from CMOs and other people in marketing roles.
- **RevGenius** provides a forum for me to ask questions about RevOps, and tooling choices, find out about a great podcast, or ping someone about deal coaching.
- **CMOlist** provides a place to reach other marketing executives to ask questions, gain insight, and share my own experiences with others.
- **Cybersecurity Marketing Society** helps me find specific resources or collaborate with other companies in my industry from a marketing perspective.
- **TMA and DCA Live**, in my local Washington, D.C. metro area, provide great opportunities to meet and connect in person with CMO peers at different times across the year.

I don't see any of these as competitive with one another. In fact, I know a number of industry friends who surf between these same communities with me. Each one provides a different but important value.

> **Don't try to corner the market in your community. Provide the best value, and people will gravitate toward you.**

Don't try to corner the market in your community. Provide the best value, and people will gravitate toward you. The stronger your community is, the higher your barriers will be to any competitors.

EXPERT TIP: BE CONSISTENT

Prioritize active and authentic engagement. To build larger and more engaged communities, you and your teams need to actively participate in community discussions, respond to inquiries and feedback, and show genuine interest in understanding and addressing community needs. Regularly providing valuable content, resources, and support further solidifies your credibility and fosters a sense of trust within the community. Remember, trust is built through consistent and meaningful engagement—not by occasionally jumping in to help someone. The more often you engage, the more likely you and your company are to be top of mind with your community members.

CHAPTER 8

Organizing Your Team

In this chapter, we will shed new light on community-led marketing to help CMOs structure, budget for, and measure their initiatives. We'll then discuss how CMOs can best align their community- and product-led marketing teams for success.

You will learn how to align community-led initiatives to your sales and product organizations for greater business impact. Failure to find these points of alignment can create cultural and organizational riffs that will lessen marketing's impact for everyone. Finding alignment between the orbits and the rest of your organization can lead to amazing experiences, energized teams, and more wins for your business.

Establish Where Orbit 3 Initiatives Live

Let's open with something that'll turn a few heads. CMOs should position the head of community-led initiatives—for Orbit 3—as a direct report. Community-led initiatives might not have the budget or staff of other direct reports to the CMO, but they represent an important piece of the overall go-to-market strategy.

For CMOs who consider themselves a "Chief Market Officer,"[61] the direct reporting structure makes even more sense. Where product and brand initiatives lie at the heart of marketing, community efforts lie at the heart of the market. Community-led initiatives provide critical insight into the market needs and its shifting requirements that make long-term planning easier. To ensure proper visibility of community interests, it is best to elevate an Orbit 3 leader to a direct report of the CMO.

That said, the right reporting structure can go wrong when strategies don't align. For example, when marketing leaders report to sales, their focus changes to closing deals and not generating pipeline. When a community team reports to marketing, the focus should not be solely oriented toward demand generation. Community-led initiatives connect marketing with the market, enhance brand awareness, and support demand generation.

The best community-led initiatives are well rounded. You will see this more— later in the book—when we walk through a number of integrated, three orbit playbooks.

> **Where product and brand initiatives lie at the heart of marketing, community efforts lie at the heart of the market.**

Even when community-led teams report to marketing, CMOs should set the expectation of operational links into product, sales, support, and customer success. At the same time, be sure the product, sales, support, and customer success teams understand the objectives and outcomes being pursued by the community-led roles and that updates are to be shared on a regular basis. If necessary, meet with your HR department to review roles and responsibilities that can improve cross-functional alignment.

While other organizational structures are possible, they are usually less efficient and more challenging to tie into specific business outcomes.

Determine Orbit 3 Community-Led Initiatives Leadership

According to the 2022 State of Community Management report, marketing is the most common reporting line for community-led initiatives. Community-led initiatives report to the marketing team 28 percent of the time.[62]

The second most common reporting line is an independent role, reporting directly to the CEO. In 2022, independent reporting lines represented 15 percent of survey organizations.[63] Community leaders taking this path will want to ensure the proper business impact and outcomes of their teams are defined. Creating a business case for continued investment becomes more difficult when impact cannot be measured efficiently.

The 2022 report shows community-led initiatives reporting into customer support as the third most popular approach—representing nine percent of organizations.[64] I would argue that community-led initiatives reporting into customer support are likely more focused on brand-led strategies where the only participants in a community are your customers themselves (i.e., Orbit 2). This organizational structure becomes more difficult when leaders want to engage non-customer members in the community and support conversations that do not pertain specifically to the company's products or services.

> **The easiest place to find the right person is to look internally for the person most connected to your community at large.**

Finding the right person to head your community is not always easy. The right candidates require the proper mix of experience and personality attributes. The easiest place to find the right person is to look internally for the person most connected to your community at large. This could be the person who is always attending and participating in industry events or perhaps loves developing new ideas and sharing them in community work spaces online.

You might also find a great candidate outside of your business that is already very well connected in the community. The person might be an individual consultant, work for a competitor, or someone who established a forum to gather community members.

Another potentially unexpected place to look for experienced community leaders is in your customer base. Individuals who are already fans of your business can make great community leaders, especially if they have already taken similar steps in the community to set up local or regional meet-up groups that foster knowledge exchange and build relationships.

More than anything, you want to identify someone who can identify themselves with your community. They don't have to be an expert in the industry or have a deep knowledge of your product or service, but they do have to have an intellectual curiosity that keeps them interested in supporting the larger cause your business is pursuing.

Community Leaders Are Connectors and Helpers

When advising business executives on the type of people they want heading their community-led initiatives, two attributes stand out more than any others. Community-led leaders are *connectors* and *helpers*.

In Malcolm Gladwell's book, *The Tipping Point*, he describes the connector as *"people with a truly extraordinary knack of making friends and acquaintances"* and a *"natural gift for making social connections."*[65]

To provide a little more context: In the book, he describes an experiment where different populations are given a list of surnames they are connected to in social circles. The average member of any surveyed group might know between 20–40 people, but the connectors were the outliers. The connectors knew more than 100 people sharing one of the 250 surnames within their social network.

Gladwell goes on to describe another type of person: The helper or "maven." He describes the maven as a person who has a lot of information about products, places, and people. The mavens like to be the helpers in community-led initiatives.

"What sets Mavens apart, though, is not so much what they know but how they pass it along," Gladwell says. *"The fact that mavens want to help, for no other reason than because they like to help, turns out to be an awfully effective way of getting someone's attention."*[66]

> **"The fact that mavens want to help, for no other reason than because they like to help, turns out to be an awfully effective way of getting someone's attention."**
> **—Malcolm Gladwell**

My close friend Mark Miller is a connector and helper, so I will share his story as a real-world example. Where most days I feel like I have a couple of hundred people in my social circles, Mark probably has a few thousand. If I ever wanted to meet or get connected with someone in the industries where Mark and I worked together, he could find a connection and begin making quality introductions within hours.

For example, one day, we were discussing how awesome it would be to have someone prominent like Bill Gates speak to a community group we were working with. To share some additional context, we had absolutely no money to pay someone like Bill Gates to speak to our community. If he were to agree to speak, it would have to be a pro bono gesture.

The very next day, Mark tells me that he's in touch with people in Bill Gates' office, and they are considering the proposal to have him speak to our community. It turns out that Mark had once worked with the Bill and Melinda Gates Foundation on an AIDS research project. He had an idea of where to start finding the connection to the right people and pursued it.

I probably have fifty such stories of Mark leveraging connections he had made over his long career as concert promoter, pasta entrepreneur, and technology influencer.

Mark is also a helper. If anything gives him more pleasure in life beyond his family, it is helping people in the community. If you want to learn something and are looking for someone who may help, Mark is your guy.

Want to know how to design that feature for your Microsoft SharePoint site? Mark can connect you with the person who wrote the book on the topic. Looking for experience in building a "DevOps" program at your business? Mark can connect you with the person who coined the term. Want to find a shop that produces the best bows for your double bass? Mark had lunch with the owner of the shop three years ago and can make the introduction.

You won't be able to measure attribution around karma, but it does pay high dividends.

The connector and helper attributes of your Orbit 3 leader are important to ensuring the scale, reach, and impact of your community. The goal of the leader is not to promote your business per se but to increase the number of connections and relationships it has in the community.

Your leader may also help many members of the community, but more importantly, you want them to connect members of the community who can help each other. These motions grow the value and recognition of your community as one that is selfless—concerned more with the needs and wishes of others than with one's own. You won't be able to measure attribution around karma, but it does pay high dividends.

The Best Community Leaders Don't Need A C-Level Title

One day, I received a call from Mary (for the sake of anonymity, I've given this person a pseudonym), an industry friend. Mary is a CMO, and her business had started a community initiative aimed at Chief Information Security Officers (CISOs). She explained that when her company started the community effort, the team thought it would be great to have their CISO lead it. On the surface, the decision seemed logical: A CISO should lead the CISO community.

While the CISO titles definitely matched, the enthusiasm to lead the effort did not. Her CISO wanted marketing to play a leading role in organizing the community because it was presented internally as part of a go-to-market strategy. He was an introvert, and this lowered his enthusiasm to engage with and respond to the initial group of community members. What had started with excitement and a grand plan was falling short of expectations because the executive wasn't truly dedicated to playing the role of the community leader.

This is a common mistake that organizations make in assigning their most senior executive to lead a community that most resembles the target persona. For example, if you were building a community of CMOs, logic would have it that you should assign yourself (the CMO) to lead that effort. If you were targeting a community of software developers, you might think that your CTO, who was once a developer, would be the perfect candidate to lead the community engagement.

In the best-case scenario, your CMO or CTO would not only want to head the community but would also bring the right personality traits of the *helper* and *connector*. They would not see the role so much as an assignment but more as a benefit to connect with and learn from others.

> **A good rule of thumb is: Don't try to find the most senior person in your organization to lead the community, especially if their heart is not into taking on the role.**

A good rule of thumb is: Don't try to find the most senior person in your organization to lead the community, especially if their heart is not into taking on the role. As another friend told me, *"You really need to find the person in your org who truly gives a f___ about the community, its values and helps make the right connections."* When you do, you know you have found the right person for the role.

Acquiring Yourself into A Community

Another option for companies wanting to accelerate their way into an external community is through acquisition. For example, in 2010, I worked for a company called Global 360 that wanted to expand its influence in the Microsoft SharePoint ecosystem. To accomplish this, we could invest more of our own time and resources toward participating in the community to gain a foothold.

But another alternative was through direct investment in an influencer who had already established a strong foundation of relationships in the industry. As such, and as you've already heard, we asked Mark Miller, who at that time ran the world's largest SharePoint community, to join our marketing team.

Our company did not purchase the End User SharePoint business that Mark operated. We simply hired him to boost our ties into the community and to help advise us on the best ways to attract attention in the market. Most importantly, we identified ways to tie Mark's community-led efforts to initiatives that boosted brand awareness and generated more leads for our business. Those efforts paid off tremendously when our company was acquired two years later—in part for the incredibly positive impact our community marketing efforts had had on brand, demand gen, and sales outcomes.

In 2020, Salesforce pursued a similar acqui-hire strategy by hiring Brian Solis. Solis is a well-known consultant and speaker with a large community following and has been writing about digital trends for over a decade. His work has been featured in publications such as *The New York Times*, *The Wall Street Journal*, and *Forbes*. Solis is an expert in digital transformation and a strong advocate for customer experience who believes that customer experience is the new competitive advantage.

Solis is a valuable asset to Salesforce's community-led efforts and will help the company to continue to lead the way in the digital age in a number of ways.

- Increasing brand awareness and thought leadership
- Gaining access to Solis's network of contacts
- Tapping into Solis's expertise in digital transformation and customer experience
- Benefiting from Solis's ability to connect with customers and employees on a personal level

CMOs venturing down the acqui-hire path need to develop clear strategies for engaging influencers. Acquiring well-known talent can provide an immediate boost to brand awareness. Community leaders can add to your bench strength of spokespeople who can confidently converse with the trade press and can produce expert content that resonates with your market. They can also accelerate your brand presence at industry events through higher-profile speaking slots. And as a knowledgeable voice of the market, they can add much-needed external perspective to strategic product roadmap decisions.

Be forewarned, not all well-known influencers in your market will make a good fit to lead your community efforts. Latane Conant, CMO at 6sense, says that, *"You need to find someone who cares about the community brand more than their personal brand."* When the influencer's personal brand is stronger than the community's brand in Orbit 3, it can be more difficult to make the needed connections back to lower marketing orbits. The community lead has to be in the role of serving the community-led orbit first and where personal brand benefits but is a secondary priority. If the community leader's brand is stronger than the community's, your business can be negatively impacted when the influencer leaves for greener pastures.

"You need to find someone who cares about the community brand more than their personal brand."
—Latane Conant

The most bang-for-the-buck results from acqui-hires will be achieved when their Orbit 3 efforts are connected with the inner demand-generation orbits. Influencers who understand and can help map their initiatives into demand-gen engines are highly sought after for their talent. This sort of multi-stage campaign mapping does not come naturally to all influencers, and therefore, may need to be complemented by team members who are better suited to connecting the dots between all three orbits. In some cases, that responsibility may fall directly upon the CMO.

Making the Right Community Hire

Sometimes, the quickest way into a community can be to buy your way into it by hiring a well-known influencer. That influencer is charged with running a community or helping further elevate the company's brand presence in a target community.

The influencers might have spent years building up their own personal brands, social media followers, and community relationships. Some of these influencers place so much value in their personal brands that when the company brand values conflict with their own, challenges crop up.

For example, imagine hiring someone who has 100,000 followers on X (formerly Twitter). They've built their brand reputation by being helpful, sharing new insights, and occasionally being very critical of social policies in your country. Their role at your global company is to help build a community in Orbit 3.

> **Sometimes, the quickest way into a community can be to buy your way into it by hiring a well-known influencer. But proceed with caution.**

Now imagine a situation that arises where the influencer shares an overly liberal or conservative view on a potentially controversial topic on their social channels. The statements they make are 100 percent aligned with the personal brand they've established for themselves. At the same time, the remarks don't align well with the community or company brand they represent as your employee. In cases like this, influencer brands that outweigh their community brands can be a distraction from the intended outcomes.

When considering hiring influencers with well-established brands, it is important to walk through expectations of where the boundaries exist for personal brands and community brands. In some cases, you may find it is better to build a trusted relationship with a well-known influencer rather than put the person on your payroll. Once an influencer is on the payroll, expectations of behavior and influence might not match the goodness you experienced when that person was independent.

You can find great influencers who are a perfect match for your culture, but it's best to learn upfront if the influencer would value their own brand over that of the company or communities.

Support Community Leaders

When crafting your organizational chart with community leadership in mind, consider the tremendous potential it holds to seamlessly integrate with your business functions. Placing the community manager as a direct report to the CMO can amplify your organization's synergy and boost collaboration across departments.

This approach streamlines the recognition of opportunities and minimizes any potential misunderstandings from other teams. For instance, the head of sales might inquire about the budget allocated to the community, driven by a genuine desire to see short-term gains. Similarly, the head of demand generation may seek ways to tap into the contacts generated by the community effort, highlighting the team's enthusiasm for the shared goal.

When everyone can clearly see how the community's value aligns with their respective spheres, these inquiries transform into productive discussions about how each department can leverage the community's strength to bolster their efforts. This unity can even lead to cross-functional initiatives that create more significant business impact.

In some cases, these departments might be so excited about the community's potential that they actively advocate for further investments. They recognize the value of community building and its role in the broader marketing strategy.

It's worth highlighting that the role of community management might be initially unclear to some within the organization. Building and nurturing a community takes time, the right people, and dedicated resources. The CMO's visionary leadership ensures that the community initiative is not only understood but also nurtured and celebrated as a vital aspect of the organization's DNA. By fostering a culture of unity and continuous communication, your organization can maximize the benefits of community-led marketing, showcasing its immense value to all stakeholders.

Budget for Success

More marketing leaders are coming to recognize the tangible benefits of community-led initiatives toward impacting top and bottom-line growth. As such, more of them have dedicated people and program budgets within their organizations to support these initiatives.

Own vs. Rent

I asked my friend Matt Heinz for advice about how to get a CEO's buy-in when it came to investing in the community. His answer was simple. *"It's better to own versus rent."*

> **"It's better to own versus rent."**
> **—Matt Heinz**

The experience of planning a marketing budget is full of investment choices about how to reach and interact with your ideal market. You might make a decision to invest $40,000 in sponsoring a large industry trade show. The event attracts 5,000 people each year. Your team's job is to attract as much interest as possible to your booth so they can scan and generate a lead list. In these moments, you are renting someone else's audience.

While valuable for demand generation, your team is actively spending time hoping to build relationships with enough trust to continue the conversation at a future time (e.g., the nurture campaign or next point of contact). The in-person experiences are fleeting and expensive.

The same goes for other outbound initiatives where you are participating in someone else's meet-ups, roadshows, or partner events. It's also the same when paying to publish content on someone else's media or industry site. You rent time with someone else's audience.

Investing in your own community is one of the best forms of inbound marketing. You can build and own the forum. The relationships built in the forum, while spontaneous in some cases, are less fleeting and more trusted because they happen in a consistent environment over time. The community is seen as a place where people can find help, get inspired, or make new connections. The more people who get involved, the more trusted relationships you can build.

When my friend Mark was running the End User SharePoint community, over 50,000 people visited his online forum each month. He built the forum, invited others to contribute, and owned the relationship with his audience.

The more his community helped people, the more they wanted to participate, share, and invite others to join.

> **When it comes to budgeting for community-led marketing efforts, pricing out *owned vs. rented* audiences is a good first step.**

When it comes to budgeting for community-led marketing efforts, pricing out owned versus rented audiences is a good first step. What would you pay to rent a 5,000-person audience at someone else's two- or three-day conference? By comparison, how would you value a community of 5,000 people who were attracted to a forum your business championed?

The reality is that you should invest in both opportunities. However, in the long run, you will get more value out of the communities you own yourself.

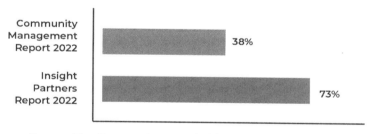

Organizations investing in community-led motions

Community Management Report 2022 — 38%

Insight Partners Report 2022 — 73%

Source: *The Community Roundtable and Insight Partners.*

Budgeting for the Community

The percentage of organizations with dedicated community budgets varies by source. At the low end, the State of Community Management Report 2022 reveals that 45 percent of marketing leaders have dedicated budgets—up from 38 percent of those surveyed for the 2020 report.[67] On the higher end, Insight Partners revealed that 73 percent of their organizations had people and program budgets for community-led motions in place.[68]

The shift toward remote work and the emergence of COVID-19 played a significant part in moving investments toward community initiatives. When marketing leaders needed to find new ways to generate qualified leads after in-person gatherings were no longer an option, community-led motions helped fill the gap. People wanted to get together in forums to exchange information and enhance their professional skills, and one of the best ways to accomplish this was by networking with their industry peers.

Marketing leaders who invested in community-led motions since the pandemic shift saw increased lead volumes, boosted brand awareness, and accelerated wins. According to the 2021 Community Industry Report, 70 percent of companies with communities increased their budget for community building as a result of being able to better attribute community-led outcomes to their top and bottom line.[69]

It wasn't that marketing executives were trading established investments in demand generation for new experiments in community-led initiatives. The best marketing teams were placing a greater emphasis on community motions that, over time, could tie directly back to demand generation. They were purposefully connecting new Orbit 3 activities to their established Orbit 1 initiatives.

As more marketing leaders report on the benefits of community-led initiatives, the industry is seeing an uptick in the percentage who are adding the motion into their go-to-market plans. For example, Insight Partners reports that 55 percent of their portfolio companies without community budgets are planning to experiment with investments in 2023.[70]

How Much Budget Should You Allocate to Community-Led Motions?

The percentage of marketing budgets invested in community-led initiatives varies. According to Insight Partners, investments ranged from seven percent on the low end to twelve percent of marketing spend on the high end.[71]

Companies that invest in working their way into more visible leadership roles within already established external communities may be on the lower end of the investment range. By comparison, companies that target investments toward building a new community forum may need to budget for higher initial start-up costs (e.g., travel, hosting dinners/events, website hosting, brand design, and paid promotions).

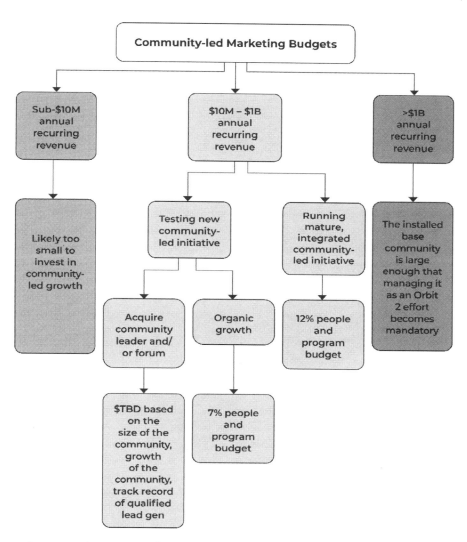

Company size matters when it comes to budgeting for community-led efforts

Not all companies should pursue community-led marketing efforts. Community-led efforts are best in organizations that have annual recurring revenue (ARR) between $10 million and $1 billion. There are always outliers, but community-led marketing and sales leaders I have spoken with agree with these guardrails.

In 2022, the percentage of marketing budgets invested in community-led activities ranged from 7 percent on the low end to 12 percent of marketing spend on the high end.

Companies below $10 million in ARR should be focused on discovering their product-market fit. At this stage of growth, the best target community for a business may be unknown. Any investment in community building will require significant time on a limited budget with a much higher risk of misidentifying the right relationships and forums. For example, suppose your business was focused on improving compliance for marketing practices. In that case, you might not know at the earliest stages of growth if the best community would be formed by engaging compliance officers or marketing leaders. Splitting time between both camps or choosing the wrong one and needing to start over is not worth the budget risk.

Companies above the $1 billion annual revenue mark have captured a significant portion of their market. They can focus more energy on building and sustaining their own product and brand communities in Orbit 2, where new and recurring revenue has specific targets for sales and marketing. At this scale, customers, partners, systems integrators, and other stakeholders require significant attention and investment. Orbit 3 community-led motions should be pursued at this revenue stage with their impact measured on brand and revenue.

Battling Short-termism

The shadows of short-termism are hard to outrun. Executive teams and Boards are looking to marketing leaders for the fastest return on investments that ensure the next quarter of growth. This problem impacts every part of the company, from product engineering to customer support and marketing.

One of the biggest hurdles CMOs will face when targeting investments for community-led motions is measuring their return on investment. While the latest marketing campaign will show results within a quarter or two, community-led initiatives can take more time to see results—especially in the formation stages. At the formation stage, relationships are being built, and trust is beginning to be established. These foundational elements of the community take time to form but pay off tremendously in time.

The longer-term marketing investments in community-led motions are similar to those made by engineering teams with product roadmaps. Some feature sets or products may take a year or more to develop before they can directly impact revenue or customer retention. Strategic long-term investments by marketing teams should be considered in a similar light, where a small portion of the budget can be applied to activities that are recognized as paying off much later.

Not all community-led marketing initiatives take a long time to pay off. Pursuing big-bang initiatives can be risky, especially if their timing crosses fiscal year boundaries. Instead, plan on short-term measures and checkpoints that help reveal the impact of content, relationships, and reach that may be leading to a much larger outcome. Incremental evidence of results will keep the budget-eating hounds at bay.

Company leaders who are unable to invest in the long term might have to be satisfied with lower-than-average future returns. While short-term profitability is important, a failure to balance this with strategic long-term investments can lead to missed opportunities and weakened competitive advantage, potentially resulting in lower-than-average future returns. Company leaders need to understand and balance the needs of the present with those of the future to ensure sustained growth and profitability. Therefore, be sure to allocate some portion of your people and program budget to these longer-term community-led motions.

Own the Tech Stack and the Data

Earlier in the book, you learned best practices for approaching the tech stack. The guiding principles in that section were to use what you have and otherwise explore free or low-cost options as you begin to invest in community-led marketing initiatives.

One important consideration for any community relates to its website and/or community platform. As you've seen, Orbit 3 initiatives are not focused on promoting your company or your products and services. Therefore, when promoting your community initiative, you will have to decide if the public-facing platform you use will be a slice of your corporate platform or if it will stand on its own. It's a matter of perspective.

Imagine you and I work for a company called SalesPlatform. Our core business is a SaaS-based CRM platform. Beyond our first and second-orbit marketing initiatives, we want to build a third-orbit community. We want the community to bring together enterprise and inside sales reps to learn from one another, share industry insights, and educate one another on best practices.

If we host the community on our core SalesPlatform.com platform—let's say at salesplatform.com/community, people who we bring to that forum may mistake the community for our company's user group, where people discuss our products and services all day. It would give the impression of an Orbit 2 initiative.

> ## Of equal importance to the branding strategy is the data strategy your marketing team will employ around the community.

As an alternative approach, we could build our community site on a different web instance called SalesExperts.com so as not to confuse it with our corporate brand. The same approach could be taken if we launched the community on Discourse, Slack, or another community platform. By dropping the corporate name from the community, you'll have a higher chance of attracting and retaining the Orbit 3 audience you plan to serve.

Of equal importance to the branding strategy above is the data strategy your marketing team will employ. Assuming you build a successful community with a growing and active base, you'll want to leverage information about them to feed and improve marketing for your core business.

The data from the community can provide terrific insights for your Orbit 1 and Orbit 2 marketing initiatives. The larger and more active your community gets, the more data and insight you will be able to gather from them, including the following.

- **Demographic:** Demographic data covers population characteristics like age, gender, income, education, and ethnicity. Your marketing team can use this data to segment audiences and create tailored marketing messages for different demographic groups, resulting in more relevant and effective campaigns.

- **Technographic:** Technographic data focuses on technology-related attributes of individuals or organizations, such as devices, operating systems, browsers, and software usage. This data will enable your marketing team to understand your audience's technology preferences, enabling them to create targeted campaigns addressing specific needs or optimizing content and user experience for popular devices and platforms.

- **Psychographic:** This type of data focuses on an individual's personality, values, interests, opinions, and lifestyle choices. Your marketing team can use psychographic data to create more targeted and personalized marketing campaigns that resonate with the audience's mindset and preferences.

- **Behavioral:** This data type encompasses information about how community members interact with content, forums, or subgroups with a specific interest. It includes browsing and purchase history, product usage, engagement with marketing materials, and customer feedback. Behavioral data will help marketers segment audiences and tailor messages to improve conversion rates.

- **Geolocation:** Geolocation data refers to the geographic location of customers. This can help your marketing team customize campaigns based on regional preferences, local events, or culture.

- **Social Media:** Social media platforms provide marketers with valuable insights into user preferences, opinions, and interactions. By analyzing social media data, your marketing team can identify trends, influencers, and sentiment to then create targeted and engaging marketing campaigns.

- **Customer Relationship Management (CRM):** CRM systems store data related to customer interactions, such as purchase history, service requests, and contact information. Analyzing this data can help your marketing team better understand community member needs, preferences, and pain points that might be expressed in their Orbit 3 activities. You'll definitely want to keep abreast of what participants are doing in the community to see if it opens insights that can accelerate or expand deals for your company.

- **Firmographic:** This type of data is used primarily for B2B marketing and focuses on the characteristics of companies, such as industry, size, location, and revenue. Firmographic data can help your marketing team identify new or potential target companies and develop tailored marketing approaches for different industry segments based on trends they observe in community forums.

- **Intent:** Intent data refers to information that suggests a potential customer's readiness to buy or their interest in a product or service. This can be derived from online search behavior, website visits, or content consumption patterns in a community forum. Your marketing team can use this intent data to identify high-potential prospects and deliver timely and relevant marketing messages that align with community interest on the topic.

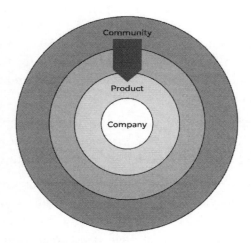

Sharing insight from community data helps improve product-led demand generation motions.

By managing data and communication platforms for the community, your company's demand-generation team can learn from it. The data will help your marketing team understand more about your ideal customer profiles and then improve the targeting of lookalike accounts. Being able to analyze hundreds— and hopefully thousands—of data points will help your team better assess and target your corporate demand generation strategies.

Imagine having on your radar what new titles are emerging in the growing market space or what industries make sense to prioritize for vertical campaigns. Your demand-generation team could then lead experimental outreach based on the data you've analyzed to see if your company could move the needle in underserved or even previously undiscovered markets.

A note of caution when it comes to data from different orbits. Data segmentation will be critical to your success.

A note of caution when it comes to data from different orbits. Data segmentation will be critical to your success. Just as your marketing team segments data by company size, customers, regions, industry, active in the pipeline, etc., you'll want to segment community-led data as well. You don't want your team to suddenly send a promotional email or invite that is targeting the product-led demand-gen prospects that also include community-led participants. This is because the community-led participants are not expecting to be pitched.

Don't worry. It's not all "hands-off" segmentation for community-led participants. Later in the book, we'll walk through a number of community-led to product-led playbooks that can help you safely shift community participants from the outer to inner orbits.

Tighten Relationships Between Orbits

I've often described marketing using an analogy of "fuel and engines." Content, connections, and stories are the *fuel* of marketing that speaks to the community, the users, and the buyers. The fuel pulls people in and creates an emotional connection with your business and the problems it can help solve. The higher the quality of fuel, the better the engine works.

The higher the quality of fuel, the better the engine works.

One of the key challenges CMOs will have to address is tightening the relationship between community-led marketers in Orbit 3 and product-led marketers in Orbit 1. Specialized demand-gen talent understands how to automate marketing outreach, plan campaigns, and measure marketing's return on investment for every dollar spent. They are *engine* experts. They know how to tune for maximum performance but don't create the fuel.

At the same time, community-led marketers serve the market's needs by building relationships, connecting members, and fostering content creation. They are fuel chemists. They know how to tune content fuel to be helpful, resourceful, and impactful, but they may know little about engine mechanics.

Community-led marketing initiatives generate some of the highest quality fuel to attract the market's attention at the top of the funnel. The content, created by your own community leaders or members, is generally helpful, neutral, and

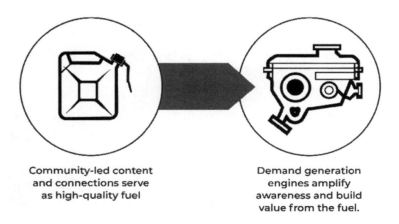

Community-led content   Demand generation
and connections serve   engines amplify
as high-quality fuel   awareness and build
                               value from the fuel.

Marketing leaders who align community-led and demand-generation initiatives create happier, higher-performing teams.

pragmatic. Examples like maturity models, community salary surveys, books, best practice guides, strategy and how-to guides, and reference architectures developed by the community can garner high levels of interest.

Demand-generation teams thrive on high-quality content. It fuels their inbound engines. Email campaigns, paid digital promotions, webinars, and websites capture more attention at the top of the funnel when the content informs and educates rather than sells or promotes. The Orbit 3 content benefits the demand-gen teams by enabling them to provide a blend of fuel: Content that pitches products, and content that is substantive and helpful.

> ## Community-led marketers serve the market's needs by building relationships, connecting members, and fostering content creation. They are fuel chemists.

The more Orbit 3 leaders understand the impact of their content and connections on Orbit 1 demand-generation efforts, the more they can optimize the fuel feeding it. For example, if Orbit 3 leaders are held responsible for tracking and reporting on the impact of their fuel in terms of leads generated, deals influenced, referrals created, and pipeline sourced, they will have a better understanding of the importance of their role toward achieving business success. They should not have to directly manage the pipeline and demand-generation efforts, but they do need to be distinctly aware of what is working and what is not. Maintaining feedback loops between engine and fuel is critical to everyone's success.

In teams I've managed, community-led marketers have been encouraged to provide weekly reports on their demand metrics. This ensures they understand the connection between their community goals and their business goals. As one of my college professors quipped, *"Keeping score improves the score."*

The better Orbit 3 leaders understand their ties to demand generation, the more they will understand that the engine cannot take an unlimited amount of fuel. Solid campaigns using high-quality content can live for many quarters in the market without the need for continuous refreshes. Orbit 3 leaders must understand that demand-gen teams don't work as well when they shift from one piece of fuel to the next, as constant shifts dilute the steady narrative in the market they have been promoting.

At the same time, Orbit 1 demand-generation leaders cannot be left to wonder what the community-led team is bringing to the table. Demand-generation teams should collaborate with their community-led colleagues to integrate content and connections into their campaigns.

For example, a community salary survey led by Orbit 3 colleagues can capture more attention through Orbit 1-led email campaigns promoting market participation. Even better, if Orbit 3 and Orbit 1 promote the survey utilizing different tracking URLs, you can compare and contrast the audiences while analyzing the survey results.

Once the survey is complete, marketing leaders in Orbit 1 and Orbit 3 should have plans to promote the findings through the demand-gen engine—email, events, and digital promotions—so they can quickly amplify attention in the market. Furthermore, Orbit 3 leaders can invite community members to speak about the salary survey results on event panel discussions, webinars, or social media channels that can expand awareness of the high-quality content.

Demand-generation leaders who champion connections and collaboration with Orbit 3 colleagues will benefit tremendously. Without high-quality fuel, their engines will show suboptimal performance.

CMOs and their marketing leaders play an essential role in shrinking the chasms that can form between orbits.

Furthermore, demand-generation leaders can help their Orbit 3 colleagues by making community-related data captured by their martech stacks more visible; data that ends up siloed can erode cross-team trust and understanding between the orbits. The more everyone is in the loop about what is happening, the more they can celebrate wins together or make adjustments when things are off-track.

CMOs and their marketing leaders play an essential role in shrinking the chasms that can form between orbits. Those chasms broaden when one group of specialists does not recognize the value brought by other specialists. The more conversations that occur between the teams, the more understanding and trust will grow. Marketing leaders can also drive alignment by establishing shared goals between the orbits. Furthermore, collaboration is a lot easier when both teams are at the table when key initiatives, projects, and business goals are being discussed.

> **Marketing leaders who fail to make, measure, and report on the value of collaboration between orbits will doom the success of their community-led initiatives.**

When business outcomes are then reported, championing the recognition of the value created by combining demand-generation engines and community-led fuel leads to happier, more productive, and more collaborative marketing teams.

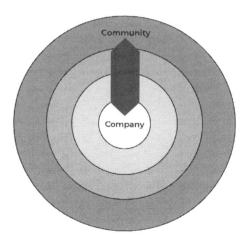

Marketing leaders can create stronger ties between orbits by fostering more conversations, establishing shared goals, and encouraging integrated go-to-market planning.

It is imperative that marketing leaders operationalize the link between their product- and community-led orbits. Marketing leaders who fail to make, measure, and report on the value of collaboration between orbits will doom the success of their community-led initiatives.

Regularly Scheduled Communications Ensure Internal Alignment

Building and growing communities is hard work. It requires a long-term commitment to building relationships and influence that will benefit the business. Communicating the impact of community-building efforts and collaborating with other teams is essential to success in Orbit 3.

In addition to having the right organizational structure, the best marketing teams ensure consistent communication across marketing and with key stakeholders across the business. The easiest place to start is with regular operational check-ins. Community-led marketers may prefer to spend most of their time in the market, but communicating their progress is essential for continued buy-in to their efforts. Consider regular check-ins with the team where they share updates on current projects and progress toward Objectives and Key Results (OKRs). Be careful not to blend community-led marketing into other functional area updates, as it may dilute or obscure the value of what they bring to the table.

The more explicit communications are between community-led marketers and other functional areas, the greater the chances are for success. Consider how to bring forward community-led marketing updates in:

- Regular marketing team meetings or stand-ups
- Pre- and post-event briefings
- Quarterly business reviews
- Product planning and roadmap reviews
- Marketing updates for the Board

For example, if Orbit 3 marketers identified three community members to participate as speakers in a field marketing event that generated 1,200 new leads for the business, make sure *both* parts of the team are credited for their contributions. You can also use the opportunity to compare and contrast results in field marketing events that did not leverage community-led efforts with those that did can help demonstrate the reach and impact.

Another important reporting opportunity comes with quarterly business reviews or Board meetings. Community-led efforts should hold a place on these agendas where they bring information about audiences reached, influence measured, participation generated, leads sourced and influenced, and data collected. The data-centric nature of many of these updates informs key stakeholders of the value community-led marketing delivers and keeps Orbit 3 marketers focused on the activities that produce the most impact.

When data on community-led influence and results are shared regularly and consistently, it builds a foundation of support for the importance of the role and investment being made in it. Everyone will better understand where the efforts are aligned with company strategy, tactics, and initiatives.

More importantly for marketing leaders and their community-led teams, when it comes to budget season, regularly reporting on the impact of Orbit 3 initiatives and impact can help ensure sufficient funds are secured.

The Importance of Feedback Loops

Community-led marketers can play two important roles in a business: Being a *voice to the market* and a *voice of the market*.

As a *voice to the market*, community marketers can drive increased understanding and awareness of trends in the market that are worthy of attention. Those trends might represent changes in industry practices, shifts in new roles being created to serve an industry, new investments being made, changes in the vendor landscape for a market, or methodologies being adopted.

Community leaders sharing these perspectives can quickly assess if the concepts resonate with the audiences they touch, if the market is not yet comprehending their importance, or if the market is addressing those trends differently than the community leader's company is suggesting.

Community marketers can also share their insights with top industry and community influencers to see if concepts resonate with them. These are the tech enthusiasts and visionaries who often lead the earliest adoption of new solutions but who also might share alternative paths to address a given problem or challenge.

> **Not all feedback is created equal. The more quantifiable and data-driven the feedback is to internal teams, the more influence it will have in changing minds.**

This is where the *voice of the market* comes into play. The more marketers can bring feedback from the community to internal teams, the more valuable they become as allies of business strategy for your executive team.

Elevating the impact of feedback to internal teams can hinge on the precision and data-centric nature of the information provided. Feedback fortified with concrete, quantifiable data can spark transformative thinking. For example, the creation of a maturity model or sentiment analysis, drawn from substantial community audiences, offers invaluable insights that can significantly influence business and marketing strategies. The introduction of data into decision-making makes the process more fact-based, minimizing emotional bias. It also ensures any counter arguments are met with actual data. As succinctly expressed by the late U.S. Senator from New York, Daniel Patrick Moynihan, *"While you are entitled to your opinion, you do not have the privilege of creating your own facts."*[72]

In contrast, feedback rooted in opinion or emotion tends to be more vulnerable to scrutiny by executives crafting their strategies. For instance, suppose your community leader suggests an alternative marketing approach based solely on a personal hunch or a few anecdotal observations. While this input may be valid, it's likely to be questioned more intensely. Without data to back it up, it becomes harder to persuade marketing and other executives who need solid evidence to inform strategic decisions.

The *voice to the market* and the *voice of the market* complement one another in the form of feedback loops that serve the business. Community leaders in your organization can play an important role as this voice, helping to build, refine, or communicate strategies your business is pursuing.

I should also add that community-based feedback is generally less biased because it is not collected through vendor-specific outreach, which may taint the audience selection or questions targeted for a response. Asking customers or active prospects in your pipeline for feedback will likely elicit different responses than when you ask the same questions in a vendor-neutral community.

Example: Product Engineering Feedback Loops

Let's look at how Orbit 3 marketers can play a critical role in feedback loops between the community and product engineering organizations. Spending so much time in the community enables marketers to see and hear of trends that may impact the long-term direction of the business. For example, they might report on their analysis of:

- Top priorities for a specific target persona they have heard in the past quarter from conference attendees, industry influencers, or community members
- Community surveys where people indicate various needs, requirements, or challenges they were facing
- Discussions trending in Discourse, Discord, Twitch, Reddit, GitHub, or Slack workspaces serving the community

- registration data from community meet-ups, conferences, webinars, or live discussions that provide insight into refining Ideal Customer Profile targets

Feedback from the community represents an important voice of the market that others might not capture through other feedback channels established by the product development organization. This feedback can be used by the engineering organization to validate new features, expand the product portfolio, determine pricing options, or eliminate offerings that are not resonating with the market.

Mary Thengvall, the author of *The Business of Developer Relations*, agrees. During a recent conversation, she shared an experience of a time she was working closely with software engineering communities in the DevOps space. The core product she was working on, Chef Software, had its roots in the Ruby on Rails programming language. She noticed a growing trend in her community where more Python developers were showing up. Her reaction was spot on.

"Hey, I see the Python community is engaging more in our DevOps community. I wonder whom we know there who could engage with our product team to help inform potential changes in our roadmap."

Mary spotted the trend and was, in essence, bringing the voice of the market back to her company's internal engineering team.

The same holds for feedback loops in product-led growth organizations. A blog post shared by Common Room states, *"A key component to running a community of products is soliciting, listening to, and responding to user feedback. Communities of products often allow users to make feature requests, test new features early, and provide feedback on existing features. This allows for real-time product development and creates a closed feedback loop between product teams and their users."*[73]

While the Common Room post may cater primarily to an Orbit 2 audience, the feedback loops you utilize within Orbit 3 will yield comparable value.

Completing the feedback loop to the community is important. Strategic directions being taken by product engineering teams can be introduced by Orbit 3 marketers as trends worth paying attention to in a market. The feedback loop in the community does not have to be company- or product-specific—even broad statements can provide insight as to what is resonating in the market with potential and current customers.

Example: Sales and Marketing Feedback Loops

Community-led marketers can also support feedback loops by collaborating with your sales organization. For example, your community marketers might host a podcast to interview people from across the industry regularly. The podcast can provide a venue where community-led marketers can ask questions that provide a source of unbiased answers to your sales teams, product marketers, and product leaders. Answers to questions like *"Why is X a priority for you now?"* or *"What tools do you use in your day-to-day?"* can provide new insights into a market, target accounts, or ideal customer profiles.

When such interactions are pursued within a community-led context—meaning no company pitches or product discussions were expected—your team can gather valuable insight that helps inform future sales and marketing activity.

Teams can pursue this same type of approach with named accounts that your sales teams might have an interest in. These efforts—initiated with a community-led approach—can begin to build relationships and trust with people in those accounts who may become customers of your business in the future. Leading with community-led relationship-building can sometimes be a more effective way to engage people at target accounts, especially if you are not sure if that account is "in the market" for the type of solutions your business is promoting.

Community-led marketers can also be great partners for product marketers on your team who are building ICP definitions. Information from community interviews, survey data, or conference presentations can reveal unbiased views of the market, the responsibilities of targeted personas, and or business priorities that are top-of-mind. Such information represents an important voice of the market when fed back to product marketers and sales teams.

Taking advantage of feedback loops like this help communicate the value of community-led efforts across your organization. Sharing the impact of wins and influence like these consistently will help smooth the path to success for community-led marketers.

EXPERT TIP: REPORT PROGRESS REGULARLY

Report on community-led initiatives regularly. Even though community-led initiatives may take longer to produce significant results, reporting smaller or milestone achievements along the way is important. Consider placing community-led marketing updates in your weekly marketing reports, quarterly business reviews, and regular team meetings.

The more community marketers are expected to provide updates, the more others on your team and across the organization will understand the value they provide. Also, don't just report on the community-specific activity; report on the longer tail of value those initiatives support. For example, if your community marketers build a survey with other people from the industry, report beyond the tactic itself. Encourage your community marketers to report on things like how many people took the survey, how data from the survey was used to improve sales enablement training, or how many earned media mentions the survey captured where community members were quoted as part of the coverage.

CHAPTER 9

Exploring Community-Led Engagement

"Reading the room" refers to the ability to understand and respond appropriately to the mood, attitudes, or overall atmosphere within a particular group, setting, or situation. It's a form of emotional intelligence or social awareness that allows a person to gauge the feelings and thoughts of others, often without explicit statements.

When marketing across orbits, "reading the room" allows your marketing team to adapt its behavior, content, and communication style to better fit the mood and expectations of the community. Doing so increases your chances of communicating effectively with them.

Crowd.dev CEO and co-founder Jonathan Reimer echoes this perspective and argues, *"The word 'community' has a broad gamut of connotations and could mean anything from social media influencers to online learning groups. Ultimately, a 'one-size-fits-all' approach doesn't work—a company laser-focused on attracting developers will probably need different tools than a company seeking to attract creators or crypto fans."*[74]

In this chapter, you'll explore how people participate, behave, and engage in communities. Continuing with the "one-size-fits-all approach doesn't work," we'll also touch on how digital natives' expectations for community engagement may differ from others. Then we will put some numbers behind those expectations to provide you with a sense of how people participate, share ideas, and create content. But first, I'll share my perspective on diving head-first into a community to best understand it.

Build Relationships in the Community

Years ago, a CEO I worked for asked me to help pivot our company from focusing on Market A to Market B. At the time, as a marketing executive, I had little idea of what Market B was, so I needed my feet to be out on the street. To learn more, I needed to dive into the community, meet people, read what was being written, and join the audiences of those out there listening to the experts. It was a similar approach to the one many CMOs and marketing leaders take when starting their role at a new company: You need to commit time to meet customers and other people in the markets you serve to understand the audience dynamics, wants, and needs.

When connecting with your community, you as a CMO or marketing leader may not be sure where to start. Communities and their participants are plentiful—if you know where to look. For example, you can find community meet-ups tied to the markets, personas, or interest groups you want to access. You can also search for Slack workspaces formed around a specific area of interest, expertise, or profession. Or you can look into books, podcasts, and online presentations that share insights into a market community. Queries to ChatGPT or similar tools can also provide you with helpful insights. Another alternative is looking at where your competitors spend time in the market.

Diving into existing communities will help you assess their priorities and needs, and the current state of maturity for various practices based on knowledge and content exchanges. It will also help you and your community leaders better assess who the smart folks are across the community with whom you'll want to build closer relationships over time.

You can also look internally for people and data that might help accelerate relationship building. For example, perhaps someone on your team or in the company is already an active member of the target community. At several companies where I've worked, we had employees leading meet-up groups in their home country or state, and as a result, had established close community relationships through them.

You might also look to your existing installed base of customers or partners to better understand what existing communities they participate in and if they can support you with introductions or share invitations to the right forums.

Finally, you can turn to your company contact database or Gong (or other similar call recording platforms used by your sales/BDR teams) to better understand who has opted-in to hear from your business and then find out the forums in which those persons gather.

Once you and your community leaders spend sufficient time identifying and participating in the right groups, you can establish trusted relationships and friendships that will deliver dividends. Through interactions with these people, you can assess if there are unfilled leadership opportunities in the community that your team might take on or if there are gaps in what the community needs that your team might be able to fill by starting a new subsegment.

You'll rarely start completely empty-handed when it comes to community relationships. A little exploration, internally and externally, can begin to open the right doors for you.

Identify Engaged Member Behaviors

"If you build it, they will come" is a famous line from the 1989 film *Field of Dreams.*[75]

However, just building your community does not guarantee that people will show up. People who join in have to find enough value in the time they spend with you to come back. They also have to discover the right cultural fit within the community to stay engaged.

Building a Safe Place for the Community to Engage

There are generally three things most community members want to do when they engage: Connect with others, ask questions, and provide insight/answers.

But before any of that, community members will likely simply observe. Their default engagement is likely going to be inactive until they determine through observation that being active is a safe thing to do. No one wants to engage in a community or forum that abuses or harasses members or blocks their participation from topics they find important. It seems like a simple thing to say, but behavior in the community is the first thing new people observe.

In several of the marketing communities I participate in virtually, we try to greet every new member who joins in. We share a wave emoji, say hi, and if they have an immediate question, we try to find them an answer or connect them with someone who can help them.

Every Friday morning, when I join the CMO Coffee Talk, the hosts cover some quick updates and then always pause to identify new members. New members are asked to provide a quick introduction and are then welcomed by our community members through exchanges in the Zoom chat. Matt Heinz or Latane Conant covers the basic ground rules of the group: No vendor pitches, be nice, share questions in the chat, and raise your Zoom emoji hand if you want to share a point. They also share that the engagements during the meeting are unscripted; if you have something to say, everyone is welcome to share. "Feeling seen" is an important part of the welcoming process in communities.

People joining your community want to know that it is a safe place to spend time. They want to observe cooperation between members and get a "sense of the room." They want to see that connections are encouraged, that poor behavior is discouraged, and that it is just as ok to share failures or challenges as it is to share insights.

Connecting with Others Like You

This is why we all join communities . . . there are others like us out there. Communities are a great source of social connection, and they give us a sense of belonging. Communities are bonded by values, attitudes, emotions, and goals.

When I join CMO and marketing communities, I recognize that the people in them are working through similar experiences and are held accountable for similar results.

The same holds true when I participate in my Facebook community of Yoder Smoker owners. Yoder is a brand of wood pellet smokers that help weekend chefs like me produce tasty barbeque for friends and family. In that forum, I am surrounded by others who share a common passion for cooking, creating, and socializing. We find pleasure in connecting, celebrating the wins of a tasty meal, or commiserating about a cooking experience that went wrong.

The more people participate in a community, the stronger their emotional ties to it become over time. They bond with other members who have shared similar experiences making their affinity for the community grow. McKinsey & Company research reinforces this sentiment, saying *"as positive emotions become deeply rooted, consumers develop permanent favorable associations with [a community] brand."*[76]

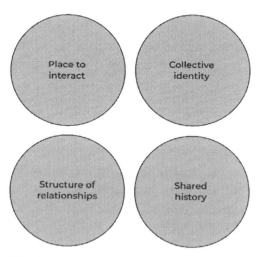

What's a community? It's where you connect.
It has an identity, structure, and shared history.

Asking Questions

Beyond joining communities just to observe what others are doing, we join them to seek knowledge and expertise from others. The simplest way to do this is to ask a question. In my CMO communities, it might be questions like:

- Who can share brand metric examples they use to report to the board?
- Who has successfully embedded ChatGPT or other AI tech into their marketing practices?
- Who knows of a good vendor for creating compelling corporate videos?
- What events are people going to that attract Chief Financial Officers?
- How should I best respond to a negative Gartner report?

When people see others asking questions and getting responses, they are encouraged to ask their own questions. As questions are answered, the knowledge body of the community grows, and that, in turn, helps attract new members.

It is also important to note that the faster questions are answered, the more likely people are to ask other questions. Imagine if you post a question in a CMO forum, and it gets a number of responses that same day. It would make you more likely to post another question in the future.

Lack of response degrades the value of a community.

Now imagine you go to a Demand-Generation community and post a different question. Let's assume no one answers that day. In fact, a week goes by, and there is still no response. You might think that either the community is unhealthy and people are seeking other forums to get answers or that the types of questions you have can't be answered by this specific community. Either way, a lack of response degrades the value of a community.

Providing Insights and Answers

This is where the real value of community explodes—answers and insights shared by community members, which naturally attract participation. Going back to the example of my Yoder Smokers community, when someone asks, *"How long does it take to smoke a 15-pound brisket?"* they will get a series of answers and perspectives.

Some might say to smoke it at 250°F until it reaches an internal temperature of 205°F. Others might chime in to say, smoke it at 400°F for the first hour and then drop the pit temperature to 250°F for the rest of the cook. Others may chime in to suggest wrapping the brisket in butcher paper after it reaches 170°F to keep it in moisture for the rest of the smoking session.

All this information and these exchanges build the body of knowledge for the community. It builds a set of content that serves to educate, inform, and inspire the community. The more answers and insights a community provides, the more its community can learn from the content over time.

When helpful answers abound, the community grows. When hurtful or misplaced content is shared, the community can suffer. For example, when someone posted pictures in the forum of Yoder Smoker t-shirts they created and wanted to sell, people in the community asked for the moderators to block them. The "sales" content did not belong in the community, based on the values it had established among the members.

> Questions beget answers. Answers beget more answers. More answers build more value for increasing the number of members.

Similarly, when I participate in CMO communities on Pavilion or CMO Coffee Talk, I find tremendous value in the content others have posted and responded to over time. I can search either of those communities for things like "salary ranges for business development reps," "integrated launch plan templates," or "top metrics to review at QBRs," and find answers that others have posted over the years. I'm either going to those communities to ask a new question or searching them for content posted minutes or years ago that may answer the question I have today. While I'm visiting the community, I often look at posts from others to see if I might be able to answer one or two of their questions.

Questions beget answers. Answers beget more answers. More answers build more value for an increasing number of members.

Ideal Community Profiles (ICP) and Keeping Your Promise

A few years ago, I joined an exclusive community for marketing executives to get an opportunity to interact with more of my peers. (*Note:* This is not a community I've mentioned previously in this book.) I joined following the recommendation of my friend Paul, who is a fellow CMO in the Washington, D.C. area.

My first interactions with the community were great. I was meeting new people, discovering new insights, and helping others through CMO challenges I had previously overcome. The more time I spent in the community, the more trusted relationships I built.

Later, the focus of that community started to shift when non-executives started to participate in the executive forums. The close-knit group of CMOs who were sharing information and insights critical to our daily work now had to weed through new posts in the forum that were originating from individual contributors who were not CMOs or those with a smaller scope of responsibilities in their work. The positive energy many of us originally felt through our participation was being sucked away by the newer participants. It felt like the original brand promise had shifted off its axis.

I don't have a problem with others gathering in communities to serve their specific needs, but when communities of different profiles collide, it's not helpful to the membership. Luckily for us CMOs in that particular group, the community moderators decided to segment the conversation channels better. This dramatically reduced the amount of noisy content we had to sift through to find the value we were seeking. It also revived the original value we appreciated, while serving more members simultaneously.

By comparison, I have had a tremendous experience with another marketing executive community you've already heard about: The CMO Coffee Talk community. The organizers promised a CMO-only participation in our Friday morning calls and have stuck with that over the years. Their effort to segment the community for this ICP makes it more valuable for all of us who participate in it.

When the Coffee Talk organizers were asked about Chief Revenue Officers, Sales Development Reps, or other roles joining the CMO community, they decided to stick with their original target audience. But with sufficient interest coming in for communities targeting other roles, they have since started different community initiatives to serve those audiences.

By contrast, at ADDO, our target ideal community profile (ICMP) had a much wider aperture. For our community, any DevOps professional was welcome. We also welcomed IT professionals, academics, and students to participate. Starting with such a wide aperture was not a problem in this case because it aligned with our initial brand promise that anyone who wanted to learn about DevOps was welcome to participate.

Moving Members from "Observers" to "Engaged"

Once members feel the community is a good place for them, the inaction of lurkers converts to the action of the engaged. These new members begin to connect with others, ask questions, and provide insight/answers. This is when the community will experience how easily information flows.

According to the Westrum model of organizational culture, good information flow is critical to the effectiveness and tempo of group interactions. Westrum characterized three aspects of good information flow:

1. It answers the questions that were asked,
2. The answers are timely, and
3. The answers are useful.

We've all been part of healthy communities where someone asks a question, and shortly afterward, someone jumps in to help with an answer or directions on where to find more information. Even better are the communities where you might have multiple people answering the question or sharing perspectives. The higher the tempo of interactions, the more likely community members are to engage. "Being heard" is one of the most important reactions that community members desire, as it invites more action and participation.

Understanding How Digital Natives Engage

People born between the mid-1970s and 2000 are more connected and comfortable using technology to connect, interact, and share than older generations. When it comes to your community-led initiatives, the engagement culture of digital natives has changed the game. They trust their community more than your company. They are engaged online continuously. They can create, exchange, and improve on ideas 24x7. And when they enter the community of their professional careers, they expect the world to operate by similar rules.

Patricia Redsicker at The Content Marketing Institute differentiates this population from more traditional consumers in that they are:

- **Multi-platform consumers:** Digital natives could be playing *Legend of Zelda: Breath of the Wild* while simultaneously sharing that experience with their friends on TikTok or Instagram.

- **Multi-device consumers:** They consume content on different devices, such as their laptops, smartphones, and tablets.

- **In charge of the conversation:** They want to determine when and how content is delivered to them—interruption marketing is offensive to them.

- **Siloed trust builders:** Disinterested in opinions of those outside their close social group but are super-interested in what their friends think.

- **Hyper-connected:** Their stories and word-of-mouth messages travel faster than any news network. Their thoughts and experiences are shared in real-time through updates, social media posts, pictures, and FaceTime videos.

- **Fans of authenticity:** They are enthusiasts of marketing that is honest and authentic.

- **Engaged:** They don't just consume content and information; they interact with it via digital expressions, such as updates, likes, shares, re-tweets, etc.

- **Digital natives:** They are used to meeting online, sharing information, and learning from one another.[77]

Digital natives have ushered in a new normal—one that accelerates the importance of community-led initiatives where engaged, helpful, and collaborative is the new expectation. Traditional marketing approaches and channels are less trusted as the first steps to engagement in this new realm. The expectation is now centered on hyper-connected communities that define their own trust parameters and seek out more authentic connections to advance their careers and make decisions.

> **Digital natives have ushered in a new normal— one that accelerates the importance of community-led initiatives where engaged, helpful, and collaborative is the new expectation.**

Marketing leaders who fail to account for these new cultural norms will struggle to connect with their markets, target buyers, and account influencers. While marketing teams can't escape the necessity of marketing products and services to those seeking them, marketing leaders must recognize that traditional product-led paths are becoming overgrown as fewer customers tread those paths first as part of their buying journeys.

The New Measure of Engagement: 55–25–20

Back in 2006, Ben McConnell introduced the tech industry to the 90–9–1 rule. The idea at the time was that, in democratized internet culture, only one percent of users on the web were actively creating content. Of the remaining population of visitors, nine percent were participating in changing or updating content, and 90 percent were simply there to consume it.[78] In your product-led orbit, the 90–9–1 rule likely still applies today when it comes to people interacting with your website and other owned content channels.

Marketing leaders should not apply that same expectation when it comes to brand- and community-led engagement. First, just by their nature, communities reward content creation and information exchange. Coupling this with the growing population of digital natives and participation in communities further amplifies the creation and reach of community-sourced content.

Analysis from the 2022 State of Community Management report reflects the change in community culture and information flow. Gone is the rule of 90–9–1; today's rule looks more like 55–25–20.[79] The report reads:

"Based on over a decade of research, a well-managed online community sees the following in a given month:

- *55 percent are inactive*
- *25 percent are validating and consuming content*
- *20 percent of members are actively creating content."*

Kathleen Booth, SVP of Marketing and Growth at Pavilion, confirms the shifting tide of community engagement. As I was writing this book, I asked her to share some metrics about their community engagement. Across a community of thousands of marketing and sales professionals during the past 30 days, she said:

- *37 percent were inactive*
- *48 percent were active and consuming content*
- *15 percent were active and creating content / initiating conversations*

How People Are Jumping into Their Community First for Answers

Today's buyers are turning first to their community of peers for advice and insight before jumping into vendor-specific paths where content is gated, phone calls from business development reps follow, and prospect tracking is part of the journey. For example, in the past week, here are some examples of questions CMOs are posting in Pavilion's Slack workspace.

- *Does anyone have any experience with a CDP or other data platform that consolidates data from your own software + Hubspot + Stripe + Jira?* (five people replied)

- *Hi everyone, I'm looking to run some experiments on the website and wondering what are some of the most recent and easiest-to-use tools to build different landing pages to showcase to new users coming to the website?* (six people replied)

- *Does anyone have recommendations on cost-effective LMS tools? I'm not sure of any pricing, but I wanted to see if anyone had experience with Lessonly, WorkRamp, or anything else for internal training.* (two people replied)

These leaders are turning to their community to research and share information on products or services they might be willing to commit budget to but are looking for independent recommendations before jumping into conversations with a vendor's sales and marketing team. The leaders are turning to a community they are active in, have built trust with, and that they know delivers strong value.

Beyond products and services, the community is also a place where they seek "how to" guidance from peers on a number of topics, like the following.

- *Would any other CMOs in a new role somewhere new want to start a little cohort? Thinking of a weekly or biweekly check-in just for a few months. A lot of us are moving into new roles at once—and joy and misery are both better with friends.* (29 people replied)

- *What metrics do you use to support conversations around a) marketing efficiency, and b) marketing is underfunded?* (four people replied)

- *I have been asked to create a Product Marketing Document/Guide to help our sales, channel, and client services team keep tight and consistent talking points around our AdTech solution. This document would also serve as a living document for all new product updates and enhancements. Does anyone have an example they could share or point me in the right direction?* (10 people replied)

Communities like this provide a safe and trusted place to ask questions, make connections, or find inspiration. Community members are sharing content, templates, best practices, worthwhile articles, and personal experiences that help one another level up or get past a challenging obstacle. Questions that arise in the CMO community often cannot be answered by vendors of tools and services because they require the expertise of someone who has been through the experience or is sitting in the same seat.

> **Interactions don't need to be facilitated by community leaders. Once community members feel they are in a safe and trusted environment, they will begin to make connections and share information naturally between themselves.**

In the Pavilion CMO community it was not uncommon for people to respond with, *"I would be happy to jump on a Zoom call to discuss my experience if that would help you."* Interactions don't need to be facilitated by community leaders. Once community members feel they are in a safe and trusted environment, they will begin to make connections and share information naturally between themselves.

Keep Members Engaged

Once you have community members engaged, keeping them engaged over the long run is a continuous process. It requires commitment, creativity, and an understanding of your members' needs and interests. There are a number of effective strategies your organization can use to keep your interest piqued.

- **Provide value:** Value can come in many forms. Content, resources, opportunities, and experiences all provide value. Pavilion offers community-training courses. CMO Coffee Talk provides forums to help people find new jobs after layoffs. And Lululemon provides opportunities to practice yoga and run training guides. People stay engaged when they feel they're gaining something from their participation.

- **Create a safe and inclusive environment:** When people feel welcomed, valued, and safe, they participate more. It's important to not only document a code of conduct for your community, but to demonstrate that you stand by it. Furthermore, inclusivity will help your community thrive. A recent McKinsey study found that *"the higher the gender diversity in businesses, the higher the likelihood of outperformance. Organizations with more than 30 percent women on their executive teams are significantly more likely to outperform those with between 10 and 30 percent women, and these companies in turn are more likely to outperform those with fewer or no women executives."*[80] Diversity and inclusion in your community helps it thrive and encourages further engagement.

- **Encourage interaction:** Build relationships among members by encouraging discussions, collaboration, and peer-to-peer learning. I experience this multiple times a week in the Slack, Facebook Group, Reddit, and Discourse workspaces I participate in online. At the Cloud Native Computing Foundation (CNCF), community members keep active in working groups like: Contributor growth, governance, maintainers circle, and mentoring. CNCF also offers free online programs, webinars, and published stories about amazing people in their communities.

- **Communicate regularly:** Believe it or not, your community members do things outside of your community. Keeping members informed about what's happening through regular updates and announcements is essential. Newsletters, email, and social media are great ways to achieve this. As I write this portion of the book, Rosie Sherry, of the Rosieland community, had just sent out her 182nd newsletter. It included updates about an "Ask Me Anything" session, how to use AI to show what members have in common, worthwhile podcast episodes, and upcoming community events. Rosie also posts regularly on X (formerly Twitter) @rosiesherry.

- **Encourage member-driven content:** When it came to ADDO, community members produced an amazing amount of content in the form of presentations, blogs, and books. At CMOlist, member-driven content is one of the primary value points of the community as peers ask questions and others provide feedback, advice, and support. The more your community members create content and information exchanges without being prompted to do so, the healthier your community will be. Member-driven content lets the community feel a sense of ownership.

- **Host events and activities:** While you might want to host a huge conference for your community, taking a moment to do small things can also build magical experiences. I've often coordinated local dinners with fellow community members when traveling on business. I've seen others organize morning walks or runs for their community members at industry conferences. Planning these activities does not always require significant commitment. I've often seen fellow community members tweet things like, *"Hey, I'm going to be in Austin, Texas for the week. Who should I meet up with while I'm in town?"*

- **Seek feedback and adapt:** There are few things more valuable than asking your members about their experiences, expectations, and needs in the community. Every chance I had to engage community members to receive feedback was a gift. *"What's working for you? What's missing from the experience? Who is doing incredible work? Who else should we involve?"* Applying this feedback let community members see that their voice mattered. Even better were the moments when the community member offered to take the lead on a change or improvement we had discussed.

- **Get personal:** *"I loved hearing Mary talk about the success of her initiative." "Thanks to Bill for bringing us all together." "Amanda ensured we got this program over the finish line ahead of time."* Communities thrive on relationships and people appreciate a personal touch. When you can, personalize communications. Celebrate member milestones, birthdays, or achievements. Avoid the temptation of mass, impersonal updates and ensure more emphasis is placed on the people in your community.

Every community is unique, so it's important to adapt these strategies to meet the specific needs and interests of your members. To keep people engaged, there is no single tactic to pursue. The best marketing teams approach community engagement more holistically. Their strategies employ many of these tactical approaches across integrated community, brand, and demand programs.

Partner with Other Communities

Over the years, people in the industry asked us to produce our all-day community conference multiple times a year. Other than pulling together a special COVID lockdown edition during the earliest months of the pandemic, we simply didn't have the resources to pull together the epic event multiple times a year. We also knew the community at large participated in other industry gatherings throughout the year; those events offered vendor-pitch-free content and excellent opportunities to collaborate with peers in person.

So rather than try to own the entire DevOps community experience, we promoted other industry alternatives like devopsdays, DevSecOps Days, and North American DevOps Group (NADOG) meetings. We also helped promote awareness of other local DevOps community groups and meet-ups on our website and encouraged people to join on a local level. Many times, these conferences or community meet-ups were looking for great speakers, and they came to us for suggestions. The work they were doing inspired us just as we had inspired them.

The team at Pavilion takes a similar approach. They have not tried to corner the entire marketing and sales community. They have established partnerships with Insight Partners, Crossbeam, Docebo, the Product Marketing Community, and Peakspan—among others—to bring more value to all their members.

Working across community initiatives enables you to thrive. Your work in the community and the relationships you build should not be centered on your success alone. Become known for helping other individuals and parallel community endeavors become successful. Unlike the commercial part of your business, you are not trying to corner part of the market when it comes to community. Aim to help the market at-large to thrive.

Cross-pollination of communities through partnerships adds significant value to member experiences. Every now and then, you might have a community member request something that is out-of-scope for the initiatives being led at the moment. However, you may be aware that another community is serving that requested need well. Making connections to other communities demonstrates inclusiveness and your openness to work with others. Forming partnerships with other communities makes your own community's value stronger. It can also minimize any potential frustration by members who might feel their request was not heard while it can also reduce the expectations placed on your community leaders to solve every problem or provide every resource requested.

Make Members Feel Welcome Every Time

The team supporting the CMO Coffee Talk also does a great job at keeping their members engaged. Every Friday morning at 8 AM and 11 AM ET, our tribe of CMOs gathers to discuss another critical topic centered around career development, strategy development, or daily operations. I've consistently made it to about 75 percent of the meetings, as travel or internal priorities sometimes get in the way. But even when I miss a couple of weeks, I know when the community will gather next and always feel welcome. The regular meeting schedule for CMO Coffee Talk is another great example of where persistence pays off.

When community members are engaged, they stick around and invite others to join them. They don't need to participate in the community every day to make an impact.

People want to know they have a forum to gather in, build relationships, and find inspiration. Sometimes that happens online, and other times it happens in person. The important thing is to schedule regular opportunities for inter-action. Schedule those opportunities at consistent times so that people know exactly where to find you when they do have time to engage. Consistency is key to community success.

EXPERT TIP: VALUE BEING HEARD

To maximize community involvement and get more out of your community members, create avenues for members to express their opinions, concerns, and ideas. Actively listen to their voices and ensure diverse perspectives are acknowledged and valued. "Being heard" is one of the best ways to move community members from occasional contributors to engaged thriving members. Being heard empowers them and boosts an individual's sense of belonging to the community.

CHAPTER 10

Building Relationships to Spark Your Movement

One of my favorite experiences in building and participating in communities is the value of relationships that are formed over time. A conversation online turns into another conversation at a conference, which leads to another conversation with industry peers at a group dinner. The relationships formed become your tribe of go-to people when you are in need of advice, a helping hand, or initiating a new connection.

Relationships forged in community-led orbits can bring significant value to lower orbits when it comes to supporting brand awareness and demand generation. The best relationships can deliver value over a long period of time across many different marketing initiatives. In the context of community-led marketing motions, we referred to these as "franchise relationships."

Franchise relationships consist of more than one-time engagements with our community. Marketing teams often employ franchise relationships with their best reference customers. Those customers will speak on their webinars, be featured in a case study, talk to the press, or present at a user conference upon request.

When extended out to the community, the franchise relationships work in a similar way. The most active community members work together in a variety of settings that help advance knowledge and connections across the greater community. The relationships do not come with requirements for company or product endorsements. If anything, endorsements pertaining to franchise relationships are implicit. The more people are seen working together in the community, at conferences, or on projects, the more it reveals a strong trust between them.

> **Relationships forged in community-led orbits can bring significant value to lower orbits when it comes to supporting brand awareness and demand generation.**

Franchise relationships that my teams and I formed supported common growth strategies, connected people with good ideas, and helped all participants succeed. The relationships were not formalized with contracts between parties. It was more a case of friends helping friends. The relationships were built on trust, respect, and mutual benefit.

Step 1: Research Key Influencers

To introduce the concept further, here is an example of how we developed franchise relationships in our community-led motions, and over time, leveraged those relationships in ways that supported demand generation and brand awareness for our business.

In 2010, my company embarked on a research effort to identify the top 50 people in the Microsoft SharePoint market that were influencing deals. This was different from a list of the most followed influencers or most vocal members of the community. We engaged a research firm that helped us identify the influencers across a number of categories that included vendors, consultants, analysts, academics, integrators, etc.

Step 2: Build A Cross-Orbit Marketing Plan

Once the research had been completed, we knew whom to pay attention to, and from them learned more about what was important and what resonated with the community. We applied those discoveries to create a go-to-market and demand-gen plan about how to best engage with those influencers and the community at large. The plan we built included a multi-stage, integrated campaign that traversed all three orbits.

I sketched out the key steps in the playbook to provide you a sense of how we started the effort in Orbit 3 with community-centric initiatives. As the plan progressed, new initiatives brought the community participants into the lower marketing orbits where our business was generating demand for our sales team.

More details about each step of the plan are covered in the following pages.

Step 3: Expose Research to the Community

The first step in the campaign would call for us to release the names of the top influencers in a series of blog articles on a large SharePoint community site. But the names would not be released all at one time. The releases would be conducted over a two-month span.

The first blog in the series informed people that we had conducted the research, explained how the research was done, and that we were planning to release the list over the next six weeks. The blog itself was released on one of the industry's most-read and respected community sites.

Following the initial blog, we then asked the community, *"Who do you think should be on the list?"* This second blog ignited a lot of conversation. For those close to the community, many obvious names were shared in comments on the blog. Thanks to community input, we also identified a few other people who were worthwhile to watch or reach out to establish new relationships.

	Activity	Result
Community-led marketing	Funded research on top industry influencers	$30,000 program cost
	Intro blog: we will reveal the top 50 influencers	Who is on your list?
	Generates very high engagement on industry news sites	5 blogs over 5 weeks reveal
	50 influencers across different categories	Generates strong buzz when people agree/disagree with the list. Identifies additional influencers to align with
Brand-led marketing	Industry survey	Create videos with top industry influencers commenting on survey results. Generates 2,500 top of funnel leads
	Industry webinar	Influencer guest host joins us to discuss the survey results. Generates an additional 1,800 leads
	Industry award	Secured Microsoft Partner of the Year Award three years in a row
Product-led marketing	Influencer dinners hosted at industry events, hosted by our field marketing team	Boosts brand and product awareness. Generates 2,500 additional leads over 12 months

Mapping out the integrated marketing playbook from Orbit 3 down into Orbit 1.

Then came the big announcements. Each week, we revealed a different part of the list. First came the consultants, then the vendors, then the systems integrators, and so on. Each time we released the list, we celebrated those who were named and even shared an "Influencer 50" digital badge that they could add to their online community profiles or websites.

Each week when a new part of the list was revealed, it not only generated a round of applause for those who were mentioned but sparked consternation from members of the community about who had not made that portion of the list. At times, some impressive people in a category were not named due to the focus of our research being who was influencing deals (vs. simply being well-known or vocal in the industry). The controversy around the list brought even more attention to our effort; however, positive sentiment far outweighed any negative remarks. It was a worthwhile initiative that paid big dividends in talking up the community and sharing information that had not been seen with that perspective previously.

The list did a number of things for our business. First, we went from being relatively unknown in the market to being very well known in a matter of six weeks. Literally, everyone at any SharePoint industry event or meet-up was talking about our company, "the list," who was on it, and who was not.

We went from being relatively unknown in the market to being very well known in a matter of six weeks.

Next, it connected our company to the top influencers in the community in a really nice way. We were celebrating them and their accomplishments. The recognition originated from us but had nothing to do specifically with an endorsement of our product or company. We did, though, get a lot of thank-yous from the industry influencers whom we named on the list, and they quickly adopted the "*I'm a top 50 SharePoint influencer*" title during their conference presentations or posts on social media or blog channels. More than a

INFLUENCER50 GLOBAL 360 & KNOWLEDGELAKE

Top50 Snapshot

1 TONY BYRNE
The Real Story Group

2 MARK GILBERT
Gartner

3 ROB KOPLOWITZ
Forrester

4 MARK MILLER
EndUserSharePoint

5 ANDREW CONNELL
Critical Path Training

6 KAREN SHEGDA
Gartner

7 TOM RIZZO
Microsoft

8 ANDREW CHAPMAN
EMC

9 TRICIA BUSH
Microsoft

10 SUSAN HANLEY
Susan Hanley LLC

11 JOHN MANCINI
AIIM

12 RON MILLER
Fierce Content Management

13 CRAIG LE CLAIR
Forrester

14 ALAN PELZ-SHARPE
The Real Story Group

15 FRANK GILBANE
Gilbane Group, Inc.

16 WHITNEY TIDMARSH
EMC

17 JOHN NEWTON
Alfresco

18 STEPHEN POWERS
Forrester

19 CARL FRAPPAOLO
Information Architected, Inc.

20 CONNIE MOORE
Forrester

21 MARK S. LEWIS
EMC Corporation

22 KEN BISCONTI
IBM

23 MIKE GOTTA
Burton Group

24 CHRIS GEIER
K2

25 JOEL OLESON
Quest Software

26 SHAWN SHELL
Consejo, Inc

27 MAURO CARDARELLI
Jornata

28 HUGH MCKELLAR
KMWorld Magazine

29 TED PATTISON
Critical Path Training

30 KARUANA GATIMU
Skechers

31 GREG CHAN
Microsoft

32 DAN HOLME
Intelliem

33 JEFF TEPER
Microsoft

34 BECKY BERTRAM
BeckyBertram.com

35 ANDREW MCAFEE
MIT Center for Digital Business

36 JOHN POWELL
Alfresco

37 JOHN ANDERSON
Bamboo Solutions

38 SCOT HILLIER
Scot Hillier Technical Solutions

39 ANDREW CONRY-MURRAY
InformationWeek

40 SHANE YOUNG
SharePoint911

41 KATHLEEN REIDY
The 451 Group

42 TYSON HARTMAN
Avanade

43 ROYCE BELL
Accenture

44 ADAM HARMETZ
Microsoft

45 ARPAN SHAH
Microsoft

46 PAUL GALVIN
Computer Generated Solutions

47 RUSS EDELMAN
Corridor Consulting

48 MIKE FERRARA
SharePointReviews.com

49 ARNO NEL
Sword Group

50 JOE MCKENDRICK
ebizQ

The SharePoint Influencer 50 campaign started as a community-led motion in Orbit 3, but integrated lower orbits in our demand generation go-to-market plans.[81][82]

decade later, you can still find remnants of the campaign by searching for influencer blogs from Sue Hanley, Becky Bertram, and Robert Bogue.[83] [84] [85]

Step 4: Run an Industry Survey

After this point, we started to get creative about how we engaged the SharePoint Influencer 50 community. We needed to bring an Orbit 3 motion into the lower marketing orbits without negatively impacting the relationships, trust, or brand awareness we had developed. Those actions took on a number of different forms.

One activity we were running in parallel was a SharePoint industry survey. The survey was to be used in creating a state of the industry report. As part of the launch preparations for the report, we shared the research findings with a number of people on the Influencer 50 list and recorded videos of their responses to specific findings. Since we had established relationships by recognizing their work in the community, they were open to working with us on making the survey initiative more robust. The influencer video clips were then used in our promotions of the survey.

As a marketing asset, we gated the survey downloads to generate leads for our business. The first year of the survey generated 2,500 downloads that added to our top-of-funnel lead-generation efforts. The survey was hosted on our employer company website, which meant we were also attracting more attention to our company's brand and solutions.

Step 5: Host a Webinar

To draw more attention to the survey results and our company, we pulled together and promoted a webinar on the findings. Once again, we invited some of the SharePoint Influencer 50 group to a panel discussion for the webinar. For speakers, we targeted the Influencer list, including analysts like Rob Koplowitz of Forrester (#3) and John Anderson (#37). More community influencer participation drew more attention and validation to our efforts and resulted in 1,800 additional leads for our demand-generation team.

Step 6: Support Field Marketing Efforts and Events

Beyond the survey and the webinar, the community-led Influencer 50 initiative also benefited our corporate event and field marketing teams. Where prior to the Influencer 50 list releases, we were just one of the many vendors participating in SharePoint industry events, we were now recognized as the company that was audacious enough to create, release, and promote the list. Those unfamiliar with what our company did were now intrigued to learn more about our firm and our solutions, and event traffic boomed. Booth traffic doubled, and we had 2,500 additional event leads in our demand-generation funnel the first year we released the report. We also hosted dinner outings for customers and prospects at the events, where we invited people like Russ Edelman (#47), Joel Oleson (#25), and Dux Raymond Sy (recognized in a future Influencer 50 report) to join us.

Step 7: Develop Reciprocal Relationships

The franchise relationships we established as a result of the initial Influencer 50 initiative were leveraged for years. The Influencer 50 report was the origin point of many relationships; however, they were not built to serve a single tactic or as a short-lived campaign cycle. Our business continued to nurture these relationships over the years through the community. As much as the Influencer 50 community did to support our marketing efforts in different orbits, we did the same for them. If there was a conference people needed help producing, a book that needed support from multiple authors, a meetup that needed an introduction to a potential speaker, or other such requests, we were eager to help. Relationships were not established as one-way streets. Our mindset was focused on creating long-lasting relationships. We're still friends with many of them to this day.

Step 8: Cultivate the Long Tail of Value

The Influencer 50 campaign transformed our position in the industry from "just another vendor" to a position of SharePoint community "tribe leadership." It's not only a great example of integrating the three orbits, but helps you understand the approach we took to achieve unfair mindshare.

The relationships we built, grew, and celebrated not only influenced our position in the community but elevated the results of our demand-generation teams operating in the inner orbits. Relationships built in the outer orbit—Orbit 3—were leveraged again and again while ensuring we never pushed boundaries on the trust we worked so hard to establish.

Building and supporting relationships in the community is a multi-year endeavor. Friends support friends. New ideas spark from conversations, and new connections are made as community endeavors expand. Just as franchise relationships pay dividends over the years, franchise content provides a similar value.

EXPERT TIP: BUILD A LEGACY

Communities are long-term initiatives. They grow, change, and evolve over time. When building and contributing to your community, take a moment to think about the legacy you are creating. Legacy refers to the contributions, values, and traditions that are passed down from one generation to the next, shaping the identity and progress of a community over time.

A strong legacy provides a shared history, values, and traditions that bind individuals together, fostering a sense of unity and pride. As people move from company to company over their careers, the shared history, values, and traditions formed through their community engagements can keep them coming back. When they experience something positive and build strong relationships within a community, they will be less willing to give up those experiences, even as their jobs and employers change.

Legacy building also serves as an inspiration for future generations. When community members see the accomplishments and contributions of their predecessors, it motivates them to carry forward the legacy and make their own meaningful contributions. This passing of the baton encourages a cycle of continuous progress and ensures that the community's values and aspirations endure.

CHAPTER 11

Mapping Out Your Community Playbook

Integrated marketing campaigns are key to building long-term trusted relationships in your community. Content that originates in the community can often be reused or repurposed over several stages of the campaign. It is what my former manager and CMO extraordinaire, Matt Howard, refers to as the long tail of content.

Great content attracts, educates, and informs the market. Marketing teams that produce great content attract larger audiences, build brand credibility, and encourage social media sharing virality. Great content is high-quality fuel for marketing engines.

When great content is used as part of an integrated marketing campaign, it can produce significantly more leads for your company. From my experience, great content that originates in the community-led orbit can easily generate 10x the number of leads compared to traditional product- and brand-led content.

Great content should not be thought of as a singular asset (e.g., a white paper, datasheet, sponsored analyst report, or webinar). Instead, great content begins in one form and is transformed to serve other purposes over its lifetime. For example, a community survey can turn into a state of the industry report, a webinar, a conference presentation, a series of blogs, interviews with the press, podcast appearances, market feedback for roadmap planning, and sales enablement tools.

Over the years, I have created a number of documents, reports, and studies that generated hundreds of thousands of leads—and were leveraged for years by the communities they served. In this chapter, we will consider an example of the "long tail" of community-originated content using a fictitious company called Crowdsource. You'll learn from the marketing playbook approach I've mapped out and used successfully so you can apply the same proven approach to your company's efforts.

Consider each playbook as a guide for inspiration. Find the approach that suits you, your team, the company, and the industry best. There are no hard and fast rules about how many initiatives need to be in each orbit. The playbooks are high level and every detail of how each of them was executed is not possible to fit in these pages. The most important thing is how you approach, plan, and execute your initiatives across the orbits. Obviously, when it comes to the results, your mileage will vary.

Think of this as an unfair mindshare playbook that leads to boosted brand awareness and significant pipeline opportunities. I'll walk you through each stage of the content's lifecycle, how to evolve it into a number of different forms, and how you can leverage similar approaches to build demand.

Playbook #1: Marketing Maturity Model

Let's imagine you're starting a new CMO role for a high-growth company in the marketing tools arena. Your software is sold to enterprise B2B clients. You're in the early stages of market creation and the current version of your software is best suited for large teams with a high level of marketing maturity.

You need to better understand how your company's tech fits into what marketing teams are doing. This can be achieved in a number of ways, including customer calls, meetings with sales and customer success teams, and self-initiated market research.

Instead of focusing solely on traditional approaches to product positioning, ICPs, and sales plays, let's consider building a community-led endeavor to support your work.

Let's start by performing blog and Google image searches. In this case, you would jump into Google to look for "marketing maturity models." You'll find many of them out there. Their focus ranges from digital marketing to content marketing, to communications, to marketing in general. You'll even find some specific to large tool category champions. For additional perspective, try turning to ChatGPT, Bard, or other AI engines where you prompt them to create a maturity model for you.

Now it's time to start building your collection. At this stage, you're effectively collecting feedback from your community about how they perceive and define marketing maturity levels. If you are doing Google image searches, be sure to click through the images further to find the blogs and other content sources where those images originally appeared. You'll want to record the author and source of each model.

You're likely to find that some of these assets are developed and shared by fellow CMOs, others by systems integrators, and still others by marketing consultants or solopreneurs. Each blog and image source will reveal a little more about marketing practices, measures, operations, team structures, and investments. It's not a sophisticated approach, but it provides a great deal of insight.

Let's say, for the sake of this example, that you find 21 maturity models. Your next step is to combine these into a slide presentation. In the presentation, make sure to recognize the author, source, and URL where you retrieved each model. Just from this collection alone, you've built something that other marketing professionals would love to see. They'll want to review each model.

What's similar in each model? What's different? Where would they rank their own team's maturity? Where do they see room for improvement at their company?

You can take the deck a step further by performing a simple analysis of the models and adding perspective to the deck. Call out the patterns you see. Comment on how many marketing teams are at each maturity level. Reflect on the elements you or other CMOs often forget to consider. You might even offer some guidance on how marketing leaders can use the deck with their own teams.

The thing about this deck that will generate the initial wave of interest is that you did not create it yourself. It represents a collection of work from the community. Others built it, but you put in the helpful effort of consolidating the information into one place.

With the deck in place, you can begin to form a strategy where your demand gen, marketing program, product marketing, social media, and content teams can begin leveraging it. From a product marketing perspective, use the content to further refine your ICP around the high-maturity marketing organization. From a demand perspective, consider ways to promote the collection of maturity models to generate interest from marketing leaders. From a marketing program perspective, consider what webinars or event presentations you might build around the topic. From a social media perspective, ask people to look at the deck and pick their favorite, or point to their own favorite example from another source. There are multiple ways the content can be used to attract attention and encourage conversations with marketing leaders.

Step 1: Helping the Community

Once the deck has been compiled, you'll want to make people aware of it. People would want to see it. As a CMO, I'd definitely want to see it.

Share the maturity model deck with your community. You can distribute it freely on forums like LinkedIn, X (formerly Twitter), and Facebook pages.

When you do, be sure to include the sample images of some of the models. When people review the deck, the first thing they'll recognize is how helpful you've been in creating the collection. The next thing they'll notice is that you are recognizing others in the community for the work they've already put into building their maturity model. You are celebrating the work of others, not taking credit for it. This move builds trust with your audience.

For example, when sharing the content, you could post something like, *"Here's a great example of how Austin Hay, a tech consultant, built his marketing maturity model. I found it useful because 1) it shared perspectives on practices I was not familiar with, 2) it revealed new ways to think about how we leverage our customer data, and 3) it gave me ideas for how we could better integrate some of our own tools."*

You don't need to promote your company's products or services at this stage. What you are doing is being helpful. You're attracting a larger audience. And you're building trust. Being helpful, building trust, and establishing a relationship with this audience will help fuel the success of your next steps. If your content is really helpful, the community will point others to it, attracting an even larger audience.

> **Expert tip:** The path to viral content shares rarely starts with the alternative approach of sharing 21 maturity models and promoting them with messages like, *"Check out these 21 maturity models that include unveiled references to our company's product."* This is self-promotional and misses the mark of leading with the "be helpful" mantra of community-led initiatives.

The key to Orbit 3 behavior is that you are doing the work to benefit the community, not to highlight your own brand or products. You can post the deck with a caption like, *"Hey, check out the 21 maturity models marketing leaders built. I found it helpful. Perhaps you will too."* Be sure to tag those marketing leaders in your posts to further celebrate the work they did.

Imagine that some time has elapsed. Three months after you released this deck, the article highlighting the deck generated 15,000 views on LinkedIn.

By month six, the article had over 35,000 views. Why? The content was help-ful to others. It was not promoting any specific company or product. It was sharing new insights from the marketing community at large. And it shared the limelight with people and companies connected to the community.

"Helpful is the new viral."
—Laura Fitton

In a world crowded with countless product and company promotions, con-tent that is produced to simply educate and inform others of best practices, or to share peer insights, attracts much larger audiences. It's the kind of mar-keting content that fits well with what one former HubSpoter, Laura Fitton, said, *"Helpful is the new viral."* [86]

Step 2: Encourage Community Involvement

One of the next things to do is to encourage more community involvement. Just because you found 21 great maturity models does not mean you found them all, or that more won't be created in years to come.

Therefore, as part of your effort to build awareness for the collection, you should also include a slide asking for community contributions. If someone out there built a really interesting maturity model and wants to include it in your collection, encourage them to do so. Provide your email address where they can send it for review and inclusion. As others submit their entries, put out the word that the collection has expanded. *"What started as 21 maturity models is now 25. Check out our latest additions from Frank, Sarah, Alexis, and Kathleen."*

Making this offer means more community-created (Orbit 3) content in the deck. When you add new content, the community benefits. When you also promote the new addition, it improves your brand perception as one that is playing a helpful role in the market. Your company is focused on serving more than its own success.

Do you have a maturity model to share?

Send it to me at weeks@unfairmindshare.com. Include the model and a link to where people can find it on the web. I'll add it to the deck and note you as the source.

Expert tip: Ask for community involvement to evolve and improve content.

I've seen other community-marketing leaders take similar approaches to creating content. For example, here are some questions someone might ask.

1. I'm writing a book on next-gen energy grids. Would anyone like to contribute a chapter?
2. I'm forming a survey on databases as a service. What questions would you ask the community?
3. We're producing a maturity model for gaming industry software development. What key differences should we document between low- and high-maturity org?
4. I'm writing a blog on community-led marketing. Is anyone available to review and provide feedback on it before I publish it?

Step 3: Boosting Awareness in Lower Orbits by Blogging

In addition to placing the maturity models online, there are other initiatives you can include that move the effort from Orbit 3 into Orbit 1.

One of the first things you could do is to begin blogging about the maturity models to draw more attention to them. The blogs can explain why you put the deck together and what value it provided. You could also highlight a couple of the maturity models and attribute them to their community creators. This would help further boost the visibility of your deck but also reiterate the vendor-neutral value it delivers. For further visibility, you could post links to the blog in places like Pavilion, RevGenius, CMOlist, Guild, CMO Huddles, and the LinkedIn CMO group.

Step 4: Promote at Conferences

Your next step could be to get the deck in front of a live conference audience. This step would further boost your company's awareness as an industry authority. You could ask one of your community marketing leaders to submit a paper on the maturity models to marketing industry conferences. It might read something like this:

Title:

"Navigating the Evolution: A Comparative Analysis of 21 Global Marketing Maturity Models"

Abstract:

The ever-changing landscape of marketing calls for robust, adaptable frameworks to guide businesses in their growth journey. Among these, marketing maturity models have emerged as essential navigational tools, outlining paths to greater efficiency and marketing efficacy. Yet, with the diversity in approach, focus, and depth among these models, the challenge lies in understanding their nuances and applicability.

In this enlightening presentation, we delve into an in-depth analysis of 21 marketing maturity models formulated by leading global marketing visionaries. This rigorous comparative study uncovers recurrent patterns, critical disparities, key attributes, and emerging trends that are reshaping the contour of marketing maturity models.

This exploration goes beyond theoretical discussions, investigating the practical implications of these models for businesses of varying scales, stages of growth, and industry types. We dissect the unique elements in each model, showcasing how geographical, cultural, and sector-specific factors influence the maturity journey.

The following are the key takeaways from this insightful presentation:

- *Gain an enriched understanding of the diverse perspectives and strategies encapsulated in global marketing maturity models and their respective strengths and weaknesses.*

- *Uncover the key trends influencing the evolution of marketing maturity models and learn how to leverage them in your strategic planning.*

- *Develop a more adaptable, nuanced approach to utilizing marketing maturity models, factoring in cultural, geographical, and industrial variances, to drive your organization's marketing evolution more effectively.*

Join us as we traverse the global marketing terrain, harnessing the collective wisdom of marketing gurus to offer a holistic understanding of marketing maturity. This session will empower you with the knowledge to enhance your marketing strategies, taking crucial steps toward optimal marketing maturity.

You could submit full-length conference abstracts (30-minute sessions), organize the talk as a CMO panel discussion (60 minutes), or submit a lightning talk (five minutes).

While the maturity models were created by others in the community, you would be able to capture credit for pulling them all together for easier access. You could encourage hundreds of people attending these conferences to use the deck as a helpful guide in their marketing journey. If they, by chance, had their own maturity model, you could encourage them to contribute it to the community deck. This would improve your company brand while celebrating the work of the community and its members.

Expert tip: *I learned this trick from an industry colleague, Gene Kim. At the end of his presentations, he would offer the content to the audience. He would approach it by saying something along the lines of:*

"Anyone in the audience who would like a copy of my slides or the research I was presenting can get it now. I've set up my out-of-office email auto reply with links to the deck and my research. If you email name@gene.com, it will automatically send you the links to the content. The links are not gated. I simply want to make sure you get immediate access to the information."

The approach is beautiful. It provides immediate value to the audience. It allows Gene to see how many people in the audience were truly interested in the content. It also allows him to see who in the audience found it valuable and offers him a glimpse as to whom he could follow up with for future conversations.

Beyond applying that expert tip, as conference speakers who took the opportunity to demonstrate their industry authority, your company would be more likely to attract attendees to your booth at the conference. Moving the content into a conference forum begins to shift its value from community-led in Orbit 3 to company-led lead gen initiatives in Orbit 2.

Let's continue the journey into Orbit 2 by organizing a webinar.

Step 5: Hosting a Webinar

Just like webinars that you would host on your company-specific topics, your marketing team could arrange a webinar on the 21 maturity models.

For the webinar, you might invite a well-known marketing industry luminary like Dave Gerhardt to join you. You might also invite a CMO peer of yours to join the webinar as a panelist.

Running your regular webinar promotion sequence and leveraging an industry media site as the webinar host, you could attract thousands of people to register. Webinars like this that aim to help the community can attract thousands of people who are looking to boost their knowledge and understanding of marketing tech stacks.

The maturity model deck would now help you generate top-of-funnel leads for your demand-generation team. You're reaching a large audience of marketing leaders who are considering ways to uplevel their maturity, while not talking about your product or services—as part of this specific motion. Think of this as Orbit 3 meets Orbit 2.

Step 6: Boosting Demand Gen Through Digital Ads and Promotions

Let's take the example even further into your Orbit 2 initiatives. Even though the initial move was to place the deck on various ungated social and content channels, there would be nothing preventing you from gating the content on your corporate website.

Imagine sending an email that promotes "21 marketing maturity models that have been viewed over 75,000 times." Invite people reading the email to register for and download the deck. You can offer even more value by highlighting the availability of the panel discussion webinar with industry experts as an additional lead-nurturing step. If the asset provides enough value, people will be willing to fill out a simple form to get access to it.

The Long Tail of Value

What you started as an effort to better serve the community transformed over time into a demand-generation opportunity for your business that could pay significant dividends for years. The content delivered immense value to a community of practitioners looking for tips on getting started or validating their own tech stacks by comparing them to what others had put together.

The 21 marketing maturity models presentation also boosted your brand awareness and generated thousands upon thousands of leads. Those leads could then be nurtured over time in motions that introduce more product-specific information. This enables your sales and marketing teams to convert some of those community members into revenue. It's where you've led people from Orbit 3 into Orbit 1.

One of the nice things about this approach is it didn't start with pitching your products and services. This approach helped balance your portfolio of marketing initiatives to include a combination of *helpful* (community-led content) and *promotional* (traditional product-specific content). The community recognized you were doing your part to be good stewards of their growth while also supporting your business growth objectives.

The long tail of value is one of the primary characteristics of community-led content. The content remains relevant for years because it aims to be helpful rather than promotional. Additionally, you did not have to waste a bunch of time creating new content every couple of months. You did your part to keep it updated, and the community supported your effort.

Now that you've experienced your first three-orbit playbook, I've helped you document the approach with this simple table. If interested, you can download this table from my blog at unfairmindshare.com. Search for the post entitled, *From Community to Revenue: A Marketing Team's Three Orbit Journey.*

Playbook #2: From Community to Demand Gen

Alice de Courcy, CMO at Cognism, shared a similar approach to developing content and executing integrated marketing plans in her post, *How to Pivot from Lead Gen to Demand Gen: a CMO's Guide.*

"We've waved goodbye to planning our content calendar a quarter in advance and taken more of an editorial mindset to what we produce for the channels our buyers are in," Alice said. *"This means producing subject matter expertise content at scale and optimizing for in-channel consumption rather than attribution."*[87]

Alice continued, *"No one is consuming that content because they have to fill in a form, and it probably just sits in their inbox, and they forget to read it. So, the value in having this ungated free-to-view content is massive."*

	Activity	Result
Community-led marketing	21 marketing maturity models created by the community	Collected community content
	Marketing maturity model deck placed on LinkedIn, Twitter, Facebook, and marketing community forums	75,000 views Ungated
	Write blogs on a variety of sites discussing the value	10,000 readers (est.)
	Invite others to contribute their models	Content grows organically with community input
Brand-led marketing	Conference presentations on the deck	500 people in the community (est.)
Product-led marketing	Webinar about the deck + thought leaders	Sourced X,XXX leads $M marketing influenced revenue
	Digital promotions about deck	Sourced XX,XXX leads (gated) $M marketing influenced revenue
	Nurture path promoting your own products to high-maturity marketing organizations	Sourced X,XXX MQLs $M marketing influenced revenue

Marketing maturity model: Integrated marketing campaign originated in Orbit 3 with a path into Orbit 1. Metrics inspired by real campaigns.

Tasks to consider?	Completed?
Create ungated resources page	☐
Take time stamps for best clips for Emily	☐
Decide on video or animated clips	☐
Decide on whether it becomes a podcast	☐
Purpose, awareness ads — Linkedin/Facebook?	☐
Share with content team for use and blogs/SEO pages	☐
Purpose slide — turtl/slide share	☐
Decide on channels to distribute with Oscar	☐
Push out through webinar speaker channels	☐
Cognition on "personal" channels parentheses (who?)	☐
Plan an email, follow up (use clips/content to entice non-attendees)	☐
Does the webinar fit into a series?	☐

Planning the long-tail of value after your core market content has been developed.[88]

When it comes to a simple marketing tactic like a webinar that generates new content, Alice has directed her team to think more like a media agency. Where they used to just measure webinar leads, they now measure engagement during the webinar and across the long tail of content that follows. Here's one example of the long-tail content considerations that Alice's team uses when planning webinars.

Alice did not document her approach in terms of marketing orbits moving from community-led efforts to brand-led efforts, but it follows a similar flow to the first playbook scenario above.

Let's map Alice's approach into the three orbits to show you.

In addition to serving up juicy, ungated content aimed at their community, Alice remarks that they also run a second, parallel nurturing funnel for the same audience that focuses more on Cognism's product portfolio that features case studies, videos, and free tools.

	Activity	Result
Community-led marketing	Create an ungated resources page for community-led content	Moved away from collecting leads by ungating some of their content and creating 'awareness campaigns'
	Produce 30 – 60 minute videos on best practices for their target ideal customer profile (ICP)	Created value-led and entertaining content that educates, delights and builds brand affinity with our ICP in the community
	Create video highlight clips to share on multiple channels	Produced content the community loved then distributed it effectively
		Social channels encouraged peer sharing
	Produce a podcast series touching on the most watched content topics from the videos	Leveraged Cognism's subject matter experts and external contributors
	Invite industry influencers as guests	Followers of B2B influencers boosted distribution of content to wider audience
Brand-led marketing	Share video content summaries on the corporate blog	Boosted declared intent inbounds
	Plan a webinar showcasing best practices and community through leaders from the video series	Gated
		Sourced X,XXX leads
		$M marketing influenced revenue
Product-led marketing	Build a multi-touch email campaign that drives webinar participants into product-specific promotions	Gated
		Sourced XX,XXX leads
		$M marketing influenced revenue

Pivot from Lead Gen to Demand Gen: A view of Alice de Courcy's, CMO at Cognism, marketing program segmented into three orbits.

Playbook #3: Industry Survey

Another easy way to start a community-led marketing effort is to begin with an industry survey. Surveys are powerful in many ways, especially when they start with the community and take a vendor-neutral approach.

For several years, I led the creation and analysis of a survey for Microsoft's SharePoint market for low-code/no-code solutions, although it was not an individual effort. Every year, we assembled a group of industry friends from different businesses to contribute to the creation of the survey. Taking this approach helped us make sure the survey and its findings would be relevant to a broader audience.

Additionally, by including others from the beginning of the process, more people and their companies were available to help promote survey participation. With more people and companies promoting the survey, it was not uncommon for us to have over 2,000 participants sharing their perspectives with us.

This same group of community friends also helped promote the survey findings once the report was published, and we included their names on the report to give them due credit.[89]

> **Vendor-neutral approaches not only appeal to a broader audience but also generate more press and analyst coverage for your business than traditional "pitches" can.**

The vendor-neutral approach not only appealed to a broader audience but also generated more press and analyst coverage for the report each year. It was not uncommon to see 40 or more pieces of press coverage on the survey in a given year. It also helped further cement our position as an industry thought leader. The community at large benefited from the survey and the trends we consistently revealed in its findings year after year.

Once the survey report was published, ungated versions were made available to the community at large. But we also promoted gated versions of the survey results through digital and emailed promotional programs. These programs fed our demand-generation efforts.

Beyond adding the survey report as another asset in our marketing arsenal, it also served to inform our demand-generation efforts better. We were able to do a much deeper analysis of the survey findings to better understand the firmographics, demographics, and technographics of our industry that we could then feed into our demand-generation engine. That analysis helped us refine our ideal customer profile (ICP), account-based marketing (ABM), search engine marketing (SEM), vertical industry targets, and geographic account priorities.

Furthermore, when enabling our sales teams, we were able to use the survey data to better inform our reps about practices, technologies, or influential roles/personas they would likely encounter in their target accounts. The data would help surface common job titles, adjacent tooling investments, process trends, and behavioral differences between smaller and larger teams.

Armed with this information, the sales reps could better target conversations with prospects while sharing insights on what other companies were investing in across our industry. We also shared more detailed survey analyses with our engineering teams to better support their roadmap planning efforts. Both these practices gave us an advantage over our competitors.

Community-led marketing efforts can create valuable assets for your organization in many ways. One comes in the value of the asset itself, supporting demand generation and brand awareness efforts. When it comes to surveys, the value of the data collected not only serves the community but also serves to better inform your marketing, sales, and engineering colleagues about what is happening in the market.

Another is that community-led marketing efforts not only boost the effectiveness of marketing campaigns and demand-gen programs but also support sales. In the next chapter, I'll share perspectives from a friend of mine, Jim Shilts. It's the story of how he pursued community-led sales. For now, let's continue with how to integrate multiple playbooks for results.

	Activity	Result (estimated)
Community-led marketing	Build a community survey for the low-code/no-code industry with help from analysts, community influencers and internal SMEs	Produced vendor-neutral survey to capture better understanding of the market and ICPs
	Promote the industry survey	2,100 participants
	Analyze results	Captured video reactions from industry influencers helping draw more attention to the survey
	Promote results	Co-branded industry survey with sales partners and influencers to drive more attention
Brand-led marketing	Release survey results from the company website	Ungated content boosted site traffic XX,XXX per month and generated thousands of views on social content sharing sites
	Generate earned media hits on survey	Produced over 40 earned media hits annually
	Share survey results with industry analysts	Survey results published by top-tier analyst firms citing our company as the source
Product-led marketing	Host webinar to present survey results	Sharing voice of the community
	Present survey results at large conferences and local meet-ups	Generated X,XXX leads

Industry survey: The integrated marketing campaign originated in Orbit 3 with a path into Orbit 1. Lead counts are kept confidential.

Playbook #4: Leverage Multiple Approaches

Let's imagine a scenario where Alex is a CMO at a business offering a SaaS-based data enrichment solution for business development reps. In his first two years in the CMO seat, community-led efforts had yielded fits and starts.

Community Without Consistency

Each time Alex's business organized a community-led initiative, the marketing team found it hard to attribute participation and leads from the activity into some meaningful measure for the sales organization.

For example, his team might run a webinar and invite a couple of industry sales luminaries to participate. They would talk about key priorities facing their industry, and the audience they attracted was often much larger than their product-specific webinars.

The same would happen with their roadshows. His team would organize events in a couple of cities. The agenda for the roadshow would include one or two executives from his firm, they would pull in a local customer, and they would do their best to pull in a local industry thought leader or analyst from their industry.

Alex aimed his team toward initiatives to engage their broader community. But their approach heavily promoted their company or products across the event agendas and content. As a result, his team failed to generate any stickiness within the community.

His question to me was, *"Why are my community initiatives not generating the audiences I want/expect?"*

The Value of Persistence

Two things were going wrong with his team's efforts: Persistence and demand gen.

First, they had no community persistence. A webinar would pop up as a community initiative once a quarter, a podcast episode made it on air every couple of weeks, and roadshows would roll into a city one day and out the next. While the efforts were attracting people in their market, there was no forum for them to keep the conversation going. Participants were not given an opportunity to stay in touch with one another and continue the good vibes they felt the first time they engaged with Alex's business.

If you take a step back and think about a monthly webinar series featuring someone from Alex's industry community, the activity would account for an investment of 12 hours a year—a far cry from the 1,000 hours of commitment we discussed earlier for community initiatives to gain proper traction.

The other thing that was happening was that Alex's team was treating every participant in these initiatives as a lead. People who showed up for what was billed as a community-led event were sent a bunch of company and product-specific emails from Alex's team as part of the post-event follow-up. For community members looking to engage with peers, learn from others, and uplevel their skills, there was no opportunity to build momentum.

Integrating Playbooks to Enable A Conversion Funnel

In an effort to build unfair mindshare, Alex decided to take a different approach to his community-led efforts. The process included elements of persistence for community engagement and integrating multiple playbooks.

The first thing he did was broaden the scope of his community-led efforts to invite anyone who touched the BDR community. This meant that account managers, sales VPs, RevOps leaders, product marketers, and demand-gen pros were welcomed. Initiatives would welcome anyone who wanted to better themselves as a sales or marketing professional. It would also aim to deliver insights on how BDRs could get more out of their relationships with their customers, account managers, and peers in marketing.

Together, he imagined a series of playbooks that would build from and feed off one another. The goal of the playbooks was to engage people first in the outer community-led orbits, and over time move the right members of the community into the inner product-led orbits.

He chose to start with a series of quarterly online conferences for sales and marketing professionals—Playbook #1. His ideal community profile for participants was much larger than a BDR-only approach. The events would feature 25 speakers who would all deliver content aimed at helping people uplevel their sales skills. BDRs, marketing pros, and sales leaders from the community would be encouraged to deliver presentations. The audience would be made up of the same persona mix.

> **The goal of the playbooks was to engage people first in the outer community-led orbits, and over time move the ideal members of the community into the inner product-led orbits.**

BDRs would learn from marketing leaders. Marketing leaders would learn from sales managers. And sales managers would learn from BDRs. In all cases, the value would be recognized from connecting members of the sales and marketing community for mutual benefit, collaboration, and knowledge exchanges. Alex and his business would benefit from the brand affinity associated with pulling this community forum together.

Offering Communities a Place to Gather

In addition to producing their event, the community marketing team would also pull together a Discourse community portal that would serve as a forum for BDRs and other sales pros to gather and interact before and following the event. Everyone registering for the Orbit 3 event was encouraged to sign up for the Discourse forum.

During the event, speakers and moderators would further promote the Discourse forum as a place to gather and share information with industry peers. Participants in the forum were promised that it was a vendor-pitch-free zone. The aim of the forum was to make them better sales and marketing professionals, not to sell products.

Some participants from the event were immediately curious about who and what company would organize such an initiative. This led those people to explore more about what Alex's company offered. They were naturally curious. They also entered the nurture sequence that Alex's demand-gen team had set up around their BDR offering.

Following the event, everyone was sent a reminder about the Discourse community. The post-event email that went out highlighted some of the great conversations already happening there that were worth checking out. It did not include product or company pitches.

Moving from One Community-Led Offer to Another

The following week, Alex's community team followed up with all the participants, informing them of a new initiative. This was Playbook #2, which aimed to create a BDR salary survey for the community. There were two asks that Alex's team made: 1) for a few community members to assist in building the survey questions, and 2) once the survey was ready, they wanted all the BDRs in the community to take it and encourage all their BDR peers to participate as well. The more people who participated, the better the results would be for everyone's insights.

Playbook #2 helped Alex's team further segment the community. Instead of trying to engage everyone, this playbook refined the focus on community participants to focus on BDR participation. The effort was still part of Orbit 3 marketing, where there was no need to promote Alex's products or company. This effort was focused on helping BDRs progress in their careers.

Once the BDR salary survey was complete, the survey was promoted to the community. BDRs took the survey and information was gathered. Alex's team analyzed the results and worked with a couple of community members to produce the report.

As the next step in nurturing the BDRs in the community, the survey participants were invited to a webinar where the results would be discussed. Alex participated as one of three panelists reviewing the findings. He invited a Director of Business Development and a VP of Sales from the community to join him for the discussion. During the webinar, the audience did not hear any product pitches. But they did hear perspectives on the report from Alex. His participation built a stronger brand affinity for his company.

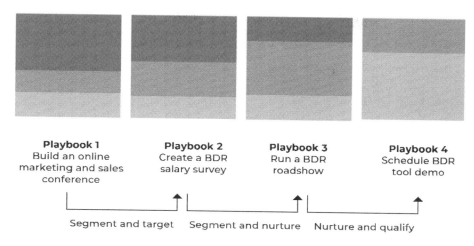

| **Playbook 1** | **Playbook 2** | **Playbook 3** | **Playbook 4** |
| Build an online marketing and sales conference | Create a BDR salary survey | Run a BDR roadshow | Schedule BDR tool demo |

Segment and target   Segment and nurture   Nurture and qualify

The best community-led marketers integrate multiple playbooks to engage, segment, nurture, and qualify audiences. These playbooks are designed to move prospects from your outer community-led orbits to your inner product-led orbits.

Those who participated in the webinar were also encouraged to join the conversations in the Discourse forum. Alex was building stickiness with the community through the forum, and participants were sharing how excited they were to interact and share insights with their peers there.

Invite Communities to Join You in Other Forums

Following these and other touch points through the nurture campaign, Alex's team reached out every once in a while with product or company-specific information. These interactions represented Playbook #3.

> ## Their approach was light on the sales voice and heavy on the community voice.

It was light on the sales voice and heavy on the community voice. For example, they would say things like, *"If you are going to be in Austin for the Forrester B2B Summit, please join us for our BDR happy hour event. While there, be sure to get one of our limited edition 'Keep BDRs Weird' t-shirts"* (playing off the Austin city theme of "Keep Austin Weird").

Over the course of several quarters, Alex's team transitioned their community-led marketing efforts away from the fits and starts initiatives of the past. They were running multiple community-led playbooks that segmented, nurtured, and better qualified the portion of the Orbit 3 community that was most aligned with their product offering.

Keep the Community Going

In parallel, Alex's team invested time in keeping the sales and marketing Discourse community running. New members were coming into the forum every week as existing members recommended it to their peers. The Discourse community became an invaluable part of his company's marketing strategy. Not only did it play a role at the top of their funnel to generate new potential leads that led to more sales, but it also provided a listening post for his marketing team to understand more about their ICPs.

Over time, the Discourse community became a go-to forum for sales and marketing professionals to assemble, ask questions, share experiences, and grow within their careers.

The Discourse community also became a source of new content for Alex's team. He gathered them each month to review an editorial calendar of content they could produce that would resonate with their target audience, yet not always serve to directly promote their products. The community exchanges would point to topics of interest that BDRs wanted to learn more about, and Alex's team could help produce and share content on those topics. HubSpot capitalized on a similar approach to this with their marketing audience over many years, and they are still active with the approach today.

The key to Alex's success was two-fold. First, he embraced the community-led initiative to serve the market more than his company. Second, he and his team came up with a plan, including integrating multiple playbooks, that moved properly qualified community members into the marketing and sales pipeline for his business.

	Activity	Result (estimated)
Community-led marketing	Broaden the scope of the community beyond Business Development Reps (BDRs)	Widen the go-to-market aperture to be more inclusive in Orbit 3
	Host a series of quarterly online conferences for sales and marketing professionals	Provide a quarterly forum for professionals to gather
	Establish a community portal for sales and marketing professionals to discuss best practices, share insights, and ask for help/advice	Provide a persistent community space for pros to gather between the quarterly forums
	Create BDR salary survey	Create helpful content for the community
Brand-led marketing	Host a webinar discussing the BDR salary survey results	Generate 1,500 top of funnel leads
	Monitor the Discourse community for topics of interest most relevant to the BDR community	Refine and organize a content editorial calendar
Product-led marketing	Build an integrated nurture campaign for BDRs active in the community to learn more about Alex's products	Nurture the lead funnel to identify high-quality MQLs originating from Orbit 2 and 3 initiatives

From quarterly forums to a salary survey to a product nurture campaign. A summary of how Alex created a community movement that built more top-of-funnel leads for his business to engage and nurture over time.

EXPERT TIP: PLAN FROM ORBIT 3 TO ORBIT 1

When planning marketing playbooks for the community, start in Orbit 3 and work your way down to Orbit 1. Beginning in Orbit 3 establishes the best relationship with your community as the value is aimed at their benefit and involvement rather than focusing on promotional content and exchanges at the beginning. Use Orbit 3 to build trust, improve your understanding of the market, and encourage participation. Once community members feel comfortable in Orbit 3, they will be more likely to venture into the lower orbits where you begin to share company and product specific content, exchanges, and opportunities to meet.

CHAPTER 12

Growing with Community-Led Sales

Years ago, Jim Shilts joined CA Technologies as a sales representative. His job was to sell software tools to the developer community in his territory. Like all reps in his position, he had a target quota to hit for both the quarter and the year. Hitting that target meant achieving his on-target earnings, and missing the mark meant the possibility of polishing his resume for the next sales role.

Any good B2B sales rep can sell almost any product put in front of them. They are extremely good at understanding the market's challenges, the problems their customers are trying to solve, and the solutions they might cobble together to address them.

The best reps, though, go a step further than the standard formula of:

your problem + my product = your solution

to make their numbers. The best sales reps establish long-term relationships in a market that will serve them well across a career—even if their employer changes from time to time. Relationship-oriented sales reps like Jim produce more bang for the buck.

Why? The relationships they establish open more meaningful doors that can lead to more sales.

Lead with Inviting Dialogue

Instead of starting with a pure product pitch in his new role at CA, Jim began building relationships in his community. He started with a simple, local networking group that would gather software developers and engineering leaders. He named the group NADOG (North American DevOps Group). In the beginning, about 20 or 30 people would show up. Jim would propose various discussion topics and invite participants to share their thoughts and experiences.

"Selfishly, I started the initiative to help build my deal funnel," Jim explained. *"But the more I engaged with the community, the movement transformed into building deeper relationships with people in my market. Even if I could not directly help someone, I often discovered opportunities to connect them with others who could help."*

Jim's approach to community mimicked the sentiment of Daniel Murray, founder of The Marketing Millennials, who tweeted in 2022: *"Most of your audience is not ready to buy. The goal of marketing is that when they are ready to buy, your brand is top of mind."*[90]

Jim listened and understood what was on the minds of community members. He then invited guest speakers from the broader developer and software engineering community to speak on topics that were meaningful to those attending. The meet-up was well-attended, and all participants raved about the value they received from participating.

There were a few set rules around community engagement that Jim imposed from the beginning of these meet-ups. First, while CA Technologies employed him, they did not talk about CA products. He also insisted on a *"no sales pitch"* policy for the meeting; there was a time and a place for those, and his meet-ups were not one of them. The meet-ups were a vendor-neutral zone where people could meet, collaborate, and learn from one another. The neutral stance of the meet-up encouraged others in the community to come and invite their friends and associates as well.

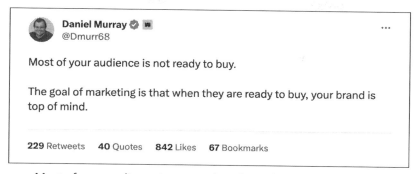

Daniel Murray ✓ 🅰
@Dmurr68

Most of your audience is not ready to buy.

The goal of marketing is that when they are ready to buy, your brand is top of mind.

229 Retweets   **40** Quotes   **842** Likes   **67** Bookmarks

Most of your audience is not ready to buy. The goal of marketing is that when they are ready to buy, your brand is top of mind.[91]

His employer did play a small part in his community-building efforts. They sponsored pizza and drinks for the attendees—usually around $150–$200 per event. Beyond being thanked as a sponsor at each meeting, there was no further mention of CA. Jim never hid the fact that he worked at the company—everyone knew. The association he needed for his day job was there, and people knew where to find him if they had a problem CA could help them address.

Experience Warm Introductions

Jim's helpful nature and leadership in the community increased his recognition within and access to his target community as a sales rep. He recounted one new prospect meeting with his sales manager at the time.

"We met the prospects in the lobby of their offices. The sales manager and I then introduced ourselves. That's when one of the prospects did a double-take."

"You're Jim Shilts? Jim Shilts, the DevOps guy?" asked the new prospect.

"Yes, that's me," Jim smiled.

"I've been sending my team all of your NADOG updates and encouraging them to participate in your meet-ups. I didn't know you were a sales rep working at CA. That's awesome."

How many sales reps would like that kind of warm introduction on a call with their manager? This is where Jim's community-led orbit was meeting his product-led sales orbit. The more he invested in NADOG, the more often this kind of experience happened.

Jim's reputation in the industry preceded him that day and on many other occasions. He was known for helping people learn more about modern software development practices. People knew he was a sales rep and worked for CA, but he never imposed those views in the community meetings. He became a trusted advisor to the community. Even though he was not a software engineer, he was welcomed as part of their tribe.

Jim extended the value of the NADOG community to his sales colleagues at CA. He also extended invites to other salespeople in the industry who he thought could benefit from the community. Getting their buy-in to attend took work.

"Do I have to go?" the reps would ask.

"No. But you should," was Jim's response.

"But why should I attend an evening event if I am not going to come away with five new leads?" they asked.

"I can't promise you five new leads from the event. But I can promise you the opportunity to forge five new relationships," Jim replied.

He advised them to approach it this way: *"Go in and participate like you are a community member. Talk about families and what they are doing. Leave your products on the sidelines. Make personal connections today that will make your future sales easier."*

> **"You don't expand through promotion.
> You expand through participation."
> —Scott Stockton**

My former colleague and sales executive, Scott Stockton, shared a similar sentiment about his sales-led community approach: *"You don't expand through promotion. You expand through participation."*

Some reps bought into Jim's approach and prospered. Others did not.

Put in 1,000 hours

When Jim started his work on what became NADOG, he did not have the advantage of communicating his approach using the three-orbit model. In his gut, he knew that to establish broader relationships in the community that would serve him well at any job, he would need to move product pitching to the side. NADOG was a community-led sales initiative for Jim. His community tribe met in Orbit 3.

Jim did not create the DevOps community at large. Instead, he created forums for those in it to gather, share information, and make connections. The NADOG forums were neutral, helpful, and local. Anyone could have done what Jim did, but he was the one who invested the 1,000 hours needed to have it catch on and flourish.

Jim summed up his investment around community-led sales with me, saying, *"Community does not have to cost that much. Just be out there and stay out there."*

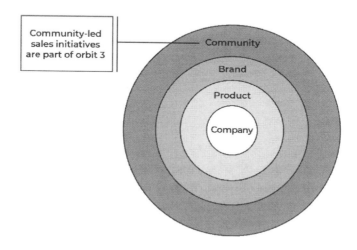

Community-led sales initiatives are part of Orbit 3. Sales professionals who lead with being helpful in their target communities can build more trusted relationships than their competition.

Connect the Orbits

Once NADOG started catching on across the DevOps community, it attracted the attention of more vendors in the space. Their employees were attending and sometimes speaking at the events. Their marketing teams were also looking for more places to connect with folks in person. At the same time, Jim was asked to extend NADOG's presence into geographies outside of his or his colleague's territories, making it less appealing for CA to fund pizza and drinks for attendees.

Every request from the community to expand into a different city or region ate away at Jim's time. He needed more resources to help. To expand NADOG more efficiently, Jim turned to others, including vendors in the community, to co-sponsor and co-host the events with him.

The vendors invited their customers and prospects in the community to attend. They recognized that not everyone in the community wanted to be "pitched" all the time. At the top of the funnel, demand-gen and field-marketing teams can benefit from being helpful. That helpful motion then builds trust and fosters new connections.

Vendors in the community often helped secure meeting spaces, managed some onsite logistics, and offered funds to feed attendees. The vendor occasionally gave away prizes through a raffle at the event that enabled them to capture leads. Community members had the opportunity to opt-in to vendor-led funnels at the event but were otherwise not spammed as a side effect of their participation.

Jim orchestrated the registration, sign-ups, and speakers for each event, keeping the community's personal data safe. Jim valued the member relationships NADOG had forged and protected them in earnest. Contact details of attendees were shared with vendors who helped organize a specific event with Jim, but everyone in the community was made aware of that practice ahead of time. For events that the group organized in Europe, lead sharing with sponsors was prohibited by law.

The approach to letting vendors participate in the community helped Jim scale its resources and reach. The vendor participation transformed NADOG into a multi-orbit community initiative. Jim could expand his community

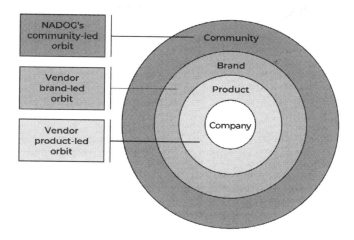

while supporting brand-led initiatives that built company awareness. Demand generation was also supported by vendors—including Jim's own employer—who collected member information from the raffles or other giveaways at the meet-ups. Community-led orbits complemented product-led orbits.

Measure Sales Outcomes

The business outcomes achieved from connecting the orbits were real. Vendors who sponsored a series of events for a couple of thousand dollars each told Jim their community investments were paying off. It was not uncommon to hear that an event series sourced over $2 million in new pipeline opportunities and influenced hundreds of thousands of dollars in closed business.

Other organizations have seen strong returns on community-led initiatives in sales as well. Erica Kuhl, former VP of Community at Salesforce, shared community engagement results in their business. Community members who participated—even in the simplest forms of engagement (e.g., ask a question or post something in an online forum)—generated more business for Salesforce.[92]

- Creating 2.5x the number of deals
- Creating 2x larger deals by dollar value
- Adopting products 33 percent faster
- Churning 3x less when it came time for renewals

Expand the Tribe

By 2019, Jim had worked closely with others in the DevOps community to grow the NADOG community to over 80 local events across multiple cities and countries with over 9,000 participants.

While the pandemic years did slow things down, the community rebounded in 2022, hosting over 50 in-person meetings. The value of the community in building relationships and sharing knowledge is something people craved and wanted to be a part of once it was deemed safe again to leave the house.

Formalize Community-Led Sales

Nobody tasked Jim to start a community-led initiative at CA. He pioneered the idea. As others in the industry begin to explore community-led sales, they are experimenting with how to best structure it.

One such firm is Commsor, a company that helps other businesses unlock the power of their communities. In November 2022, the company blogged

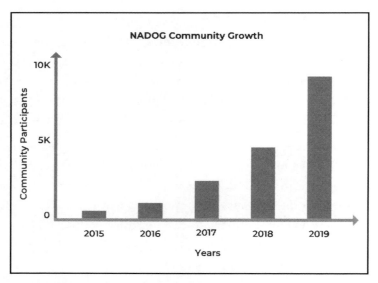

Growth of the NADOG community was exponential. It grew from a brand promise of being helpful to IT professionals in local communities.

about bringing community-led thinking to its sales organization by hiring Community Development Representatives (CDR). They would primarily focus on building relationships and encouraging engagement.

As part of this move, Commsor explained, *"There's nothing worse than joining a community and having your first touchpoint being a salesperson reaching out because joining the community triggered some alert in their sales system. Sales teams should not run or set community strategy, nor should communities exist solely to drive sales."*[93]

They structured the community-led sales positions to transform the typical approach from this:

> *"Hey, I'd love to set up a call to talk you through our product. Oh, you're not ready just yet? No problem."*

To more helpful engagements like this:

> *"Hey, this discussion popped up in our community, and it made me think of that problem you're having. There might be some useful advice in here for you."*

They summarized their organizational structure, emphasizing that salespeople continue to follow a traditional product-led path to deals, but their CDRs would take a community-first approach.

No matter how your organization structures it, we can all agree that fostering deeper relationships in the market through more helpful engagements results in better business outcomes.

Leverage All Orbits to Meet Sales Goals

To people like Jim, the value of community-led sales has been evident for a long time. No one asked him to do it. He just knew he needed to do it. He saw value in relationship building where others didn't.

Where he invested his time was regularly met with questions from marketing and sales leaders who were always eager to measure results. Initially, it was harder to identify specific numbers because communities don't form and build close ties overnight or even over a quarter. Trust takes longer—especially when you have "sales" in your title.

Over the years, Jim continued to invest in NADOG, even as his employer changed from one company to another. When new managers would inquire about the value of community initiatives, he would say, *"I knew we were doing the right thing if 80 percent of the audience we are building intersects with our potential customer base."*

> **"I knew we were doing the right thing if
> 80 percent of the audience we are building
> intersects with our potential customer base."
> —Jim Shilts**

He could also share his track record of meeting or exceeding quota each year and anecdotes from other companies that shared influenced and sourced pipeline figures with him. For Jim, community-led sales were not an alternative to the traditional product- and brand-led initiatives many of his colleagues pursued over the years. Instead, the community-led orbit complemented the product and brand orbits, supporting his sales goals year after year.

EXPERT TIP: FOCUS ON THE CONVERSATION

Community does not have to cost that much. Building trust is free. Encouraging people to collaborate, share, and educate brings value to every participant. If you create something of real value for people, they will seek it out again and again.

"Buying friends" in the community by giving away swag, hosting fancy parties at cool venues, or creating other materialist exchanges erodes the authenticity of interactions. Buying friends often results in shallow and superficial relationships. The focus is primarily on material gain rather than genuine emotional connection. Such relationships lack depth and may not provide the support, understanding, and empathy that true community friendships offer.

My teams would frequently host dinners or evening get-togethers at industry events, but we did so in very approachable locations. We would get more value out of hosting a dinner at a decent restaurant with good food and a great atmosphere for fostering conversation, than we could have from organizing a five-star formal dinner or inviting people to a club where the music was so loud that no one could hold a conversation.

When it comes to community, keep your focus on the conversation and away from compensation.

CHAPTER 13

Measuring Your Impact

"I interviewed 25 senior-level community builders last year, and almost all of them (96 percent) reported the number one struggle they faced: not getting buy-in from leadership," said April MacLean, Founder of Wondry.[94]

One of those community builders she interviewed added, *"Everyone wants community but, in the end, they don't want to invest in it."*

> **"Everyone wants community but, in the end, they don't want to invest in it."**

This is where collaboration between marketing leaders and their community leaders is critical. Without proper measures, investment in communities is challenging. And communities that fail to drive business outcomes face much higher scrutiny when it comes to reviewing investment priorities.

When initiating community-led marketing initiatives, community leaders can't set fluffy or hollow expectations for the outcomes they are setting out to achieve for the business. At the same time, marketing leaders need to establish with the community leader what success will look like, how it will be measured, and over what period of time. Without this alignment, community efforts inside a business are doomed to fail.

Connecting Orbit Leaders to Improve Reporting

When community-led marketing is done well, the links between Orbit 3 and Orbit 1 are pronounced and measurable. Community leaders on your team will benefit from establishing close ties with your demand-generation leaders to help them understand, track, and report on outcomes of their efforts. Community leaders and their efforts may represent the very top of many demand-generation funnels, but it is often the demand-gen leaders who have invested in the tools and reporting that track any leads into and through the funnel.

> **When community-led marketing is done well, the links between Orbit 3 and Orbit 1 are pronounced and measurable.**

As expected, community-led motions mostly occur at the top of the funnel, often representing first-touch attributions in a demand-generation funnel. However, for marketing and demand-generation leaders who focus on last-touch attributions before qualifying a lead or an account, reporting community-led efforts might require additional effort to tie into revenue outcomes.

Measure Your Progress

"In the game of gains, keep count," is something I often share with my teams as a reminder to measure progress. In community-led marketing, keeping

count is critical to support continued investment in the effort for any marketing executive.

Community-led activity can be measured in a number of different ways. Community impacts brand awareness and grows brand affinity. It accelerates sales, creates obstacles for competitors, and improves customer loyalty.

Early in your community-led journey, measurement is hard. Communities don't form overnight, and normal weekly, monthly, or quarterly metrics used by product-led demand teams might not be directly transferable to the community-led realm. But make no mistake—if you want stakeholders to invest in community-led marketing initiatives year after year, you will need to keep score.

In cases where community leaders have less experience with marketing metrics that matter, you might need to help them create the proper dashboards. In other cases, your community-led marketers responsible for leading or inspiring content creation might not have direct access to the demand-generation reporting tools that track their impact on the sales pipeline; this is where you need to foster the right culture of information transparency between team members.

> **Make sure your demand-generation teams that are promoting the community content don't take all the credit for the pipeline generated simply because they manage the tools.**

For example, make sure your demand-generation teams that are promoting the community content don't take all the credit for the pipeline generated simply because they manage the tools. As discussed previously, demand generation is a combination of high-quality fuel (content) and powerful engines (amplification) that need to be reported on holistically.

Monitor Goals, Outcomes, and Cost

The first thing you will want to consider is program spend. Community-led motions can have little to no cost or require significant investments, depending on how you approach and structure the activities. Regardless, it is essential community-led marketers understand the costs associated with programs they are running. Supporting awesome initiatives in the community is not free, and tracking spend is an essential first step in understanding your return on investments.

Consider applying a basic tracking model to community-led efforts that include the objective, measurable goal, tactic, and cost.

For example, let's say you work at a FinTech organization that builds software and APIs (application programming interfaces) that enable small businesses to accept payments, send payouts, and manage inventories online. For your community-led initiative, let's say the objective is to start a new forum for CFOs who work at start-up and scale-up organizations with under $100M in annual recurring revenues. You want to provide an online forum for them to gather, share experiences, and ask peers for recommendations and insights.

Your goal will be to engage 10,000 participants, starting with 2,000 people in your first quarter of the program's operation. The tactic will be to provide an online forum of educational content and a conversation space to exchange ideas. Your program budget to start things off is $40,000.

After building the conference and online forum, you'll engage the community in an annual survey—The CFO FinTech Survey. The survey will explore CFO perspectives on fintech adoption, top challenges, investment priorities, risk management strategies, and impact on financial operations while gauging collaboration with start-ups and expectations for future innovation in financial services.

The survey will be developed as a collaboration between several different companies, university professors, analysts, and industry thought leaders. The tracking and business outcomes might look something like the following.

Objective	Survey our CFO community on fintech adoption, top challenges, investment priorities, risk management strategies, and impact on financial operations
Measurable Goal	Engage 2,000 participants in Q4'2023
Tactics	Build a survey with the community, promote it across different forums, collect results, analyze results, and report on them
Cost	Program cost <$10,000
Outcomes	**Community-led** · 6,000 participants completed the survey **Brand-led** · 25 earned media opportunities secured from survey results · 12 earned conference speaking slots secured for our employees · 15,000 survey downloads over 12 months; 65 percent from community members **Product-led** · 1,500 marketing qualified leads from survey campaign · $3.5M in marketing sourced deals over 12 months, originating from community members

Set goals for your three-orbit programs and measure the outcomes achieved.

Report on Outcomes

Reporting on community-led outcomes is critical to support continued investments in Orbit 3. Reporting is not only important for holding community-led leaders on your team accountable, but it serves as a reminder that community motions are serving a greater purpose—not just for the members—but for your company.

There's no denying that much of what happens in community orchestration is qualitative in nature (e.g., fostering relationships), but that does not relieve Orbit 3 leaders of the need to measure and report on quantifiable outcomes.

Reporting also helps bring a realistic versus an emotional measure to results. For example, a community-led marketer might be excited that 50 people participated in a vendor-neutral meet-up event they had organized. But when the opportunity came to engage some of those people in more community-led motions or even company-specific endeavors, none of the attendees took the next step. Therefore, as exciting as the work might have been, the business community outcome wasn't realized from the community investment. A one-time engagement did not result in longer-standing relationships with the community or the business.

I've also seen community marketing leaders get excited about a small audience of practitioners engaging in an event that took a lot of time and investment to pull off. When measured against the time and investment of a company's other marketing initiatives or campaigns, the activity fell woefully short by comparison. Measuring and reporting activities can provide an important reality check on whether or not the business should double down on repeating an activity or simply recognize that it would not be worth further investment.

Create a Salesforce Campaign

Campaigns in Salesforce can help track and attribute community engagement to a specific contact, company, or lead. Just as you would measure a lead's engagement in a conference, webinar, banner ad, or landing page, community engagement can be added as another campaign category.

As your community initiatives grow, you might develop multiple campaigns from community efforts that can be attributed to a sales cycle. For example, conferences, meet-ups, surveys, live-streamed meetings, book downloads, or dinner events could all be registered as different campaign interactions.

Tracking engagement in your community initiative for an individual or an account can provide valuable insights to your sales team about what topics, content, and opportunities their prospects and customers are interested in exploring further.

Link Orbit 3 to Tangible Business Outcomes

"Measuring the value of something that is inherently relational is almost impossible," said April MacLean, Founder of Wondry, an agency dedicated to launching and scaling impactful communities.[95] While she did not have the perfect answer for how to measure the value of community-led efforts, she offered two pieces of advice to marketing leaders responsible for community-led efforts.

> **"Measure stickiness, not engagement.** *Engagement is a bad goal because it only measures how many people showed up once. The more important measure is how often an audience member returns to the community. She suggests a common community measure like Daily Active Users (DAU) divided by Monthly Active Users (MAU) with the following benchmarks:*
>
> - *DAU/MAU = 10 - 20 percent (good)*
> - *DAU/MAU = 20-25 percent (strong)*
> - *DAU/MAU = 26 percent+ (outstanding)*
>
> **Drive business outcomes.** *Outcomes should usually fall into one of four categories: acquisition, retention, support/success, and user-generated content."*

April suggests picking one primary goal for the community and measuring against it. She also advises marketing leaders to give community-led efforts sufficient runway—especially when you are starting off. April notes, *"If a community is new, it will take 6–12 months to get any meaningful data."*

Expert tip: *I dive into this topic in more depth on my blog at unfairmindshare.com. Head there to read* "How to Measure Community-led Growth and Participation." *In this blog, I point to the problem with DAU and MAU is that it suggests measuring "users." This is often how brand-led marketers think of and measure the activity of people in their product or service communities (Orbits 1 and 2). When it comes to true community-led marketing in Orbit 3, not all community members are "users" or "customers." Therefore, I am proposing a new metric to measure the health of the community-led orbit. That is, measuring Daily Active Community (DAC) and Monthly Active Community (MAC).*

It's critical to your annual budgeting and planning process to connect community participation to tangible business outcomes. While not every element of participation will be measurable, there are plenty that can be measured. To identify them, marketing executives need to work closely with their community leadership and demand-gen teams.

According to the 2022 State of Community Management report, the most reported business outcomes driven by community efforts were: Increased customer loyalty/retention (68 percent reported the benefit), improved awareness

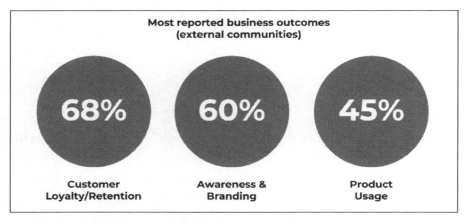

Examining tangible business outcomes achieved from community-led efforts.
Source: *The State of Community Management Report 2022,*
from The Community Roundtable

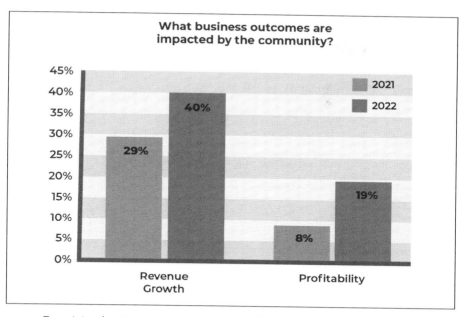

Examining business outcomes impacted by community-led efforts and revealed that revenue and profitability were both positively impacted. Source: The State of Community Management Report 2022, from The Community Roundtable.

and branding (60 percent), and improved product usage (45 percent).[96] The report also noted that, while revenue growth and profitability weren't prevalent enough to crack the top three outcomes, their year-over-year jumps were noticeable.

Worry less about how many people are showing up in your community. Focus more on how many people are sticking around and what they are doing when they do.

Survey participants recognized improvements in revenue growth from the community jumped from 29 percent to 40 percent between 2021 and 2022. Marketing teams measuring improvements in profitability jumped from eight percent to 19 percent during the same period.[97]

Track Engagement and Participation

Next, your team will want to focus on engagement targets. This area requires meaningful review to help community marketers distinguish important business metrics from fully vanity metrics.

Tracking engagement targets can be as simple as measuring how many people:

- Attended a presentation at a conference
- Registered for webinar hosting a community panel
- Downloaded a whitepaper
- Listened in on a webinar
- Tuned into a live stream event on Twitch
- Participated in a survey
- Attended a meet-up event
- Requested presentation slides following a conference session
- Signed up for or contributed content to a collaboration forum

Each of the activities above can be organized or led by Orbit 3 marketers. Orbit 3 marketing leaders should also track and measure participation and engagement to understand how their investments pay off. When engagement is high, it indicates activity types that should be repeated. When there is low engagement, it represents activities requiring adjustment, or perhaps not worth repeating.

Report on Lead Generation

Working with their demand-generation counterparts, Orbit 3 marketers can determine how and when to best engage participants with company- or product-specific offers. Moving community participants from vendor-neutral community-led orbits into company-specific demand-gen orbits must be done in a natural, not forced way. Forced movements may erode the trust and relationships built over months or even years of community engagement in a matter of days or even hours.

Not all community participants are or will become leads for the business. But depending on their role and/or relationships with others, they may be active

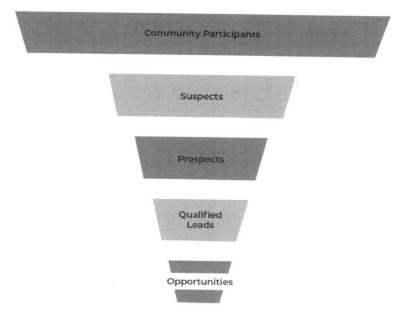

Community-led initiatives can build a massive set of top-of-funnel leads for your business. But not all leads from a community need to be placed into a nurture cycle. Further segmentation and rules of engagement can help ensure trust is maintained with community members.

influencers within deals. In addition, relationships in the community take time to mature. That said, when large communities are built and sustained, a five or ten percent conversation rate can represent a significant upside for your business.

I'll share some examples of how marketing leaders might track and report on community-led initiatives. Let's start with a few simple ones your organization can track.

1. **Delivering a conference presentation**

   Your community-marketing leader might be signed up to give a vendor-neutral talk at an industry conference. You can immediately measure how many people attended the session; some events might even share the specific badge scans of those who attended the presentation session with your team.

The community leader might offer to send a copy of the presentation to anyone in the audience, where you can then track whether the audience was engaged enough to want a copy of the information.

> **Expert tip:** *At the end of your community conference presentations, tell the audience they can immediately get a copy of your slides by emailing yourname@companyname.com.*

Set up your out-of-office email message to include a link to the slides and then monitor what percentage of the audience took me up on it. You can then nurture and track those people as part of our engaged community.

If memory serves me correctly, I once got 80 percent of an audience numbering in the hundreds to request my slides using this approach.

Following the presentation, you should also coordinate with your event team to understand how many people attended the community-led session and visited your company booth at the conference.

So, some event measures you can include are:

- How many people attended the session?
- How many people requested the slides?
- How many people from the presentation visited your company booth?
- How many of those accounts converted over time?

2. Community Survey

I ran a low-code/no-code community survey for three years that studied application creation and operations. The survey was put together with the help of several friends at different companies around the industry. The survey itself was vendor-neutral and did not promote our company or products. We had about 900 people participate in taking the survey every year.

One of the questions in the survey requested feedback from community members on what they thought were the most important priorities for the industry at large or in their organizations that year. We asked them for permission to include their response in the survey analysis report.

Later, we distributed copies of the survey findings report that always included a number of quotes from community members who represented the overall results.

We often presented the survey results at industry conferences and invited our friends at other companies who helped us with the survey to do the same; it was not uncommon for someone to ask for a copy of my deck to present at their local or regional event. This effort helped inform the industry of the current practices and trends we were observing to help them make better decisions on people, tools, and approaches at work.

The survey served our community well, but it also supported demand generation and brand promotion efforts. Our demand-gen teams would use the study to attract people to local field marketing events. Our digital promotion team would build ad campaigns featuring survey results that drove community members to landing pages. And our communications team promoted the survey results to industry media to increase coverage for our company and thought leaders.

Each year, we could track millions of dollars in revenue back to marketing-sourced leads that came from the survey.

Some of the measures you can use to monitor interest and progress:

- How many people participated in the survey?
- How many speaking sessions at different conferences were secured on the topic?
- How many people registered for demand gen-led webinars discussing the survey results?
- How many people clicked through digital promo ads featuring survey statistics?
- How many articles in industry trade publications or analyst reports referenced the survey results?

- How many account leads from events or digital promotions converted to becoming customers over time?

Upgrade Lead Gen Reporting

Regarding large communities and engagement, the investment model and measures can be more sophisticated. One significant activity can lead to multiple lead-converting channels over time. For example, large community conferences that we ran when I was CMO at the Linux Foundation, can generate future participation in working groups, community surveys, industry panel webinars, market landscapes, best practice guides, topical training courses, and local meet-ups. Your team can organize and report on these engagements as they approach multi-touch, integrated campaigns.

As plans are laid out, it is critical to establish budgets and goals for each activity. Community-led endeavors—especially the larger ones—require budgets to operate. Orbit 3 marketing leaders who understand the cost of activities can decide better what to invest in and how often to make those investments. Additionally, those marketing leaders who can show a strong return on investment are more likely to secure funding for their activities during the next budget planning cycle.

When establishing conversion goals for community-led motions, you can apply your traditional MQL and SQL percentages to community initiatives for the first couple of initiatives/events. However, as you gather more data on the community's behaviors, new operating benchmarks for them can be established.

Here is a more sophisticated view of how a large community initiative may be measured by your marketing team.

You will notice that the reporting starts with goals and tracks actuals alongside them. The community initiative not only tracks engagement but tracks conversions through to bookings for marketing and sales teams. Investment returns are then calculated by comparing the influenced bookings to the program spend.

Admittedly, this form of reporting may represent a bridge too far if you are just getting started with community-led marketing initiatives. Like all marketing

Community-led Motions	Goal	Actual As %
Total Program Spend	$$$	91%
Marketing contribution to pipeline creation (pre-opportunity creation)	X,XXX	111%
Target accounts engaged	##	##
Contacts at target accounts engaged	###	###
Conversion to MQL	7%	110%
Account Qualified Leads	Y,YYY (7%)	117%
Conversion to AQL	1.5%	103%
Marketing contribution to pipeline acceleration	ZZZ (1%)	108%
Marketing contribution to renewal	NNN	101%
Marketing Sourced Pipeline (MSP) at 3 months	$5M	107%
Marketing Sourced Pipeline (MSP) at 6 months	$15M	107%
Close rates on MSP	20%	105%
Marketing Influenced Bookings	$3.0M	140%
ROI on community-led motions	Every $1 invested returns $X in revenue	Every $1 invested returns $Y in revenue

A more sophisticated view of how a large community initiative may be measured by your marketing team.

practices, maturity levels in tracking and reporting can evolve over time. By partnering with demand generation and marketing operations leaders, community-led marketers can advance the state of their reporting faster.

EXPERT TIP: SET MEASURABLE GOALS

Setting measurable goals is essential for any marketing or business activity. Community-led marketing is no different. Setting measurable goals for community-led marketing is crucial for tracking progress, ensuring accountability, assessing return on investment (ROI), making data-driven decisions, aligning efforts, and fostering communication and collaboration.

Measurable goals enable the monitoring of initiatives, hold teams accountable, compare costs and outcomes, optimize marketing efforts, align with organizational objectives, and create a common language for collaboration. Ultimately, measurable goals enhance the effectiveness and success of community-led marketing initiatives.

CHAPTER 14

Improving Your Intent Signals for ABM Programs

Community-led marketing initiatives are a powerful ally in enhancing Account Based Marketing (ABM) programs. As we've discussed, community-led initiatives can attract a much larger audience than product-led initiatives. Therefore, examining data gathered from community-led initiatives is akin to seeing more of your total addressable market.

Tap into the Rich Data of Community

Imagine how much insight we gathered at Global 360 after thousands of people participated in our community surveys. Imagine how much of the market Jim Shilts' NADOG initiative exposed him to when his efforts attracted over 10,000 people. Imagine how much 6sense and Heinz Marketing learned about their market by attracting more than 3,000 people to their CoffeeTalk community or when RevGenius drew over 30,000 to its community.

Data-rich community-led initiatives can help you tap into a vast pool of potential customers, providing a 10–100x larger perspective on market participants, target accounts, geographies, and ideal customer profiles. By leveraging data gathered from community-led engagements, you can gain insights into demographics, technographics, firmographics, and geographic information. Then you can use this to refine your target account list and personalize your marketing efforts.

Analyze Community-Generated Content for ABM

Regarding content required to support ABM programs, community-generated content is more likely to attract eyeballs. Community-generated content, such as training courses, maturity models, community surveys, newsletters, reference architectures, books on best practices, and live-streamed best practices sessions led by community members, can serve as valuable resources for identifying prospects and target accounts that might now or in the future express purchase intent.

Even before the content serves to attract new audiences to ABM programs, the community production process can reveal insights that your marketing team might not have recognized about the market. Analyzing data tied to community-led content can help marketers pinpoint trends and use the new understandings to tailor their messaging, ad copy, and engagement strategies.

You can incorporate data and content from community-led initiatives into your ABM programs to:

- Segment your target audience more effectively based on demographic, technographic, firmographic, and geographic information, which allows for more precise targeting and personalization.
- Identify high-intent prospects and accounts by monitoring community discussions and content consumption and then prioritizing these accounts in your ABM efforts.
- Leverage user-generated content, like maturity models and training courses, to create tailored marketing collateral that resonates better with your audience and generates more engagement.

- Encourage community members to share the content with people in their professional circles. In this way, they act as both community-led and brand-led advocates, amplifying your reach within the target market and bolstering the credibility of your marketing messages.

Refine Your Understanding of the Market

Orbit 3 marketing initiatives are instrumental in helping marketing professionals fine-tune their Target Account Lists (TAL) and create account lookalikes lists, which play a pivotal role in the success of ABM programs. In addition, by attracting large audiences through these initiatives, marketers gain access to a wealth of data, allowing them to identify trends and better understand their target market.

For example, at the Linux Foundation, the LFX platform was used to track community engagement of over 500,000 developers across different initiatives.[98] Every activity a developer participated in helped us better understand our ICP and community member interests.

With an expanded data set, marketers can:

- **Identify similarities among high-value accounts:** Marketers can create lookalike lists based on shared characteristics by analyzing key attributes of accounts where community members work. This information enables them to target accounts with similar traits, increasing the likelihood of marketing success.

- **Discover untapped market segments:** Larger data sets can reveal patterns in the market that may have been previously overlooked. This enables marketers to identify new potential customer segments and refine their TALs to include these newly discovered targets.

- **Enhance segmentation and personalization:** By leveraging the wealth of account data obtained through community-led engagements, marketers can segment their TALs more effectively. This allows for highly personalized marketing campaigns tailored to each account's unique needs and preferences, which can lead to higher conversion rates.

- **Adapt to evolving market conditions:** As the data set grows, marketers gain a better understanding of market trends, enabling them to make data-driven decisions and adapt their TALs and ABM strategies accordingly. This agility helps businesses stay ahead of the competition and capitalize on emerging opportunities.

- **Validate and refine Ideal Customer Profiles (ICPs):** The insights gained from larger account data sets can be used to validate and refine existing ICPs. By continuously updating ICPs based on real-world data, marketers can ensure that their ABM programs consistently target the most relevant and valuable accounts.

Community-led marketing initiatives provide a rich data source that can significantly improve the creation of Target Account Lists and account lookalikes lists for ABM programs. The larger data sets enable marketers to better identify new brands or accounts to target, ultimately expanding their potential customer base and increasing the effectiveness of their ABM strategies.

Align with Sales Teams and the Community

Community-led marketing initiatives not only improve ABM programs but also lead to better business outcomes by empowering sales and customer success teams with valuable insights. The benefits derived from these initiatives are multifaceted and interconnected.

Enhanced lead quality is a significant advantage, as marketing teams can provide sales with better-qualified leads by leveraging insights from community initiatives to develop more accurate TALs. This improves sales efficiency, as they can focus on high-potential prospects, resulting in a higher lead-to-customer conversion rate.

The data and insights from community initiatives can also better inform efforts led by product marketing teams who are responsible for developing sales enablement content. With in-depth knowledge of prospects' pain points and preferences, product marketers can guide sales teams to better tailor their approach to address these market needs, fostering trust and rapport. Better knowledge of market needs and trends can lead to more personalized engagements that increase the likelihood of closing deals.

Insights from community-led marketing initiatives enable sales teams to better understand prospects' readiness to buy, allowing them to prioritize opportunities and engage with prospects at the right time. This can lead to reduced sales cycles and increased revenue.

Even when prospects aren't ready to buy, sales teams can keep the accounts warm by encouraging them to participate in your company's community-led initiatives. Instead of moving on to the next opportunity, sales reps can introduce the prospect to specific conversations, content, or members of the community. It moves their prospects out of vendor-pitch territory with the sales team to a non-vendor-pitch zone with the community-reminiscent of the Community Development Reps that Commsor put in place which we discussed in an earlier chapter. Sales reps who make these connections are viewed as more trusted partners by prospective customers over the long run.

In summary, Orbit 3 marketing initiatives provide valuable data and content that can significantly enhance your ABM programs, enabling more accurate targeting, increased engagement, and ultimately, higher conversion rates. In addition, by incorporating community-generated insights and content into your ABM marketing efforts, you can foster more substantial alignment among marketing and sales teams, leading to improved business outcomes.

EXPERT TIP: SEEK OUT USER-GENERATED CONTENT

By integrating ABM with community-led efforts, you tap into the community's power to create relevant content, build relationships, and increase conversions. Work within your community to create content that addresses its most pressing discussions and challenges. The more you can encourage user-generated content the better the opportunity it has to generate buzz that attracts more potential buyers. Content that resonates more with people's true needs or challenges should create higher levels of engagement for your ABM campaigns.

CHAPTER 15

Growing Affinity Matters

The truth is that all community-led efforts cannot be quantified. One of the most essential things community-led marketing teams will do is establish relationships, connect people, and build trust. Without investing time in fostering and nurturing relationships, you won't have a community to engage. However, in the absence of metrics, there is no way to monitor or report progress and achievements either.

Measure the Basics

There are many things you can measure across a community that might not impact the bottom line. For example, you can track how many community members:

- Joined a Slack workspace
- Followed a code repository

- Visited a community website
- Registered for a community conference
- Attended a community dinner at an in-person event
- Signed-up for emails
- Read a blog

When starting up your community-led initiatives, measuring this type of early engagement is important. Actions taken by community members are representative of awareness-building efforts. But marketers need to be aware that, in the long run, these are vanity metrics.

When community members take an action that does not automatically signal a commitment to participate further or indicate that the members have received value from their engagement, they may just be in the early discovery stage of community engagement. The discovery stage is where community members get their first feel of the community, its culture and structure, the content and exchanges, and the quality and type of interactions with and between members.

When someone new engages in this discovery, they might decide they like it and stick around. Or they might be someone who ended up on a path that didn't make sense or support the value they were seeking. For those members who stick around, you want to help them through the initial onboarding.

Well-established communities can be a daunting experience for new members. So, you'll want to consider ways to welcome them, connect them with others, or point them to areas where most new members find value quickly. The sooner you can orchestrate these experiences, the more engaged those community members will become and more likely to become contributors.

Carrie Melissa Jones does an excellent job of describing the stage of community engagement in her Commitment Curve diagram. The diagram reflects how early, simple engagement doesn't immediately equate to a commitment from the community. Over time, as more initiatives and actions are taken, commitment and contribution to the community grow.

Commitment Curve

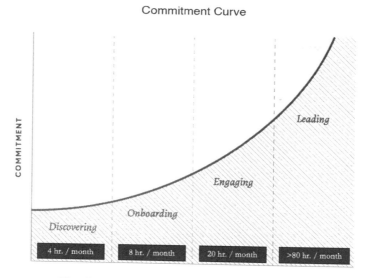

The Community Commitment Curve, as shared by Carrie Melissa Jones, with added emphasis on suggested time commitments for community participation.[99]

Identify Trends in Community Engagement

Once the community has a healthy level of engagement, it is essential to begin tracking more about what's happening.

It is more important to look at the trends associated with interactions in the community and if momentum is building around specific activities. For example:

- How many monthly active users are in our community, and are members returning regularly after they sign up?
- How many people are joining Slack weekly, and are numbers trending positive or negative?
- Are podcast listeners growing month over month, and are we releasing more episodes regularly?

- How many people registered for the community conference, and how does that compare to the goal we set for the conference?
- How many more people subscribed to the newsletter? Are unsubscribes trending down?
- How many people visit our blog, and how long are they staying on the site? Are they reading more than one blog, and do they share links to the content on social platforms?

The trends are more important than the metric itself as it helps reveal momentum behind the community. The trends are especially significant if you are experimenting with several different ways to engage the community. For example, you might have a Discourse workspace, a meet-up series, and a podcast channel set up as mechanisms to engage your community. If Discourse and the meet-ups attract more people and show positive engagement while the podcast is slower to get off the ground, you might shift resources to the higher-performing channels. You can always revisit the lower-performing channels as community initiatives further mature.

Track Action and Engagement in Community-Led Initiatives

Beyond the trend, you will next want to track action and engagement. This is where the real power of community-led efforts comes into play. You can think of actions and interactions as gaining resources for community-led initiatives. Where in the earliest stages your team may be doing all the work, in the later stages of the community commitment curve, the community contributes greater efforts.

When we first started organizing the ADDO community, there were only two of us in the marketing team dedicating effort to the Orbit 3 motions. We also engaged five people from the community to support us in organizing the community. As the community grew, more people outside of our company took on leadership positions or assignments that benefited the community.

In all, we had around 50 very active people in the community doing work part-time that would have otherwise been performed by one of our employees.[100] I can't imagine going to our CEO or CFO and asking to add 50 people to our community-led marketing team. That would have been a very tricky business case to establish.

Luckily, thriving communities don't require a ton of headcount. Instead, the best communities attract more people. Those people engage in community activities. And some community members decide they want to take on roles that lead specific initiatives, create valuable content, or encourage new members to join. At the same time, those behaviors take the onus off your marketing team and budget for payroll.

You will know that your community is working when you start measuring changes in activities like:

- What trend do we see for people regularly contributing to our community blog?

- How many people actively answer questions in our Discourse, Discord, and Slack workspace communities?

- Do we have more inbound than outbound requests for people speaking at our community meet-up events?

- Are we seeing an increase in the number of people volunteering to contribute to or build a new part of the community?

You will begin to identify trends associated with people engaging and leading activities in the community. Once you have sufficient participation from engaged members and community leaders, you can focus on what Leslie Greenwood of Chief Evangelist Consulting calls *"mobilizing the middle."*

How many people do you see engaging regularly and sharing meaningful content or information—and can you move them up the ranks into a leadership position? Actively listening to, watching, and participating in the community enables you to identify members who, with the right encouragement, can become leaders.

Support Brand Affinity for Organic Sales Conversations

"The more we spoke about DevOps, the more our brand affinity in the market grew," shared Mary Engvall, author of *The Business Value of Developer Relations and former community builder at Chef.*

"People would come up to us at our event booth and say, 'I have problem X. Can you help me solve it?'" Mary continued. *"Sometimes that problem was related to software we sold, and other times it was not."*

"People were surprised but also impressed when we sometimes admitted that our company's product could not solve that specific problem, but we knew a competitor's product was well-suited for that use case. At that early growth stage in our market, we recognized that a rising tide lifts all boats and that being a good steward of the community would benefit us in the long run."

Like many others running community-led motions, Mary understood there was a direct correlation between her activities in the community and a growing interest in her company's products. The challenge was that she could not always measure it.

> **Emotional ties not only build trust between community members but also extend to the corporate brand represented by the community marketer.**

This is where brand affinity plays a role in community-led motions. Relationships and connections form in a community organically. People in the community help one another. Those people who help more often build stronger reputations in their community.

For community-led marketers who build connections and share knowledge, the relationships they form become personal and hold strong emotional ties. Those emotional ties not only build trust between community members but also extend to the corporate brand represented by the community marketer.

The brand affinity that grows from these relationships can have a positive impact on company performance. It has long been said that people want to do business with people they know, like, and trust. Your best sales reps know this, and so do your best community marketers.

Brand affinity also supports greater brand loyalty. Where loyal customers may be used to purchasing the same product repeatedly, their relationship with a brand can be easily swayed by newer, cheaper, or faster alternatives. When community relationships link brand affinity to loyalty, the product/customer relationship becomes harder to break.

For example, in the CMO Coffee Talk community, many participants are customers of 6sense or Heinz Marketing. After spending months or years building relationships with marketing leaders in the Coffee Talk community, it would be more challenging for me and others to walk away from their products or services in search of a competitive alternative. We not only like their products, but we also like them as people. As such, if we did have an issue or challenge, we would be more likely to bring it to their attention first to find a solution rather than abruptly severing the relationship.

Another element of brand affinity that works well in community-led settings is what Dr. Robert Cialdini, author of *Influence: The Psychology of Persuasion*, refers to as peer-suasion. He describes this as, *"an action coming from similar others [e.g., community peers] increases our confidence that it will prove valid, feasible, and socially acceptable should we perform it [e.g., buying a product]. Therefore, we are more inclined to follow the lead of our peers in a phenomenon we can call peer-suasion."* [101] In an earlier chapter, I referred to this as the herd effect.

Social connections are, therefore, a tremendous lever for brand affinity. The more we see others taking action, the more likely we will be comfortable taking the same action. As the community grows, so does the number of people taking action.

When I look across businesses that are leading great communities, it is easy to see that more people do business companies because of the work they are doing in the community. The challenge is—and has been for a long time—

that brand affinity is very difficult to measure precisely. Measuring the first or multiple touches in a community of hundreds or thousands of people is challenging to tie directly into marketing- or account-qualified leads. The practice works better at the smallest of scale, but tracking becomes nearly impossible beyond the earliest stages of growth.

That said, when it comes to community-led marketing, CMOs cannot ignore the power of brand affinity just because it is difficult to measure. Affinity is not created overnight and therefore won't show results after one activity or engagement. For CMOs who do want to measure it, it is vital to take a longer-term perspective by measuring affinity over a series of events and activities.

The power of brand affinity shows up in a number of the sample playbooks shared in this book. The four playbooks leverage relationships built in Orbit 3 to influence or encourage participation in lower orbits.

For example, imagine that you manage a local meet-up for business development reps (BDRs). You're doing this because your business is selling solutions that help BDR's gather account intelligence better, engage prospects, and close more deals. At this meet-up, you invite different speakers to present to the community. Mary, a Direct of Sales Development, presents her best practices for breaking into key accounts. Mary does an incredible job and really engages the audience.

Even though Mary does not work for your business, you believe she would be great on a panel discussion webinar that your team is organizing. You invite Mary to speak on the webinar, and because of the relationship you formed in the community, she accepts. With Mary on the webinar, your business attracts a larger audience and generates more leads for your business. Mary benefits as she grows her own personal brand as a sales expert. When your brand does good things for the community, more people are eager to work with your business.

When you are just beginning to measure affinity associated with community-led motions, keep your initial measure simple. For example, Insight Partners says that affinity can be measured by *"collecting data against the key activities that create value for your community."* For example:

- Attended the user conference
- Hosted a virtual event
- Contributed technical documentation
- Engaged in the community forum."[102]

They also recommend tracking those activities over time to get more sense of the strength of the relationship. For example, if I attended the CMO CoffeeTalk 80 percent of the time over the past six months, shared social media posts that indicated I was interacting with other community members, and then attended an in-person meeting of the forum, my affinity score would be higher than someone who attended 90 percent of the CMO Coffee Talks last year but had not participated in any of them for the past nine months.

Calculating the affinity score for an individual could be as simple as:

Activity A x Recency (days/months/years) = Affinity Score

Activity B x Recency (days/months/years) = Affinity Score

Activity C x Recency (days/months/years) = Affinity Score

= Total Affinity Score

Insight Partners goes a step further in tracking key performance indicators across community member engagement. In her blog, *Measuring the Impact of a Community-Led Growth Motion*, Whitney Rothe shares, *"Your organization's ability to report on relevant KPIs will evolve in sophistication as the community grows. Remember that community is additive and should not be considered a separate sourcing engine for business value."*[103]

Whitney shares the following KPIs across community, prospect, and customer engagements that can measure engagement for reporting to stakeholders and investors.

	KPI	DEFINITION
Community	% new active member growth	% increase in new active members compared to prior periods
	% member growth by level	% increase in members by level compared to prior periods
	% community gravity score Affinity x Influence = Gravity	% increase in community gravity score compared to prior periods
SEO	% organic session growth (documentation, forums)	% increase in traffic to community relevant web pages compared to prior periods
	# keyword ranking increases (non-branded keywords)	# increase in keyword rankings for relevant non-branded keywords
Prospects	% active user growth	% increase in active users of the product compared to prior users
	$ community influenced new logo pipeline	$ value of new logo opportunities influenced by community
	% community influenced target accounts	% of target accounts that have active community members
Customers	$ community influenced expansion pipeline	$ value of expansion opportunities influenced by community
	% community influenced retention	% increase in retention of customers with active community members
	% community influenced NPS score	% increase in NPS of customers with active community members
	% ticket backlog reduction	% decrease in open support tickets compared to prior periods

Performance KPIs to consider as described by Insight Partners, "Measuring the Impact of Community-driven Motion" (2021)[104]

As community-led resources and tooling at your company grow, brand affinity can be tracked in new sales and renewals. For example, 6sense keeps track of how many members are active in their CMO Coffee Talk community and reports internally on how many of them become customers of the business over time. They measure the power of brand affinity from this community when it comes to recommendations from its community members to other non-member CMOs who are considering making a new 6sense purchase. 6sense can also track that community members are X times more likely to renew their contract for the company's products—a direct correlation to their brand affinity.

> **"Remember that community is additive and should not be considered a separate sourcing engine for business value."**
> **—Whitney Rothe**

Brand affinity through community-led marketing efforts tie to three outcomes for your business. The affinity reduces sales cycles, increases the number of qualified leads from your community, and leads to higher customer retention rates.

According to the 2022 State of Community Management report, brand affinity builds trust between your organization and community members. When high levels of trust are built in the community prior to any engagement by your sales organization, familiarity with your brand will accelerate the sales cycle. Without the support of community-led engagements, sales teams would have to commit more time to build trust with economic buyers and influencers within a target account.[105]

Community-led engagements also improve the quality of leads entering the sales pipeline. Activity in a community can be tracked over time and provide more insight into the interests of key accounts and stakeholders. The number and frequency of community conversations, content sharing, event participation, and referrals can be used to identify stronger intent signals for the purpose of lead scoring.

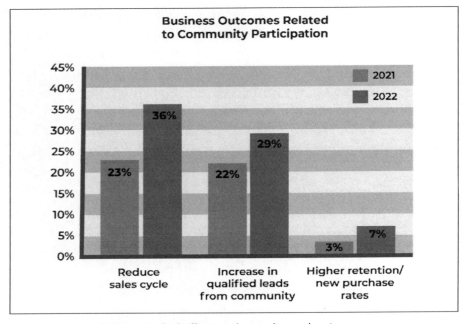

Community-led efforts reduce sales cycles, increase
qualified leads, and support higher customer retention.
Source: *The State of Community Management Report 2022,*
from The Community Roundtable

As discussed in the CMO Coffee Talk example above, community members who spend more time with people from your company are more likely to renew or expand their investments with you. Community members want to do business with people they know, like, and trust.

EXPERT TIP: BOLSTER BRAND AFFINITY

Cultivating strong community relationships is a savvy move for businesses seeking to bolster brand affinity and nurture customer loyalty. By fostering a sense of belonging and facilitating engaging interactions among like-minded individuals, brands can forge deeper emotional connections with their customers. Actively listening to customer feedback and customizing offerings accordingly further strengthens this bond. Investing in community relationships creates a loyal customer base that is less likely to be swayed by competitors, making it harder to break the product/customer relationship.

What's Next?

"Sometimes you take a trip, and sometimes the trip takes you." [106] This was an inspiration I picked up years ago from filmmaker Eric Saperston.

When I reflect on my experiences championing community-led marketing, it has been the trip that took me—along with my teams and thousands of friends.

Building a thriving community is one of the most rewarding things a CMO can do in marketing. You not only get the reward of the business growth that comes with it, but you also create incredibly meaningful relationships across a market. Those relationships offer a friend to call when you are looking for a candid piece of advice, open doors to new opportunities, and build wider trust circles that can accelerate your business and career.

My aim through these chapters has been to share perspectives on the investments CMOs can make to accelerate sales, boost demand gen, and elevate their brand above competitors. It was not intended to persuade you to scrap your traditional marketing approaches in favor of a novel tactic but, instead, to add a new and very powerful orbit to your playbook.

The concepts we covered were simple. You first have to understand the marketing orbits you are already operating in for product, brand, and community. Before jumping into the community-led orbit, you need to do some homework to understand its purpose, positioning, approach, and investments required. Then it's a mix of taking the time to embed yourself or the right members of your team in the community to build trusted relationships and provide a forum for content and information exchanges that people value for their benefit.

Following the rules of community engagement will help you avoid stumbles that other less-experienced marketers have collided with on their failed attempts to reach into higher orbits.

The most successful CMO will not only lead their teams into the community-led orbit, but they will ensure the proper feedback loops between all three orbits to keep their teams, programs, and businesses in sync.

The stories and playbooks shared throughout this book are meant to educate and inspire. They don't prescribe your next action as much as they provide a glimpse into the right mindset with which to pursue the journey.

After you've read this book, I encourage you to share it with your teams. Community is not a journey you travel alone. I'll also leave you with a simple reminder of the question Mark Miller asked me years ago in London:

"Would we be doing anything different today if we wanted 15,000 people to participate in the community?"

Use this question to challenge your thinking and inspire your teams. You might be going after two, ten, or a hundred thousand people. Whatever the size, I only ask you to dream bigger. Take a risk. Be audacious. And most of all, have fun.

THANK YOU FOR READING MY BOOK

By now, you've seen the value of community-led marketing for business growth. While you get it, many others don't know how this could revolutionize their go-to-market strategy.

If this book enriched your understanding of community-led marketing, why not pass it on? Share it with a colleague, your team, or community peers.

We all benefit when knowledge is shared. I'd be truly honored if you would take a moment to share a specific insight you've gained from this book in a review on Amazon. Your shared wisdom could be the beacon that guides future readers toward more effective outcomes for their community, brand, and demand-generation initiatives.

HELPFUL RESOURCES

If you're interested in elevating your marketing strategy, enhancing team skills, or inspiring your community with Derek's deep insights and proven methodologies, feel free to reach out. Direct message him on LinkedIn (linkedin.com/in/derekeweeks/) to discuss speaking engagements, tailored workshops, or consultancy services tailored to your specific needs.

Looking for more resources to help with community-led marketing initiatives? Be sure to check out Derek's blog at unfairmindshare.com. Here are a few topics there you may find interesting:

- **The art of integrating community and demand gen** (rebrand.ly/artofdemand)

- **The importance of empathy in marketing** (rebrand.ly/empathymarketing)

- **The CEO asked, "Do we need a community?"** (rebrand.ly/ceoasked)

- **Numbers don't hug back: why marketers must rekindle relationships** (rebrand.ly/numbershug)

- **How we started All Day DevOps and attracted 13,000 people** (rebrand.ly/13000people)

- **Top 5 community-led marketing books you need to read today** (rebrand.ly/top5book)

- **What to do when community conflicts arise**
  (rebrand.ly/conflicts)
- **Community-led growth: spotting the imposter**
  (rebrand.ly/spotting)
- **Community-led growth: time to scale**
  (rebrand.ly/timescale)

NOTES

CHAPTER 1

1. Derek Weeks and Mark Miller, Introduction to *Feedback Loops: Voices of All Day DevOps: Volume 1*. (Amazon.com, 2019), xi.

2. "Mark Miller and Derek Weeks – All Day, Every Day, DevOps," Cloudbees, February 27, 2018, https://www.cloudbees.com/resources/devops-radio/episode-28-mark-miller-and-derek-weeks-all-day-every-day-devops.

3. Geoffrey A. Moore, *Crossing the Chasm,* 3rd edition. (New York: HarperCollins Publishers, 2014) https://www.harpercollins.com/products/crossing-the-chasm-3rd-edition-geoffrey-a-moore.

4. All Day DevOps, "All Day DevOps: How We Did It – Mark Miller," YouTube (video), 31:25, April 9, 2017, https://www.youtube.com/watch?v=TqY1aVkhdB8.

5. Derek Weeks, Introduction to *Feedback Loops: Voices of All Day DevOps: Volume 1*. (Amazon.com, 2019), xi.

6. Derek E. Weeks, "All Day DevOps," Devops.com, October 26, 2016, https://devops.com/all-day-devops/.

7. All Day DevOps, "All Day DevOps: How We Did It – Mark Miller," YouTube (video), 31:25, April 9, 2017, https://www.youtube.com/watch?v=TqY1aVkhdB8.

8. David E. Sanger and Nicole Perlroth, "Hackers Used New Weapons to Disrupt Major Websites Across U.S.," *The New York Times*, October 21, 2016, https://www.nytimes.com/2016/10/22/business/internet-problems-attack.html.

9. All Day DevOps, "All Day DevOps: How We Did It – Mark Miller," YouTube (video), 31:25, April 9, 2017, https://www.youtube.com/watch?v=TqY1aVkhdB8.

10. All Day DevOps, "All Day DevOps: How We Did It – Mark Miller," YouTube (video), 31:25, April 9, 2017, https://www.youtube.com/watch?v=TqY1aVkhdB8.

11. Manuel Pais, "Everyone is Part of Continuous Delivery @ All Day DevOps Oct 2017)," Slide 77, Slideshare.net (slideshare presentation), October 25, 2017, https://www.slideshare.net/ManuelPais/everyone-is-part-of-continuous-delivery-all-day-devops-oct-2017.

12. All Day DevOps, "All Day DevOps: How We Did It – Mark Miller," YouTube (video), 31:25, April 9, 2017, https://www.youtube.com/watch?v=TqY1aVkhdB8.

13. All Day DevOps, "All Day DevOps Live – A Conversation with Helen Beal," YouTube (video), 9:56, Sept 8, 2017 https://youtu.be/qAwmaYAK18I.

14. "2019 All Day DevOps Conference Plays to a Record 36,000 Participants," *GlobeNewswire*, November 5, 2019, https://www.globenewswire.com/en/news-release/2019/11/05/1941731/0/en/2019-All-Day-DevOps-Conference-Plays-to-a-Record-36-000-Participants.html.

15. "How to Engage 4000 Developers in One Day," Apple Podcasts (podcast audio), November 14, 2019, https://podcasts.apple.com/de/podcast/how-to-engage-4000-developers-in-one-day/id300769012?i=1000456824185&l=en.

16. "How to Engage 4000 Developers in One Day," Apple Podcasts (podcast audio), November 14, 2019, https://podcasts.apple.com/de/podcast/how-to-engage-4000-developers-in-one-day/id300769012?i=1000456824185&l=en.

17. "Club 20," All Day DevOps, November 2020, https://www.alldaydevops.com/2020-club-20.

18. "2019 All Day DevOps Conference Plays to a Record 36,000 Participants," *GlobeNewswire*, November 5, 2019, https://www.globenewswire.com/en/news-release/2019/11/05/1941731/0/en/2019-All-Day-DevOps-Conference-Plays-to-a-Record-36-000-Participants.html.

19. Tom Goodwin, "The Battle Is For The Customer Interface," *TechCrunch*, March 3, 2015, https://techcrunch.com/2015/03/03/in-the-age-of-disintermediation-the-battle-is-all-for-the-customer-interface/.

20. Derek Weeks. Introduction to *Feedback Loops: Voices of All Day DevOps: Volume 2*. (Amazon.com, 2020), xiii.

CHAPTER 2

21. Scott Brinker, "2023 Marketing Technology Landscape Supergraphic: 11,038 solutions searchable on martechmap.com," chiefmartec.com, May 2023, https://chiefmartec.com/2023/05/2023-marketing-technology-landscape-supergraphic-11038-solutions-searchable-on-martechmap-com/.

22. Jessica Stillman, "Your Self-Promoting Is More Annoying Than You Think," Inc.com, October 27, 2014, https://www.inc.com/jessica-stillman/your-self-promoting-is-more-annoying-than-you-think.html.

23. "3 Statistics That Show How Customer Reviews Influence Consumers," Dixa.com, accessed May 25, 2023, https://www.dixa.com/blog/3-important-statistics-that-show-how-reviews-influence-consumers/.

24. Natalia Zanuto, "Community-led Growth: what is it & why is it important for business growth?" Zapnito.com, accessed May 25, 2023, https://zapnito.com/insights/community-led-growth-what-is-it-why-is-it-important-for-business-growth/.

25. Corinne Marie Riley, "Community-Led Growth: The Product-Led Growth Expansion Pack," Medium, January 28, 2021, https://corinneriley.medium.com/community-led-growth-the-product-led-growth-expansion-pack-b474ab9a7940.

26. Derek Weeks (@weekstweets), "We have a community-led growth strategy," X (formerly Twitter), November 1, 2022, https://twitter.com/weekstweets/status/1587519768076046336.

CHAPTER 3

27. Phil Fersht, "You've got to start with the customer experience and work back toward the technology – not the other way around," *Horses for Sources* (blog), August 8, 2020, https://www.horsesforsources.com/steve-jobs1997_080820/.

28. Sonatype, " DevOps and Continuous Delivery Reference Architectures (including Nexus and other popular tools)," Slideshare.net (slideshare presentation), March 18, 2015, https://www.slideshare.net/SonatypeCorp/nexus-and-continuous-delivery.

29. Sonatype, "DevOps and Continuous Delivery Reference Architectures - Volume 2," Slideshare.net (slideshare presentation), July 27, 2015, https://www.slideshare.net/SonatypeCorp/devops-and-continuous-delivery-reference-architectures.

30. Sonatype, "2019 DevSecOps Reference Architectures," Slideshare.net (slideshare presentation), April 1, 2019, https://www.slideshare.net/SonatypeCorp/2019-devsecops-reference-architectures-139154951.

31. Carrie Melissa Jones, "Creating a Community Commitment Curve," *Carriemelissajones.com* (blog), June 18, 2022, https://www.carriemelissajones.com/blog/community-commitment-curve-jddmt?rq=curve

32. Insight Partners, "Establishing, Scaling and Measuring the Impact of Community-Led Growth," YouTube (video), 1:01:08, posted May 19, 2022, https://www.youtube.com/watch?v=vEhM3Nrsz9s&t=427s.

CHAPTER 4

33. "Had Gandalf not challenged the Balrog in Moria, would it have left Moria to give chase to the Fellowship?" *Quora*, September 29, 2017, https://www.quora.com/Had-Gandalf-not-challenged-the-Balrog-in-Moria-would-it-have-left-Moria-to-give-chase-to-the-Fellowship.

34. Derek Weeks (@weekstweets), "The community management industry needs to evolve beyond tactical community management and embrace strategic community leadership. Our audiences have evolved. Our strategies must too. #AllDayDevOps," X (formerly Twitter), December 16, 2022, https://twitter.com/weekstweets/status/1605251815611584513

35. All Day DevOps, "All Day DevOps Live – A Conversation with Helen Beal," YouTube (video), 9:56, Sept 8, 2017 https://youtu.be/qAwmaYAK18I.

36. Adrian Speyer, *The Accidental Community Manager: A Guide to Building a Successful Community* (Adrian Speyer, 2022). https://www.amazon.com/Accidental-Community-Manager-Building-Successful/dp/1778294219

37. Adam M. Grant, *Give and Take: Why Helping Others Drives Our Success* (New York: Penguin Books, 2014).

38. All Day DevOps, "All Day DevOps Returns November 12th," YouTube (video), 0:09, posted October 12, 2021, https://www.youtube.com/watch?v=PU6BzQ5XzAk.

39. All Day DevOps, "All Day DevOps Returns November 12th," YouTube (video), 0:09, posted October 12, 2021, https://www.youtube.com/watch?v=PU6BzQ5XzAk.

40. "With great power comes great responsibility," Wikipedia, accessed May 25, 2023, https://en.wikipedia.org/wiki/With_great_power_comes_great_responsibility.

41. Christina Brodzik, Nathan Young, Sarah Cuthill, Nikki Drake, "Authentically inclusive marketing: Winning future customers with diversity, equity, and inclusion," *Deloitte Insights*, October 19, 2021, https://www2.deloitte.com/us/en/insights/topics/marketing-and-sales-operations/global-marketing-trends/2022/diversity-and-inclusion-in-marketing.html.

42. Sonia Thompson, "Data Shows Consumers Want Diversity In Marketing—Why Many Brands Struggle to Get It Right (And How to Fix It)," *Forbes*, February 5, 2020, https://www.forbes.com/sites/soniathompson/2020/02/05/data-shows-consumers-want-diversity-in-marketing-why-many-brands-struggle-to-get-it-right-and-how-to-fix/.

43. "A level playing field: how inclusivity breeds innovation," *Financial Times*, accessed May 25, 2023, http://www.ft.com/partnercontent/servicenow/a-level-playing-field-how-inclusivity-breeds-innovation.html.

CHAPTER 5

44. Rosie Sherry (@rosiesherry), "The community industry, needs more women in senior leadership roles. what tangible actions can we take to enable this? #cmgrchat," X (formerly Twitter), February 15, 2023, https://twitter.com/rosiesherry/status/1627715969744240665.

45. Jono Bacon (@jonobacon), "The world is filled with stupid vanity numbers," X (formerly Twitter), October 24, 2022, https://twitter.com/jonobacon/status/1584576212373884928.

46. Jono Bacon, "A Strategy For Making the Most of Community Health Metrics," *Discourse* (blog), July 6, 2022, https://blog.discourse.org/2022/07/a-strategy-for-making-the-most-of-community-health-metrics/.

47. Jono Bacon, "A Strategy For Making the Most of Community Health Metrics," *Discourse* (blog), July 6, 2022, https://blog.discourse.org/2022/07/a-strategy-for-making-the-most-of-community-health-metrics/.

48. Seth Godin, *Purple Cow: Transform Your Business by Being Remarkable*, New Edition, (New York: Portfolio, 2009).

49. 3G4G, "Advanced: 5G Service Based Architecture (SBA)," Slideshare.net (slideshare presentation), February 4, 2018, https://www.slideshare.net/3G4GLtd/advanced-5g-service-based-architecture-sba-87217349?from_search=0.

50. 3G4G, "Advanced: 5G Service Based Architecture (SBA)," YouTube (video), 20:50, February 4, 2018, https://www.youtube.com/watch?v=LotQ1RwXdoE.

51. David Spinks, "The Best Community Technology Stack," Unfairmindshare.com (blog), February 17, 2023, https://unfairmindshare.com/blog/f/the-best-community-technology-stack.

52. Susan Fournier and Lara Lee, "Getting Brand Communities Right," *Harvard Business Review*, April 2009, https://hbr.org/2009/04/getting-brand-communities-right.

CHAPTER 6

53. David Spinks, "Should You Ditch Your Community Job Title?," *Davidspinks.Substack.com* (blog), March 16, 2023, https://davidspinks.substack.com/p/should-you-ditch-your-community-job.

54. "Meet the Lululemon Global Yoga Ambassador Who Transforms Communities with His Practice," Enroute.aircanada.com, December 20, 2019, https://enroute.aircanada.com/en/interviews/ryan-leier-lululemon/.

55. Chantal Fernandez, "Inside Lululemon's Unconventional Influencer Network," *Fashionista*, November 2, 2016, https://fashionista.com/2016/11/lululemon-ambassadors.

CHAPTER 7

56. "Developers Tel Aviv," Meetup.com, accessed May 25, 2023, https://www.meetup.com/developers-tel-aviv/.

57. "Israeli Unity3d developers," Meetup.com, accessed May 25, 2023, https://www.meetup.com/israeli-unity3d-developers/.

58. "Node.js Israel," Meetup.com, accessed May 25, 2023, https://www.meetup.com/nodejs-israel/.

59. "A Better Way to Build a Brand: The Community Flywheel," McKinsey & Company, September 28, 2022, https://www.mckinsey.com/capabilities/growth-marketing-and-sales/our-insights/a-better-way-to-build-a-brand-the-community-flywheel.

60. Jay Peredo (@jayperedox), "Marketing isn't always about acquiring customers immediately…," X (formerly Twitter), February 24, 2023, https://twitter.com/jayperedox/status/1629066132681330688.

CHAPTER 8

61. Kimberly A. Whitler, "A New C-Suite Role: The Chief Market Officer," *Forbes*, June 6, 2020, https://www.forbes.com/sites/kimberlywhitler/2020/06/06/a-new-c-suite-role-the-chief-market-officer/.

62. "State of Community Management 2022," The Community Roundtable, accessed May 25, 2023, https://communityroundtable.com/what-we-do/research/the-state-of-community-management/state-of-community-management-2022/.

63. "State of Community Management 2022," The Community Roundtable, accessed May 25, 2023, https://communityroundtable.com/what-we-do/research/the-state-of-community-management/state-of-community-management-2022/.

64. "State of Community Management 2022," The Community Roundtable, accessed May 25, 2023, https://communityroundtable.com/what-we-do/research/the-state-of-community-management/state-of-community-management-2022/.

65. Malcolm Gladwell, *The Tipping Point: How Little Things Can Make a Big Difference* (Boston: Little, Brown, and Company, 2000), https://www.gladwellbooks.com/titles/malcolm-gladwell/the-tipping-point/9780759574731/.

66. Malcolm Gladwell, *The Tipping Point: How Little Things Can Make a Big Difference* (Boston: Little, Brown, and Company, 2000), https://www.gladwellbooks.com/titles/malcolm-gladwell/the-tipping-point/9780759574731/.

67. "State of Community Management 2022," The Community Roundtable, accessed May 25, 2023, https://communityroundtable.com/what-we-do/research/the-state-of-community-management/state-of-community-management-2022/

68. "The ScaleUp Guide to Community-Led Growth," Insight Partners, April 26, 2022, https://www.insightpartners.com/ideas/the-scaleup-guide-to-community-led-growth/.

69. "The 2021 Community Industry Report," CMX Hub, accessed May 25, 2023, https://cmxhub.com/community-industry-report-2021/.

70. "The ScaleUp Guide to Community-Led Growth," Insight Partners, April 26, 2022, https://www.insightpartners.com/ideas/the-scaleup-guide-to-community-led-growth/.

71. "The ScaleUp Guide to Community-Led Growth," Insight Partners, April 26, 2022, https://www.insightpartners.com/ideas/the-scaleup-guide-to-community-led-growth/.

72. "About the Daniel P. Moynihan Papers," Library of Congress, accessed May 25, 2023, https://www.loc.gov/rr/mss/moynihan/moynihan-about.html.

73. "Community of Practice vs. Community of Product," *Commonroom.io* (blog), November 29, 2022, https://www.commonroom.io/blog/community-of-practice-vs-community-of-product/.

CHAPTER 9

74. Paul Sawers, "Meet Crowd.dev, an open source user-led growth platform for fostering developer communities," *TechCrunch*, November 1, 2022, https://techcrunch.com/2022/11/01/meet-crowd-dev-an-open-source-user-led-growth-platform-for-fostering-developer-communities/.

75. "Field of Dreams," Wikipedia, accessed May 25, 2023, https://en.wikipedia.org/wiki/Field_of_Dreams.

76. "A Better Way to Build a Brand: The Community Flywheel," McKinsey & Company, September 28, 2022, https://www.mckinsey.com/capabilities/growth-marketing-and-sales/our-insights/a-better-way-to-build-a-brand-the-community-flywheel.

77. Patricia Redsicker, "Digital Natives: How They Are Changing the Content Marketing Game" Content Marketing Institute, April 12, 2012, https://contentmarketinginstitute.com/articles/how-digital-natives-are-changing-content/.

78. "1% Rule," Wikiwand, accessed May 25, 2023, https://www.wikiwand.com/en/1%25_rule_(Internet_culture).

79. "State of Community Management 2022," The Community Roundtable, accessed May 25, 2023, https://communityroundtable.com/what-we-do/research/the-state-of-community-management/state-of-community-management-2022/.

80. "Diversity Wins: How Inclusion Matters," McKinsey & Company, May 19, 2020, https://www.mckinsey.com/featured-insights/diversity-and-inclusion/diversity-wins-how-inclusion-matters.

CHAPTER 10

81. "Influencer50 Snapshot," KnowledgeLake SharePoint, November 2012, https://joeshepley.files.wordpress.com/2012/11/i50_identificationsnapshot_knowledge lake_2012.pdf.

82. "Influencer50 Snapshot," KnowledgeLake SharePoint, November 2012, https://joeshepley.files.wordpress.com/2012/11/i50_identificationsnapshot_knowledge lake_2012.pdf.

83. Susan Hanley, "Honored to Be Named to the 50 Top SharePoint Influencers List," *Computerworld*, September 21, 2010, https://www.computerworld.com/article/2227237/honored-to-be-named-to-the-50-top-sharepoint-influencers-list.html.

84. Becky Bertram, "Named to SharePoint Influencer 50 Again," *Savvy Technical Solutions* (blog), November 19, 2012, https://www.savvytechnicalsolutions.com/2012/11/19/named-to-sharepoint-influencer-50-again/.

85. Robert Bogue, "On Influencer50 and the SharePoint Influencer50," *Thorprojects.com* (blog), October 21, 2010, https://thorprojects.com/blog/2010/10/21/on-influencer50-and-the-sharepoint-influencer50/.

CHAPTER 11

86. Laura Fitton, "Laura Fitton's Guide to Twitter," Slideshare.net (slideshare presentation), July 8, 2015, https://www.slideshare.net/HUGAtlanta/laura-fittons-guide-to-twitter.

87. "How to Pivot From Lead Gen to Demand Gen: a CMO's Guide," Cognism, February 28, 2023, https://www.cognism.com/blog/how-to-pivot-from-lead-gen-to-demand-gen.

88. "How to Pivot From Lead Gen to Demand Gen: a CMO's Guide," Cognism, February 28, 2023, https://www.cognism.com/blog/how-to-pivot-from-lead-gen-to-demand-gen.

89. Global360PersonaBPM, "SharePoint Survey Results," YouTube (search results), 2011, https://www.youtube.com/results?search_query=sharepoint+survey+results%2C+global+360.

CHAPTER 12

90. Daniel Murray (@Dmurr68), "Most of your audience is not ready to buy...," X (formerly Twitter), July 8, 2022, https://twitter.com/Dmurr68/status/1545414143485923329.

91. Daniel Murray (@Dmurr68), "Most of your audience is not ready to buy...," X (formerly Twitter), April 3, 2021, https://twitter.com/Dmurr68/status/1378381913371541505?lang=en.

92. Erica Kuhl, "Road to Chief Community Officer," YouTube (video), 25.57, posted by CMX, December 21, 2021, https://youtu.be/cadGKe5iIwQ?t=1130.

93. Mac Reddin, "Sales Leaders – Your SDRs Should Be CDRs," Commsor, March 16, 2022, https://www.commsor.com/post/community-development-representative-sales.

CHAPTER 13

94. April MacLean, LinkedIn, March 2023, https://www.linkedin.com/feed/update/urn:li:activity:7037083870864822272/

95. April MacLean (@mizmaclean), X (formerly Twitter), accessed May 25, 2023, https://twitter.com/mizmaclean.

96. "State of Community Management 2022," The Community Roundtable, accessed May 25, 2023, https://communityroundtable.com/what-we-do/research/the-state-of-community-management/state-of-community-management-2022/.

97. "State of Community Management 2022," The Community Roundtable, accessed May 25, 2023, https://communityroundtable.com/what-we-do/research/the-state-of-community-management/state-of-community-management-2022/.

CHAPTER 14

98. "Explore the LFX Collaboration Platform," The Linux Foundation, accessed May 25, 2023, https://lfx.linuxfoundation.org/.

CHAPTER 15

99. Carrie Melissa Jones, "Creating a Community Commitment Curve," *Carriemelissajones.com* (blog), June 18, 2022, https://www.carriemelissajones.com/blog/community-commitment-curve-jddmt?rq=curve

100. "Mark Miller and Derek Weeks – All Day, Every Day, DevOps," Cloudbees, February 27, 2018, https://www.cloudbees.com/resources/devops-radio/episode-28-mark-miller-and-derek-weeks-all-day-every-day-devops.

101. Robert B. Cialdini, *Influence: The Psychology of Persuasion*, rev. ed. (New York: HarperCollins, 2021).

102. "Measuring the Impact of a Community-Led Growth Motion," Insight Partners, December 21, 2021, https://www.insightpartners.com/ideas/measuring-the-impact-of-a-community-driven-motion/.

103. "Measuring the Impact of a Community-Led Growth Motion," Insight Partners, December 21, 2021, https://www.insightpartners.com/ideas/measuring-the-impact-of-a-community-driven-motion/.

104. "Measuring the Impact of a Community-Led Growth Motion," Insight Partners, December 21, 2021, https://www.insightpartners.com/ideas/measuring-the-impact-of-a-community-driven-motion/.

105. "State of Community Management 2022," The Community Roundtable, accessed May 25, 2023, https://communityroundtable.com/what-we-do/research/the-state-of-community-management/state-of-community-management-2022/.

WHAT'S NEXT?

106. Eric Saperston, "Award Winning Film: The Journey," EricSaperston.com, accessed May 25, 2023, http://www.ericsaperston.com/award-winning-film-the-journey/.

ABOUT THE AUTHOR

Derek Weeks is the founder and CEO of Unfair Mindshare, a leading marketing consultancy renowned for crafting boundary-pushing go-to-market strategies that capture the attention of markets, win more deals, and create remarkable brand experiences. As a four-time CMO and VP of Marketing with more than thirty years of experience, Derek has shaped marketing at Fortune 100 technology powerhouses and scaled growth for innovative venture-backed start-ups alike. Honored as one of the top CMOs in the Washington, D.C. metro area by DCA Live and snag-  ging the coveted Marketing Department of the Year award from the Business Intelligence Group, Derek strives every day to make a positive impact in the community of marketers worldwide.

Derek is the pen behind *Unfair Mindshare: A CMO's guide to community-led marketing in a product-led world*, and a co-author of the insightful *Feedback Loops: Voices of All Day DevOps* trilogy.

Born in Philadelphia and raised in Silicon Valley, Derek now lives in beautiful Bethesda, Maryland with his wife, children, and tail-wagging Labradoodle.

Stay updated with Derek at unfairmindshare.com. Follow his insights on LinkedIn: linkedin.com/in/derekeweeks. And keep up with his musings on X: @weekstweets.